Health Operations Management

As governments and other health care financing agencies are increasingly requiring health care providers to 'modernise' their services in order to make more intensive and efficient use of existing health care resources, health care providers are facing growing pressures to change the ways in which they deliver services. These pressures have meant that health operations management has become an increasingly important aspect of managing health services.

Health Operations Management is the first text to address operations management within the context of health services. This exciting text offers readers the opportunity to reflect on the direct application of the principles of this important subject by illustrating theory with real-life case studies. In addition it contains a discussion of related fields including health care quality assurance and performance management. The case studies cover:

- analysis of hospital care processes
- scheduling outpatient appointments
- admission planning
- master scheduling of medical specialist
- aggregate production and capacity plan
- services for older people.

D1421904

This is an original and timely textbook and essential reading for students of health care management, health care managers and clinicians alike.

Jan Vissers is Professor in Health Operations Management at the Institute of Health Policy and Management of Erasmus University Medical Centre in Rotterdam, the Netherlands. He is also affiliated to Eindhoven University of Technology and Prismant, Institute for Health Care Management Development in Utrecht.

Roger Beech is Reader in Health Services Research, Keele University and the Academic Lead for Research, Central Cheshire Primary Care Trust.

ROUTLEDGE HEALTH MANAGEMENT SERIES

Edited by Marc Berg, Robbert Huijsman, David Hunter, John Øvretveit

Routledge Health Management is one of the first series of its kind, filling the need for a comprehensive and balanced series of textbooks on core management topics specifically oriented towards the health care field. In almost all western countries, health care is seen to be in a state of radical reorientation. Each title in this series will focus on a core topic within health care management, and will concentrate explicitly on the knowledge and insights required to meet the challenges of being a health care manager. With a strong international orientation, each book draws heavily on case examples and vignettes to illustrate the theories at play. A genuinely groundbreaking new series in a much-needed area, this series has been put together by an international collection of expert editors and teachers.

Health Information Management

Integrating information technology in health care work
Marc Berg with others

Health Operations Management

Patient flow logistics in health care
Edited by Jan Vissers and Roger Beech

Leadership in Health Care

A European perspective
Neil Goodwin

Performance Management in Health Care

Improving patient outcomes, an integrated approach
Edited by Jan Walburg, Helen Bevan, John Wilderspin and Karin Lemmens

Health Operations Management

Patient flow logistics in health care

Edited by

Jan Vissers and Roger Beech

Routledge
Taylor & Francis Group

LONDON AND NEW YORK

First published 2005
by Routledge
2 Park Square, Milton Park, Abingdon, Oxon OX14 4RN

Simultaneously published in the USA and Canada
by Routledge
270 Madison Ave, New York, NY 10016

Routledge is an imprint of the Taylor & Francis Group

Typeset in Perpetua and Bell Gothic by
Florence Production Ltd, Stoodleigh, Devon
Printed and bound in Great Britain by
MPG Books Ltd, Bodmin

British Library Cataloguing in Publication Data
A catalogue record for this book is available from the British Library

Library of Congress Cataloging in Publication Data
Vissers, Jan.
   Health operations management: patient flow logistics in health care /
   Jan Vissers and Roger Beech – 1st ed.
      p. cm.
   Includes bibliographical references.
   1. Health services administration. 2. Hospitals – Administration.
   3. Operations research. I. Beech, Roger. II. Title.
RA971.V54 2005
362.1′068–dc22   2004030799

ISBN10: 0–415–32395–9 (hbk)   ISBN13: 9–78–0–415–32395–6 (hbk)
ISBN10: 0–415–32396–7 (pbk)   ISBN13: 9–78–0–415–32396–3 (pbk)

Contents

CONTENTS

Figures

Tables

Notes on contributors

Ivo Adan is Associate Professor in Stochastic Operations Research at the Department of Mathematics and Computer Science of Eindhoven University of Technology. Received his M.Sc. Mathematics in 1987 and his Ph.D. from EUT in 1991. Currently member of the editorial board of Statistica Neerlandica and Queueing Systems. His main areas of interest are: Markov processes, queueing models, stochastic fluid flow models, inventory control and performance analysis of production and warehousing systems.

Roger Beech is a reader in Health Services Research in the Centre for Health Planning and Medicine, University of Keele, and the Academic Lead for Research for Central Cheshire PCT. He is also an honorary member of the Faculty of Public Health Medicine. He has a M.Sc. in Operational Research and Management Science (University of Warwick, 1981) and a Ph.D. in Industrial and Business Studies (University of Warwick, 1988). His research can be categorised as having four main but overlapping themes: the economic and organisational aspects of health services and in particular services for elderly people, for intermediate care, and for patients with stroke; the development and application of methodologies for planning health services and in particular services for intermediate and emergency care; health needs assessment and in particular needs for renal services; and the use of models to evaluate changes in the delivery of health care.

Will Bertrand is Full Professor in Production and Operations Management at the Department of Technology Management of Eindhoven University of Technology since 1988. His main areas of interest are: production control in engineer-to-order manufacturing management, supply chain control, hierarchical control of production and inventory systems, planning and control of new products development processes.

Tom Bowen has degrees in Mathematics and Operational Research, and an extensive background of projects in the fields of health care planning and information systems spanning two decades. After analytical and management posts in both the Department of Health and the NHS, he has been operating in consultancy for the NHS and in other European countries for the past nine years. Special interest areas include the development of service plans for patient groups with chronic care needs, in particular services for older people. He has been involved with developing and applying the Balance of Care approach for several years; originally as an analyst at the Department of Health and, more recently, through the activities of the Balance of Care Group. He is an active member of the Operational Research Applied to Health Services Working Group.

Gijs Croonen is Quality Coordinator at Rivierenland Hospital in Tiel in the Netherlands. Received his MA Industrial Psychology and Social Psychology from Katholieke Universiteit Brabant in 1989. From 1989 to 1993 he was a management consultant at Rivierenland Hospital, from 1993 serving in several functions at the same hospital. His main areas of interest are: quality management, patient safety, patient flow management and management information.

Miriam Eijdems has been a management consultant at VieCuri Medical Centre for North Limburg since 1994. Before this she worked as a registered operating theatre assistant and studied Industrial Engineering and Management Science at the Polytechnic in Eindhoven. During the years she has been involved in many projects in the area of patient flow logistics, also applying simulation models.

Paul Forte has degrees in Geography and Planning and worked in health services research at the University of Leeds obtaining his Ph.D. in 1990. He was with the Department of Health Operational Research Service from 1985–91 and, since then, has worked as an independent consultant in health planning and management and as a member of the Balance of Care Group. He has also been closely associated with the Centre for Health Planning & Management at Keele University, England since 1991 and he is currently an honorary senior lecturer on the MBA and Diploma programmes. Throughout his career Paul has focused on the development of decision support systems for health service management, and their application: how and why people use information to support planning and management decision making.

Steve Gallivan is Professor of Operational Research at University College London and Director of the Clinical Operational Research Unit. He also acts as a scientific advisor to the National Confidential Enquiry into Patient Outcome and Death, UK. He received his B.Sc. and Ph.D. from University College London in 1971 and 1974 respectively. He spent many years applying Operational Research techniques in the context of traffic engineering before switching to address problems in health care. The majority of his research involves developing and applying analytical methods to generate insight concerning a wide range of health care problems, from the clinical management of patients to the structure and organisation of health service delivery.

Richard Goulsbra is an Operational Research analyst at the Department for Work and Pensions. Current projects include analysis of the appointment systems in Jobcentre Plus offices in an attempt to increase the proportion of advisor time spent with customers, reduce the occurrence of clients failing to attend their appointments, and to lead to better management of the problem as a whole. He received his M.Sc. in Operational Research from Lancaster University in 2003 having obtained a B.Sc. in Mathematics, Statistics and OR at UMIST a year earlier. His summer project in 2003 was an operations management study of ophthalmology clinics at the Royal Lancaster Infirmary.

Miguel van den Heuvel is an actuarial employee at Delta Lloyd General Insurances, Amsterdam, NL. He received his M.Sc. Applied Mathematics, with a specialisation in Statistics, Probability, and Operations Research, from EUT in 2003. He is currently involved in a study of Actuarial Sciences at the University of Amsterdam.

Mark Jit is a research fellow in the Clinical Operational Research Unit, University College London. He received his Ph.D. from University College London in 2003. His Ph.D. consisted of building mathematical models of cell signalling. His research is now focused on applying modelling techniques to problems in health care, particularly those associated with capacity planning.

Anne de Kreuk is a research analyst and model developer at ABN Amro Bank in the department Asset Management. She received her M.Sc. Applied and Industrial Mathematics with a specialisation in operations research from Eindhoven University of Technology in January 2005. During her studies she became involved in a project concerning health operations management.

James Rankin is a member of the Business Modelling Team at Tribal Secta. Current projects include developing draft HRG Version 4 at the NHSIC, Activity and Capacity Modelling for Papworth NHS Trust and working with Secta Starfish on Supporting People Programme needs analysis for a variety of Local Authorities. He received his M.Sc. in Operational Research from

Lancaster University in 2003 having previously obtained a B.Sc. in Operational Research at the University of Hertfordshire. His summer project in 2003 was an operations management study of ophthalmology clinics at the Royal Lancaster Infirmary.

Martin Utley is a principal research fellow and Deputy Director of the Clinical Operational Research Unit at University College London. He also holds an honorary research post at Guys Hospital London and acts as a scientific advisor to the National Confidential Enquiry into Patient Outcome and Death, UK. Martin received his B.Sc. from the University of Manchester in 1993 and his Ph.D. from the University of Glasgow in 1996. His interest is in developing and applying Operational Research techniques to improve the quality of information available to those planning, delivering or evaluating health services.

Jan Vissers is Professor in Health Operations Management at the Institute of Health Policy and Management at Erasmus Medical Centre Rotterdam, and also Assistant Professor in Health Operations Management at the Department of Technology Management of Eindhoven University of Technology, Eindhoven, NL. He is also a senior management consultant at Prismant – Institute for Health Care Management Development in Utrecht, NL. Received his M.Sc. in Industrial Engineering and Management Science from EUT in 1975 and his Ph.D. from EUT in 1994. Member and current chairman of the European Working Group on Operational Research Applied to Health Services and member of the editorial board of Health Care Management Science. Received the 1995 Baxter Award for his thesis 'Patient Flow based Allocation of Hospital Resources' for its contribution to Health Care Management. His research focuses on the analysis, design and control of operational health care processes and systems. Special interest areas are the development of the process concept and the allocation of shared resources within a hospital setting and beyond.

Guus de Vries is Professor in Health Operations Management at the Institute of Health Policy and Management at Erasmus Medical Centre Rotterdam. He is also a partner in DamhuisElshoutVerschure Management Consultants in Den Bosch, NL. He received his M.Sc. in Industrial Engineering and Management Science from EUT in 1979 and his Ph.D. from EUT in 1984. Editor of a book (in Dutch) on patient flow management and co-editor of a series of books (in Dutch) with case studies on applications of industrial engineering to health care settings. His research interest areas are: staffing and workload control, patient flow management, analysis and (re)design of health care processes in hospitals and other health care institutions, including organisational development and change management topics.

Karin Wiersema received her Master's Degree Health Sciences, specialisation Health Policy and Administration, in 2002 at Maastricht University. Since 2002, she is Management Consultant at Elkerliek General Hospital in Helmond. Between 1989 and 2001 she was a nurse at an intensive care department at the same hospital. Her practice experience is very useful for the projects she is currently involved in. Main areas of interest are: patient flow logistics, management information, general management and innovation. She is a member of the board of the national society NVOG (Dutch Society for Organisation in Health Care).

Erik Winands received his M.Sc. degree in Industrial and Applied Mathematics from Eindhoven University of Technology in 2003. Currently, he is doing research for his Ph.D. thesis at the same university. His main research interests are in queueing theory and its applications to the performance analysis of production systems, which is also the focus of his Ph.D. study.

Dave Worthington is a Senior Lecturer in Operational Research in the Department of Management Science, Lancaster University Management School, UK. He is trained as a mathematician at Birmingham University and then as an operational researcher/statistician specialising in health and social services at Reading University. He also did his Ph.D. thesis at Reading University, investigating hospital waiting lists as queueing systems with feedback. His research, project work, consultancy and publications are in two main areas: the health care applications of management science; and queue management – including the development and use of queueing models. As in the case of this book, these two research interests sometimes overlap.

Preface

This is the first book with an explicit focus on health operations management (health OM) and its development. There are two main reasons why we and our contributing authors – often educated in operations management (OM) but working in the field of health care – felt that the time was right to produce a dedicated book on health operations management. The first reason surrounds the current and evolving 'climate' in which health services are delivered. The second surrounds the need to make operations management theories and techniques more accessible to heath care professionals and practitioners and to those studying health care management.

We define health OM as 'the analysis, design, planning and control of all of the steps necessary to provide a service for a client'. In other words, health OM is concerned with identifying the needs of clients, usually patients, and designing and delivering services to meet their needs in the most effective and efficient manner. It can be argued that the importance and complexity of this agenda of responsibilities is increasing.

Health care providers are having to respond to changes in patient demands for health care. In many countries the proportion of the population aged over 65 is increasing. This demographic change will increase overall demands for health care and it is also likely to affect the ways in which health care is delivered: for example, in the United Kingdom there is increasing emphasis on developing services in the community as an alternative to acute hospital-based care. Regardless of changes in overall demand, individual consumers of health care are becoming more 'vocal'. For example, they are less willing to accept 'long' waiting times for treatment and the development of the internet and initiatives such as 'expert patient' programmes mean that they are more aware of the types of care that they should receive.

Health care providers are also facing pressures to change the ways in which they deliver services. Governments and other health care financing agencies are increasingly requiring health care providers to 'modernise' their services such that they make more intensive and efficient use of existing health care resources. In the UK a government-funded department, the Modernisation Agency, has been established to facilitate the adoption of improved approaches to analysing and managing health services. In addition, initiatives such as the development of clinical guidelines and the promotion of evidenced based care are encouraging health care providers to increase the effectiveness of their services. Although such initiatives have a clinical focus they often require a change in the organisation of services: for example, changes in the organisation of radiography departments may be needed if guideline targets in terms of access to CT scan facilities by stroke patients are to be met.

Hence the relevance and importance of health OM principles and approaches are increasing. Up until now, health care professionals, practitioners and students wanting to find out more about operations management would have had to turn to general textbooks, which describe the application of operations management principles and approaches in the manufacturing and service sectors. When your interest lies in health care, this implies that you first have to familiarise yourself with 'general' operations management and then translate general principles and approaches into the health service setting. Not everyone will have the time or patience to follow this route and there is a danger that some of the key messages may be lost in translation. A dedicated health OM textbook therefore has the advantage of a health specific introduction of OM principles and approaches, with possibilities for direct application. In addition, as health care application is the focus of this book, it also contains a discussion of related fields of development, such as health care quality assurance and performance management. As the prime orientation of health care students and health care managers is health care management development, this will help them to identify how to position health OM within the context of these other initiatives and disciplines.

In the initial chapters of the book a conceptual framework is developed in which to position health OM theories and techniques. A series of case studies then follows. In addition to reinforcing the messages of the early chapters, these case studies offer practical illustrations of the situations and settings in which health OM theories and techniques have been used. They also help to generate an awareness of how the approaches and techniques described might be used in other areas of health care. Taken overall, the book allows us – and our co-authors – to share our experiences in health OM with others working in the same area of application. Our aim is that the book should help to promote a more widespread understanding of health OM theories and approaches. In turn, the adoption of these theories and approaches will help to facilitate improvements in the delivery of services for patient care.

December 2004
Jan Vissers
Roger Beech

Abbreviations

A&E	accident and emergency
ABACUS	Analysis of Booked Admissions and Capacity Use
AEP	Appropriateness Evaluation Protocol
AVGs	ambulatory visit groups
BAWC	booked admission with coordination
BAWOC	booked admission without coordination
BOM	bill of materials
BOR	bill of resources
BPR	business process redesign
BWW framework	framework by Bertrand, Wortmann and Wijngaard
CAGs	coronary angiographies
CCU	cardio care unit
CNA	could not attend
CT scan	computerised tomography scan
CVA	cerebrovascular accident
DC	day case
DNA	did not attend
DRGs	diagnosis related groups
ECG	electrocardiogram
EEG	electroencephalogram
ERP	Enterprise Resource Planning
FTE	full time equivalent
GF	goods flow
GP	general practitioner
HCRPS	health care requirements planning system
HRGs	health related groupings
HRP model	Hospital Resource Planning model
IC	intensive care

ICD	International Classification of Diseases
IIASA	International Institute for Applied Systems Analysis
ILP	integer linear program
IQP	integer quadratic program(ming)
JIT	just-in-time
MPS	master production schedule
MRP-I	Material Requirements Planning
MRP-II	Manufacturing Resources Planning
MRU	maximum resource use
NHS	National Health Service
NP	nursing capacity
OM	operations management
OP	outpatient
OPD	outpatient department
OPT®	Optimized Production Technology
OT	operating theatre
OTD	operating theatre department
PAV	peripheral arterial vascular
POA	pre-operative assessment
PSU	pre-operative screening unit
PTCAs	percutane transluminal coronary angiographies
PU	production unit
SCM	supply chain management
SCOR	Supply Chain Operations Reference
SHO	senior house officer
SMED	Single Minute Exchange of Dies
SOM	Schedule Optimisation Model
SP	specialist
TCs	Treatment Centres
UTA	unable to attend
VBA	Visual Basic for Applications
WTEs	whole time equivalents
ZWT	zero waiting time

Chapter 1

Introduction

Jan Vissers and Roger Beech

DEFINING HEALTH OM

The term operations management refers to the planning and control of the processes that transform inputs into outputs. This definition also applies to health OM. Consider the individual doctor/patient consultation. The input to the consultation process is a patient with a request for health care. The output of the consultation process might be that the patient is diagnosed, referred to a further service, or cured. The resources that have to be managed to transform inputs into outputs are those associated with the care provided by the individual doctor: for example, their time and any diagnostic or therapeutic services that they use.

In this illustration the role of the health OM process was to ensure that adequate resources were in place to provide an 'acceptable' service for the patient. Hence, health OM focuses on the individual provider that produces a health service and on the tasks involved to produce this service.

In the above illustration the individual provider was a doctor. However, the 'individual' provider might be, for example, a hospital department (e.g. an X-ray department), a hospital, or a network of hospital and community-based services (e.g. services for the acute care and rehabilitation of patients who have suffered a stroke). At each level both the scale and scope of the resources to be planned and controlled increase, as does the complexity of the OM task.

Figure 1.1 presents an example of a health OM view of an individual hospital provider, adapted from a meta-process model of a health care delivery system described by Roth (1993). The agenda for health OM is covered by the central box.

The central function of the hospital is to provide patient care. Hence, patient demand for care is the key input that influences the planning and control of the resources required to transform inputs into outputs. However, as Figure 1.1 illustrates, other 'inputs' influence both the types and levels of patient demand and the ways in which the hospital delivers care. These other 'inputs' include the overall

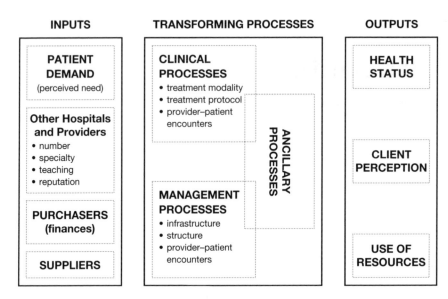

Figure 1.1 *Meta-process model of a health care delivery system.*
Adapted from Roth (1993)

level of finance available to provide care, the availability of goods from suppliers, and the nature and actions of other hospitals.

Figure 1.1 highlights three generic processes for transforming inputs into outputs: clinical, management and ancillary. Clinical processes are probably the most important as they are directly associated with the planning and control of those resources used for the diagnosis and treatment of patients. However, management processes are needed to support the clinical processes. These management processes include those for organising the payment of staff and for purchasing goods from suppliers. Finally, ancillary processes are needed to support the general functioning of the hospital. These processes include the organisation of services for cleaning hospital wards and departments and for maintaining hospital equipment.

The resources to be planned and controlled within each of these processes include staff (e.g. doctors, nurses), materials (e.g. drugs, prostheses), and equipment (e.g. X-ray machines, buildings). Inadequate planning and control of resources within any of the processes can have an impact on the others. For example, deficiencies in the management processes for ordering materials may affect the quality of care that can be delivered by the clinical processes (e.g. a shortage of equipment to support care at home may lead to delays in patient discharge from hospital). Similarly, if services for the cleaning of hospital wards are inadequate, the potential for hospital acquired infections will be increased, as will the likelihood of subsequent ward closures.

Hence, when planning and controlling the resources that they use, an 'individual' provider must also consider the ways in which their actions might impinge upon other 'individual' providers, for example other hospital or community-based departments. In this sense, their actions represent 'inputs' to other processes for transforming inputs into outputs.

Finally, Figure 1.1 illustrates the outputs of the OM processes that must be monitored. Health status markers (e.g. mortality rates, levels of morbidity and disability) are relevant to the success with which clinical processes are transforming inputs into outputs, as are measures of client perception/satisfaction where the client (and/or their family) is the patient. In addition, the client of a process might also be a hospital doctor who requires a service from a diagnostic department or a hospital manager who requires details of patient activity levels from doctors. Similarly, 'resource' performance output measures are relevant to all three generic processes as they are needed to monitor the efficiency (e.g. patient lengths of stay, response times of ancillary support services) and effectiveness (e.g. use of 'appropriate' or 'modern' procedures) with which resources have been used to transform inputs into outputs.

Again, there are relationships and potential conflicts between the different types of output. For example, measures to increase patient satisfaction by reducing patient waiting times might require additional investment and mean that the hospital is unable to achieve its budgetary targets. Similarly, budgetary pressures may mean that a hospital is unable to invest in all of those services that are known to be effective in improving health status: examples might include expensive treatments for rare conditions. Hence, in its attempts to ensure that there is an effective and efficient organisation of the delivery of services, the role of health OM is to achieve an 'acceptable' balance between different types of output.

Having illustrated the nature of health OM it is now possible to offer a definition of health OM:

> Health OM can be defined as the analysis, design, planning, and control of all of the steps necessary to provide a service for a client.

CONTEXT OF HEALTH OM

This section discusses the context of health OM decision making: drivers for change and factors that influence decision making. The previous section demonstrated that the system of 'inputs', 'transforming processes' and 'outputs' is subject to its own internal dynamics and influences. Efforts to improve the outputs from one process might have an impact on the inputs and outputs of others. Here, we will discuss some of the key 'external' factors, and additional 'internal' factors, that influence health OM decision making. Again, for the purposes of illustration, we will take the perspective of an individual hospital provider.

Probably the main external factor that affects the behaviour of individual providers is the overall health care system setting in which they function, for example, market and 'for profit', national health system or government regulated. In a 'for profit' setting, the emphasis for providers is on profit maximisation. As a result, providers will want to maximise the number of patients whom they can treat at 'acceptable' standards of quality but at 'minimum' costs per case. The market environment, therefore, creates the incentives for providers to ensure that the processes for transforming inputs into outputs are functioning in an effective and efficient way. Providers must continually review and invest in their trans-forming processes as a means of maintaining their market share, attracting new patients or reducing costs. For example, the market creates the incentives for providers to invest in new health care technologies in order to either attract more patients or reduce costs per case.

In a national health system or government regulated system, providers are budgeted by the contracts annually arranged with purchasers (government related bodies or insurance organisations). In such a system the main incentive for providers is to ensure that budgetary targets are not exceeded. Hence, provid-ers need to invest in mechanisms for monitoring the use of key resource areas such as the use of beds and theatres. Beyond the need to ensure that 'cost' performance targets are achieved, relative to the market environment, providers probably have lower incentives to continually review and update transforming processes or to ensure that other 'output' measures, such as client perception are 'satisfactory'.

However, this situation is changing and, in the absence of market incentives, regulation is being used as a vehicle for change. For example, in the National Health Service (NHS) of the United Kingdom (UK), National Service Frameworks are being developed for key disease areas (e.g. diabetes) or patient groups (e.g. older people). These frameworks specify the types of services that should be available for patient care: hence, they have a direct influence on clinical processes. The NHS of the UK is also setting performance or 'output' targets for providers, for example, maximum waiting times for an outpatient appointment or an elective procedure. Again, to ensure that such targets are met, providers will need to review and modify their processes for transforming inputs into outputs.

In Europe, government regulated health care systems are still dominant but gradually more market incentives are being introduced. In the US, although health care is shaped as a market system, the level of regulation is increasing through developments such as the development of Health Maintenance Organisations.

Beyond the health care system, and the actions of governments, other external factors are affecting the context in which health OM decisions are made. For example, most western countries are experiencing changes in the demographic mix of their populations such that there is an increasing proportion of older people. Both the scale and nature of hospital resources (and those in other settings) will need to be adjusted to meet this demographic change. For example, the NHS of the UK is currently expanding its services for home-based care as an alternative to hospital care.

In addition, advances in medical technology (for example, new drugs and other forms of treatment) are either changing or expanding the options that are available for patient care. Providers will need to decide if and how they should respond to these advances. Again, government regulation is likely to be used as a vehicle for change.

Finally, via the internet and other outlets of the media, patient knowledge of health care treatments and expectations of heath care providers are increasing. Providers are having to adjust their care processes to address this change in consumer expectations.

Up until now, this discussion of the context of health OM has focused on external factors that affect the environment in which decisions are made. In comparison to other service or manufacturing organisations, the internal environment for decision making is in itself unusual.

Often, the roles and responsibilities of those involved in decision making are either not very clearly defined or are overlapping. Health care management often takes the form of dual management, in which clinical professionals share management responsibilities with administrative staff and business managers. Finding out who is actually managing the system can therefore be a real issue in health care organisations.

In addition, health care management decision making often takes the form of finding consensus among the different actors involved: managers, medical professionals, nursing staff, paramedical disciplines, administrative staff. These actors often have different interests along the dividing lines of quality versus costs or effectiveness versus efficiency. As health care does not have the possibility of defining profit as an overall objective, it is often difficult to find the right trade-off between these two perspectives of managing organisations.

Hence, there is a range of 'external' and 'internal' factors and challenges that influence health OM decision making. This book presents a scientific body of knowledge and reflection to support the planning and control of health care processes.

RELATED FIELDS

Health OM activities are complemented by and related to other areas of 'management' activity that focus on the core processes of the organisation. These other areas include:

- quality management, which aims to improve and maintain the quality of services delivered by processes;

- performance management, which concentrates on measuring and monitoring the performance of the organisation in terms of the outcomes of processes;
- information management, which concentrates on the development of tools for providing and handling information about processes; and
- operational research, which offers analytical techniques and approaches that can be used to investigate and improve processes.

Often the boundaries between health OM and these other areas of 'management' might seem somewhat 'fuzzy'. However, it could be argued that health OM creates the broad agenda that is then addressed, in part, by these other fields of management.

OUTLINE OF THE BOOK

This book is the first to focus explicitly on health OM and its development. Chapters 2–6 therefore offer conceptual contributions to the development of health OM theories and techniques. The main body of the book then consists of a number of case studies that illustrate health OM at work in health care settings. The concluding chapter of the book discusses future challenges and further areas of development for health OM.

Scientific interest in the development of theories and techniques to support OM originated in the manufacturing and service environment. The supply of health care is often seen as a special type of service industry. Hence, many health care researchers and managers have turned to OM literature from the industrial and service sectors when seeking answers to the many problems faced in delivering health services. In chapter 2, Will Bertrand and Guus de Vries offer a critical discussion of key theories and techniques that originated in industrial and service sectors and the ways in which they might contribute to health OM. It will be demonstrated that many theories and techniques developed in industrial and service sectors are not directly applicable to health OM, but that nevertheless the underlying principles may still hold and need to be translated to health care.

Health OM, therefore, requires a specific approach. Chapters 3–6 develop a conceptual framework for positioning health OM theories and techniques. An overview of this framework is given in Figure 1.2.

Earlier the health OM process was considered from the perspective of an 'individual' provider. The potential breadth of the health OM task was indicated by the fact that the 'individual' provider might be, for example, a doctor, a hospital department, a hospital or a network of hospital and community based services. Figure 1.2 illustrates the potential depth, or differing aspects, of the health OM agenda of responsibilities. Again, for the purposes of illustration, this agenda will be discussed from the perspective of an individual hospital.

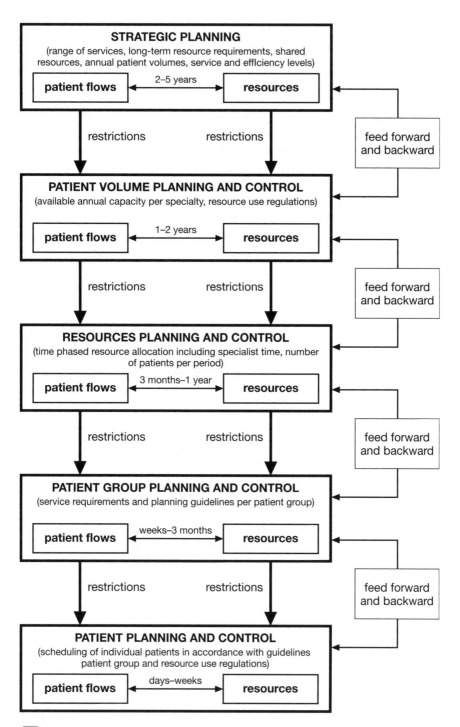

Figure 1.2 Conceptual framework of health OM planning and control processes.

Strategic planning decisions create the long-term vision of the hospital and the types of services that it should provide. However, this vision then needs to be implemented and sustained. This is the function of health OM processes: turning strategic visions and directions into reality.

'Patient volume planning and control' represents the start of the process of deciding how best to transform 'inputs' into 'outputs'. This represents an initial check that the hospital has the correct types and amounts of services (or transforming processes) in place to meet the needs of the patients whom it plans to treat. This check will need to be remade at more detailed levels of planning further down the framework. The concepts used for elaborating the various aspects of the health OM agenda of responsibilities are discussed in chapter 3.

The process of checking that the hospital has the correct types of services in place is described in terms of an assessment of the types of 'units' or departments required, the types of 'resources' that they will use and the types of 'operations' or activities that they will undertake. For example, hospital admissions are cared for on wards (units) that require nursing staff (resources) who provide general medical care (operations). Similarly, surgical patients are treated in operating theatres (units) where surgeons (resources) undertake surgical procedures (operations).

Checking that the hospital has the correct amount of services in place is more complex and requires an understanding of the relationships between patients, operations and resources. Chapter 3 begins this process of understanding by introducing the concepts of 'unit' and 'chain' logistics.

Units undertake similar types of operations for (usually) different types of patient: for example, operating theatres are used by patients requiring orthopaedic procedures, urological procedures, general surgical procedures etc. Unit logistics aims to ensure that the resources used by a unit are allocated in an appropriate and efficient way. Hence patients might be treated in 'batches', for example, general surgery theatre sessions on Monday and Wednesday afternoons. Alternatively, patient access to resources might be prioritised in a way that smoothes peaks and troughs in terms of demands for resources: for example, delaying the admission of elective patients means that a hospital requires fewer beds than if a decision is made that all patients (elective and emergency) should be admitted on the day that their needs for care are identified.

Chains cross unit boundaries and represent the total range of resources required to produce a product or to treat a patient. Hence, a chain might be regarded as a patient pathway: for example, the chain of care for stroke might consume resources provided by imaging departments, general and stroke specific hospital wards, and physiotherapy departments. Chain logistics is concerned with coordinating the appropriate and efficient allocation of resources along patient pathways or product lines, for example, scheduling patient flows in order to avoid delays or 'bottlenecks' in patient care.

Unit logistics is discussed in greater detail in chapter 4: in the planning framework this is referred to as 'resources planning and control'. The discussion of the allocation of resources within units considers issues such as: whether or not resources can be 'shared' by more than one patient group; whether resource use in one unit 'leads to' or 'follows' resource use in another unit; and whether or not a resource is scarce and as a result might represent a 'bottleneck' in the delivery of services. For example, CT scanning facilities can be used by more than one patient group and represents, therefore, a shared resource; the use of resources in an intensive care unit (often a bottleneck) is influenced by the allocation of resources in operating theatres (leading resource) and the use of resources on general wards (following resource); and access to the time of clinical specialists for decisions about patient discharge might represent a scarce or a 'bottleneck' resource that influences the use of beds on wards. Chapter 4 also discusses methods that can be used to monitor the efficiency with which resources are utilised within units, for example, the proportion of allocated operating theatre time that is used for patient care.

Chapter 5 then focuses on chain logistics: in the planning framework this is referred to as 'patient group' and 'patient' planning and control. Key issues discussed include: identifying the 'products' to be represented by chains; clarifying the types of resources that they use; and coordinating and scheduling access to these resources.

As the planning framework indicates, 'products' might be classified as 'patient groups' with similar care needs: for example, in the NHS of the UK the patient pathway for 'older people' is being re-designed such that non-acute nursing and social care needs will be met by services for intermediate care rather than an admission to, or an extended stay in, an acute hospital bed. Alternatively 'products' might be 'patients' with specific diagnoses (for example, stroke patients) or requiring specific types of procedure (for example, hip replacements). The need for such precision will be increased by initiatives such as patient booking systems, which allow patients to select the date of their admission for an elective procedure. Such initiatives mean that resources must be coordinated and scheduled to meet the requirements of 'individual' patients.

For some patient groups or types, the chain or pathway might reach beyond the acute hospital. For example, in the UK, National Service Frameworks are being used to both improve and standardise care for common conditions. The one developed for stroke demonstrates that although the pathway might start with an acute admission, it ultimately continues with rehabilitation and secondary stroke prevention in the community. Similarly, efforts to coordinate and schedule care might stretch beyond the boundaries of the hospital. For example, a shortage of resources for community based social care might lead to delays in the hospital discharge of patients.

The conceptual framework developed throughout chapters 2–5 is summarised and discussed in chapter 6. This chapter also acts as a prelude to the main body of the book: a range of case studies that illustrate OM at work in health care settings. The conceptual part provides a reference framework for positioning the different case studies; moreover, the case studies can also be used to reflect on the framework and show the way for its further development.

Most case studies have the hospital as setting. This is logical as processes in hospitals are most complex, have a shorter throughput time and a higher volume, compared to other sectors of health care, such as mental health, care for disabled persons and home care for the elderly. Therefore, one could state that hospitals are a perfect development ground for health OM. Nevertheless, the principles of the examples can be easily translated to these other health care sectors. Hence, as part of the case studies we will reflect on the relevance of the approaches and ideas expressed for other health care organisations, as many processes of patients do cross the boundaries of single health care providers. This is an area for future development of health OM approaches, as a parallel with supply chain management in industry.

The case studies will be rich in description of the features of health care processes and illustrated with diagrams and quantitative data. They will provide excellent material for cases that can be used for the education of future health care managers and researchers. The book is therefore relevant for Masters' students and postgraduate students, and health care professionals looking for support for improving the logistic performance of health care processes. Though health care systems vary much between different countries and have a major impact on the way health organisations are managed, there is more similarity in the underlying processes of providing care to patients. A description of the primary process of a hip surgery patient, in terms of the steps taken and the resources required in each step, does not differ much between countries and is easily understandable in an international context. This is an advantage of the focus of this book on health OM.

The book concludes with a chapter that discusses the further extension of both the scope and content of health OM approaches. This reflects the fact that the hospital was, primarily, used as the setting in the development of the conceptual framework and throughout the case studies. However, health OM philosophies and approaches are equally relevant in other settings, for example, when planning the delivery of services for primary care. This chapter considers areas where more work is needed to further develop health OM skills and techniques: in other words, the need for health OM is clear but the ways forward are not. These other areas include ways of responding to some government initiatives: the translation of these strategic visions into reality might represent a difficult and complex task.

QUESTIONS AND EXERCISES

1   What are the main differences between a national health care system or
    government regulated system versus a market regulated or 'for profit' health care
    system, and what is the impact on the operations management of the hospital?
2   Given the decision-making process on managerial issues in a hospital, what will
    be important aims for health OM?

REFERENCES AND FURTHER READING

Brandeau M.L. *Operations Research and Health Care: A Handbook of Methods and Applications*. Berlin, Heidelberg, New York: Kluwer Academic Publishers, 2004.

Delesie L., A. Kastelein, F. van Merode and J.M.H. Vissers. Managing health care under resource constraints. *Feature Issue European Journal of Operational Research*, 105 (2), 1998, 247–370.

Meredith J.R. and S.M. Shafer. *Operations Management for MBAs*. New York and elsewhere: John Wiley & Sons, Inc. Second edition, 2002.

Roth A.V. World class health care. *Quality Management in Health*, 1 (3), 1993, 1–9.

Young T., S. Brailsford, C. Connell, R. Davies, P. Harper and J.H. Klein. Using industrial processes to improve patient care. *British Medical Journal*, 328, 2004, 162–164.

Part I

Concepts

Chapter 2

Lessons to be learned from operations management

Will Bertrand and Guus de Vries

INTRODUCTION

From an operations management point of view, hospital care processes are considered to be rather complex as compared to processes in industry or most other types of service organisations. This may explain the difficulties that often are encountered during efforts to apply operations management principles and techniques in hospital care settings. However, complex operational processes also exist in industry, and operations management principles and techniques have been successfully applied to many of them. The question, therefore, is to identify the assumptions underlying the operations management principles that have been developed over the last decades in industry and to find out which of these assumptions are justified in hospital care.

In this chapter we present a number of operations management principles and techniques and discuss their applicability to hospital care processes.

OM PRINCIPLES AND TECHNIQUES

Over the last decades the management of operational processes has evolved at a rapid pace. The forces driving these evolutions were the fierce competition between companies on a more and more global scale, the acceleration in product innovation that resulted from the increased competition and the revolution in information technology. These factors created a high pressure on operational processes in terms of quality, efficiency and flexibility, and stimulated research into ways to improve the performance of these processes. As a result, principles and techniques have been identified that can support operations managers in identifying opportunities for improving the performance of their operational processes. Operations management concepts that have experienced wide applications in industry are:

- the focused factory concept
- the just-in-time concept
- the production control concepts MRP (Material Requirements Planning) and OPT® (Optimized Production Technology®)
- hierarchical production control.

The focused factory concept

The focused factory concept, developed by W. Skinner (1985), is the idea that an operational process should be designed to support optimally the production and delivery of a homogeneous group of products or services. Homogeneity refers to the quality and requirements for the products or services in the market and the resources needed for their production. The concept is based on the observation that differences in quality and service requirements and differences in resources needed for production require the production organisation to maintain different modes of operation, and to switch frequently from one mode of operation to another. It even might require a production organisation to simultaneously operate in two or more different modes. Such requirements are difficult to fulfil, and there-fore often imply poor quality, poor service and, perhaps even more important, lead to high production costs. Poor quality, poor service, and high production costs are caused, on the one hand, by the lack of knowledge in the internal organisation about the requirements in the market and, on the other hand, by the decreased possibilities of making use of learning-curve effects. The learning-curve effect refers to the phenomenon that the time required to perform a task declines at a decreasing rate as the number of times that the task has been performed increases.

The focused factory concept should not be equated with the much older concept of specialisation that is also based on learning-curve effects. Specialisation refers in general to functional specialisation, e.g. the use of resources that have been designed for performing a special function in a very efficient way. Specialised resources may be used in a focused factory, but in principle resources in a focused factory have been designed or selected for the optimal functioning from the perspective of the performance of the group of products or services that the factory delivers. The essence of a focused factory can be found in the way in which the various resources in the factory are coordinated in order to achieve the required operational performance. The larger the variety in products, in services or in per-formance requirements is, the larger the required variety in resources and modes of operation will be and, as a result, more effort will be needed to coordinate the resources. The large variety in products, services and resources will also result in less opportunity for learning, which takes place with the repeated execution of similar processing steps and repeated interaction with similar customers.

An excellent review of early learning curve literature can be found in Yelle (1977). Empirical research on learning has revealed that the learning effect depends on the technology used in the process. Generally the use of technology leads to a decrease in the amount of time needed for a task (this is the purpose of using the technology). However low-technology tasks show higher learning effects than high-technology tasks. Learning effects occur at the individual level as well as at the group level. For instance, Kelsey *et al.* (1984) showed that the success rates of surgeons increased as their experience increased. The performance of small groups also seems to fit the characteristic learning curve, and even at the organisation level, learning-curve effects are found.

Argote *et al.* (1990) found substantial learning-curve effects in the data about the production of a standardised ship at sixteen different shipyards in the US during the Second World War. However they also found lack of persistence in organisational learning, implying that the conventional measure of learning, cumulative output, overrates persistency of learning. They speculate that lack of persistency may be due to product changes, process changes and inadequate organisational records. Interruption in performing a task may also lead to deteriorating performance.

The negative effects on performance of task interruptions have also been observed at the individual level (Globerson *et al.* (1989), Bailey (1989) Shtub *et al.* (1996)). This has been named the 'forgetting' effect. Forgetting can lead to a substantial reduction of the 'learned' task efficiency, and this also applies to organisational learning. Thus the variety of products and processes that a production system must be able to handle should be carefully considered in relation to the number of switches to different products or processes that would result from such a choice. Based on data collected in a number of consultancy projects Stalk and Hout (1990) concluded that lack of focus degrades the operational efficiency of a production system, even to the extent that a firm loses its competitive edge. In their book they introduce the concept 'cost of variety' and argue that increasing volume by adding more products rather than by aiming to increase sales of existing products may effectively lead to a decrease of efficiency of the resource use due to the increased change-over costs and the forgetting effects, and an increase of overhead costs due to increased data handling, planning and communication activities. Figure 2.1 illustrates the opposing effects of production volume and product variety on total production unit costs.

The just-in-time concept

Just-in-time refers to the product and process-engineering principles that were developed at the Toyota factories in the 1960s for the design and control of the production system (for an overview see Schönberger (1984)). These principles are completely in line with the focused factory concept but also include a number of other ideas that allow a large variety of products to be produced without incurring excessive product variety costs. The main principles underlying just-in-time

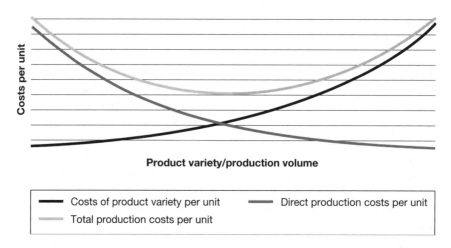

Figure 2.1 *The effects of production volume and product variety on production costs.*

are zero-defect production, set-up reduction and stockless production. These principles were implemented via product design, process design and organisation of work. The aim of just-in-time production was to produce a variety of end-products with short lead-times (response time to fulfil demand) without having to invest in stocks of end products. It was observed that product defects have a devastating effect on productivity and on delivery reliability: a defective product needs repair, or has to be rejected, implying losses of resources and materials; moreover it leads to unreliable supply to the next production phases causing unplanned idle times on resources. The only way to avoid such resource idle times is to have high work-in-process, which in turn leads to long lead-times to the market or high investments in inventory.

The just-in-time concept implies that the production system is first of all organised for the elimination of the causes of product defects. This is mainly achieved by the shop floor employees, who are organised in teams that are trained, equipped and empowered for this purpose. Collecting knowledge about causes of product defects can be considered a learning process that can be accelerated by focusing on a limited set of products requiring a similar range of processes. Thus focused factories have the advantage that they can decrease their product defect rate at a higher rate than non-focused factories. The obvious disadvantage of focused production is that it limits product and process range, implying limited product flexibility to the market. The just-in-time concept minimises this effect by having a strongly modular product design and a process design that avoids large set-up costs or change-over times. A modular product design enables the development of a wide range of functionally different end-products out of a limited number of different components or subassemblies, with many components and subassemblies requiring the same or very similar production processes. This leads to the fortunate combination of high external product variety and low internal material and process variety. The internal variety can be further reduced by choosing manufacturing technologies that require no or very small change-over times when changing production from one item to another. This principle has become known as SMED (Single Minute Exchange of Dies – see Shingo (1985)). If this principle is implemented, production can take place in small batch sizes, which makes it possible to adapt production to actual demand, and avoid the 'nervous' patterns in capacity requirements that are generated when producing in large batch sizes. Smooth patterns of capacity requirements are much easier and cheaper to fulfil than nervous patterns.

The last principle underlying just-in-time production is to install sufficient capacity for demand to be fulfilled without any delay other than manufacturing time. This implies that at some times some resources are idle, the advantage of this being that the production system can run with a very low inventory and work-in-process (also known as zero-inventory). Implementation of all these principles in the Toyota factories resulted in the creation of the famous Kan-Ban system, a very simple way (by using cards as production signals) of controlling production activities in a chain (Monden, 1993).

Production control concepts

It will be clear from the previous description that just-in-time is completely rooted in engineering and work organisation. In fact, the idea is to realise, through product design, process design and organisation of work, a lean production system that can respond with high reliability to varying demand for a pre-specified range of products. However, in many production environments it may be impossible or not economically justified to achieve this ideal. For instance, certain manufacturing processes operate at the edge of current technological knowledge, and therefore have high product defect rates (for example, integrated circuit manufacturing, special steel manufacturing) or are impossible to change over from one product to another without high change-over costs or change-over times (glass manufacturing). This leads to production in batches and the need for keeping stocks. Also, in some production environments market demand is volatile or shows high seasonality. In such environments installing sufficient capacity to cope with the maximum demand that can occur cannot be economically justified. As a result, anticipating stocks are used, which decouple production from demand, or dynamic lead times are quoted to customers when manufacturing to customer order. In such an environment the coordination of successive production phases becomes a complex problem, complexity which cannot be avoided and has to be dealt with. A number of methods and techniques have been developed to cope with this complexity, such as Material Requirements Planning (MRP) and Optimized

Production Technology (OPT®). These techniques take the product and process design as a given, and heavily rely on information technology to model the material supply relationships in the supply chain, the operational characteristics of the manufacturing processes and the state of the supply chain in terms of inventories, outstanding orders and work-in-process.

Material Requirements Planning

Material Requirements Planning has been developed for production environments where a range of related end-products (featuring subassembly and component commonality) is produced that experience dynamic demand, and where subassemblies and components are manufactured in different batch sizes with substantial lead-times. Using bill of materials (BOM) information, information about batch sizes and lead times, and information about the current inventories, work-in-process and outstanding purchasing orders, the Material Requirements Planning mechanism calculates for each item (subassembly or component) in the BOM the time-phased patterns of production orders to be released in order to 'fulfil' the current master production schedule (MPS). The MPS is a statement about desired future time-phased output at end-product level (Orlicky, 1975). The Material Requirements Planning mechanism provides good decision support if demand is dynamic but not (very) stochastic, and production capacity can be easily adapted to the capacity requirements following from the production order release patterns. If demand shows substantial stochasticity, actual demand deviates from expectations, and the MPS must be frequently updated. As a result the production order release patterns can change drastically over time (the notorious 'nervousness' property of Material Requirements Planning systems). If capacity cannot be easily adapted, or high capacity utilisation is a required factor, anticipation stocks should be built up at some points in the chain. Material Requirements Planning does not support these possibilities.

Material Requirements Planning, referred to as MRP-I, evolved in the 1980s into Manufacturing Resources Planning, referred to as MRP-II. MRP-II is not a control mechanism like MRP-I, but a hierarchical conceptual framework for controlling goods flows in a factory, also including the planning and control of production capacity. However the hard core of MRP-II retains the MRP-I mechanisms for calculating production orders and purchasing order release patterns based on the MPS, a fixed bill of materials and fixed production lead-times. Thus material control is the dominant dimension and capacity control is driven by the needs derived from material control.

Optimized Production Technology®

OPT® is similar to MRP in that it provides decision support for the coordination of production decisions for production environments where a range of related end-products that experience regular demand is produced in a configuration of sequential and parallel production units. The system is different from MRP in that it assumes that some manufacturing resources have essentially constrained capacity, and in that it recognises the dynamic interaction between batch sizes, capacity utilisation and lead-times. OPT® calculates a production plan that aims at maximising some measure of throughput (output rate of the production system as a whole) under some constraints on work-in-process. Unlike in MRP, batch sizes are explicit decision variables and lead-times are not a given, but result from the scheduling process. OPT® therefore simultaneously considers the material and capacity aspect of the production-planning problem (for details see Goldratt (1988)).

The essential assumption underlying the OPT® mechanism is that there exists a stable bottleneck resource in the production system; in other words, which resource acts as the bottleneck (constraining the output rate over time) should not depend on the mix in demand for the various end-products. The performance of the OPT® mechanism, however, is quite sensitive to changes in the bottleneck resource, in that it can generate totally different production plans for two different resources as a bottleneck, even if the two sources are quite close with respect to available capacity relative to required capacity. This is a type of nervousness similar to that of MRP-I. Just like MRP-I, the OPT® mechanism is based on deterministic planning concepts and therefore cannot deal with the intrinsic uncertainties in real-life production systems, other than by introducing static buffers (such as safety time and safety stock).

Both MRP-I and OPT® should be applied with care; the concepts available in both techniques do not cover all aspects of the coordination problem and must be complemented with planners who are aware of these deficiencies and who can compensate for them by a correct interpretation of the planning results (see also Bertrand *et al.* (1990)).

Hierarchical production control

MRP-I, OPT® and the Kan Ban system are different mechanisms to control production in complex production situations where complex products are produced via a network of production processes. As has been discussed in the previous section, each of these mechanisms is based on specific assumptions regarding the production system and the processes. For instance, the just-in-time approach aims at creating the conditions for which the Kan Ban control mechanism can work. However, as mentioned before, creating such conditions may not always be possible. In the majority of current production environments one or more conditions for the Kan Ban system (or MRP-I or OPT®) are not realised, in particular having sufficient capacity available for production. In this case, capacity decisions should also be considered and should also be coordinated with production decisions and order material decisions. From the product perspective, capacity and capacity-use decisions are aggregate decisions; they generally do not constrain individual items or products but constrain groups of products, i.e. aggregates. Also, capacity and capacity-use decisions often have to be taken earlier in time than the decision about how much of a specific item or product to produce. Hierarchical production control concepts have been developed for the coordination of the aggregate level of decision making (capacity, capacity-use) and the detailed level of decision making (items, production orders). Most of these hierarchical planning systems have been developed for specific types of production environments (see e.g. the hierarchical planning system for a paint factory, developed by Hax and Golovin (1978), or the hierarchical planning system for a maintenance and repair shop developed by Schneeweiß and Schröder (1992)). For general principles, see Bitran and Hax (1977). In the next section we discuss the principles for designing hierarchical control systems that were developed by J.W.M. Bertrand, J.C. Wortmann and J. Wijngaard (Bertrand *et al.* 1990). These principles, further referred to as the BWW framework, are intended as guidance for identifying a proper hierarchical control structure in the function of the operational characteristics of the production system and the market it operates in.

PRINCIPLES FOR PRODUCTION CONTROL SYSTEM DESIGN

In this section, we present a condensed description of the BWW design framework for production control systems. The framework has been applied successfully to production control system design in many manufacturing environments. The design principles state that for a proper design the following issues should be dealt with:

- how to coordinate demand and supply
- where to position decoupling points in goods flow
- which variables to be controlled centrally (at the goods flow level) and which variables to be locally controlled (at the production unit level)
- which variables to be controlled as aggregates and which variables to be controlled in detail.

Coordination of demand and supply

Given the boundaries of the operational system considered, the demand for resources should be balanced with the supply of resources. Resources are used here in a broad sense and can include capacity, materials or services. Coordination of demand and supply takes place at two levels:

1   structural coordination: this refers to the setting of arrangements and condi-
    tions that allow for operational coordination, including the target service
    level, resource utilisation, batch sizes and lead-times;
2   operational coordination: this refers to the customer order acceptance and the
    ordering of materials, capacities and services, such that these are in balance
    with the orders accepted.

Structural coordination is part of the tactical level of decision making, and uses
models that relate the performance or service that can be obtained at the operational level to the resources that can be made available, and to the rules and
regulations regarding the resource-use, resulting in the positioning of decoupling
points in the flow of operations. In industry, regulations regarding resource-use
include batch size rules, overtime rules, outsourcing rules and safety stock rules.
In a hospital setting, resource-use regulations include length of operating theatre
sessions and rules regarding the sharing of expensive resources such as intensive
care beds and wards. The resources made available and the rules and regulations
regarding their use put restrictions on the performance that can be realised,
performance being defined as the amount of products that can be delivered and
the delivery reliability. In a hospital setting, the performance could be expressed
in the number of patients that can be treated, the flexibility and speed of access to
the hospital, and the speed of treatment and the delivery reliability of the treatment. It will be clear that the quality of the operational control will also have an
impact on the performance that is realised. However, operational control must
work within the constraints given by the available resources and the resource-use
rules. Therefore, at the tactical level, a trade-off must be made between the available resources and resource-use, on one hand, and the market performance, on
the other. As a result of this trade-off a set of constraints on future customer orders
is available, as expressed in a master production schedule. The specific amount of
resources available and these resource-use rules will impose constraints on the
performance that can be obtained by the operational control.

Goods flow control versus production unit control

Within the boundaries of the operational system, decoupling points can be distinguished in the flow of operations that are needed to satisfy demand. Decoupling
points can be introduced in the flow for the following reasons:

■   differences in batch sizes or combinations of work orders at different places
    in the flow;
■   differences in specificity of material or activities (common materials
    upstream, more specific material downstream);

- differences in capacity flexibility; a highly loaded or relatively inflexible resource often is preceded and followed by a decoupling point in order to protect the resource against variations in work supply;
- reduction of demand uncertainty or manufacturing uncertainty; decoupling points are introduced at points in the flow where a large change in uncertainty occurs.

Decoupling points lead to dynamic inventory levels or dynamic work order backlog levels. These levels are controlled at the goods flow (GF) level. Between adjacent decoupling points production phases exist and these are dealt with at the production unit (PU) level; this is local control that applies within the boundaries of the production unit, and that governs the progress of the production orders in the unit. Each production unit is characterised by its operational characteristics; these state the volume and timing of output that can be delivered by a PU, in relation to available resources and the load on the resources. Given the inventory and backlog levels in the decoupling points, work orders are released to the production units by goods flow control (see Figure 2.2). Goods flow control aims at realising the accepted customer orders taking into account the operational characteristics of the production units.

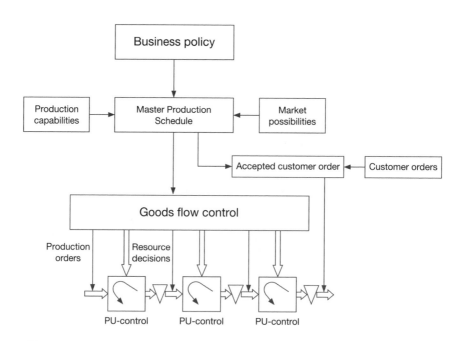

Figure 2.2 *Production control functions for production-to-stock.*

Aggregate versus detailed control

Aggregate control should be carefully distinguished from detailed control. Often materials and/or resources can be used for many different items or end-products. This provides much flexibility in customer order acceptance, since many different combinations of customer orders can be dealt with by the same set of resources. However, in order to be able to use this flexibility, two issues should be dealt with:

1   Aggregates of products (or product groups) should be related to common materials or resources and their time-phased availability. This identifies the production capacities that are available and informs the demand–supply match.
2   Given the market possibilities for aggregate products or product groups, sales plans should be brought into agreement with supply possibilities and vice versa.

Detailed control, i.e. control that couples individual customer orders or work order to resources, is necessary as soon as the order is generated at the goods flow level. In general, many different types of commonality exist in production systems and – more important – can be designed into a production system (e.g. the use of multi-functional work force and the principles of specificity postponement). Both at the goods flow level and the production unit level, aggregate and detailed control should be distinguished, although in general, aggregate control is more likely to be found at the goods flow level. Figure 2.2 illustrates the relationships between the production unit level, the goods flow level and the coordination of production and sales.

The BWW framework does not provide direct guidelines for design but identifies the issues to be dealt with when designing a production control system and in so doing generates the questions to be answered. From the description of the framework, it will be clear that its application assumes a well-defined production system, i.e. a homogeneous product range and a primary process that is geared to this product range. In other words, it assumes a 'focused factory'. If a company produces a variety of product ranges, a different control system should be designed for each range of products. Often this leads to splitting up the organisation into a number of business units, each dealing with one product range and having (in part) a dedicated production system (the business unit as a focused factory). The organisation as a whole, of course, facilitates the different business units, and the different business units have to follow the company policies. The BWW framework outlined above applies at the business unit level and has no direct implication for company control. For instance, the planning of product ranges and the financial and investment policies are outside the system boundaries of production control. However, product planning does have an impact on the production control problem and should therefore be an input to the design of production control systems, but only as a conditioning factor, not as a decision variable.

The principles of production control discussed in this section raises the question of the extent to which the 'focused factory' concept applies to hospitals. Can we distinguish, within a hospital setting, product ranges with reasonable homogeneity in terms of underlying production processes and market characteristics in order to approach them as a 'focused factory'? We will return to this in a later section, after we have described in more detail the characteristics of hospital care processes.

SIMILARITIES AND DIFFERENCES BETWEEN INDUSTRIAL OM AND HEALTH OM

In manufacturing industry, competition between companies was one of the driving forces for evolutions in operations management. Competition creates a high pressure on performance in terms of quality, efficiency and flexibility. Production control or logistics can be defined as the coordination of supply, production and distribution processes in manufacturing systems to achieve specific delivery flexibility and delivery reliability at minimum costs (Bertrand et al., 1990). Related objectives are to decrease the lead-times, delivery times and costs and to increase throughput, revenues and profit of the organisation. Logistics-oriented manufacturing has contributed in many circumstances to improvements in customer performance (delivery times, delivery reliability) as well as efficiency by the better balancing of delivery performances and efficiency.

Health care is confronted with similar challenges (see for instance Royston (1998) and Delesie (1998)), such as:

■ increased complexity of processes by shorter lengths of stay of patients, a shift from inpatient treatment towards ambulatory treatment and day care, use of new technology and increased specialisation;

■ need for efficient utilisation of resources and reduction of costs: first, because treatment is concentrated in a shorter time-space, and second, because of the political pressure to control national health care expenditure;

■ increased pressure to improve the quality of services by, among other things, decreasing waiting lists and in-process waiting times;

■ need to control the workload of nursing staff and other personnel in order to avoid adverse impacts on their working conditions.

However, a hospital is not a manufacturing organisation, but rather a special kind of service organisation. The major differences with a manufacturing environment are:

■ Production control approaches in manufacturing organisations are focused on material flows. The core process of health care organisations is concerned with the flows of patients who need treatment, while the flows of material are secondary.

- In health care there is much less price-performance interaction than is present in most production environments.
- Production control approaches presuppose complete and explicit specifications of end-products requirements and delivery requirements; in health care, product specifications are often subjective and vague.
- Health care organisations do not have a simple line of command, but are characterised by a delicate balance of power between different interest groups (management, medical specialists, nursing staff, paramedics), each of them having ideas about what should be targets for production performance.
- The key operators in the core process are highly trained professionals (medical specialists) who generate requests for service (orders) but are also involved in delivering the service.
- Care is not a commodity that can be stocked; the hospital is a resource-oriented service organisation.

Table 2.1 summarises these similarities and differences between manufacturing and health care organisations.

Taking these similarities and differences into account, we can define production control in health care organisations – analogous to the definition of production control in an industrial setting – as:

> the design, planning, implementation and control of coordination mechanisms between patient flows and diagnostic & therapeutic activities in health service organisations to maximise output/throughput with available resources, taking into account different requirements for delivery flexibility (elective/appointment, semi-urgent, urgent) and acceptable standards for delivery reliability (waiting list, waiting-times) and acceptable medical outcomes.
>
> (Vissers, 1994)

Table 2.1 *Similarities and differences between manufacturing and health care operations*

Characteristics	Manufacturing	Health care
Object	Material flow	Patient flow
Specification of end-product requirements	Up-front specified	Subjective and fuzzy
Means of production	Equipment and staff	Equipment and staff
Buffers	Stock or lead-times	Waiting times and lead-times
Financial goal	Profit	Cost control
Market environment	Market competition	Limited market competition

APPLICABILITY OF OPERATIONS MANAGEMENT PRINCIPLES TO HEALTH CARE PROCESSES

The focused factory concept

The focused factory concept entails the idea that an operational process should be designed to support optimally the production and delivery of a homogeneous group of products or services. Traditionally, hospitals are focused on the groups of specialties that are delivering their services to patients. This is not an approach based on the principle of homogeneity, because generally there is a large variety in resources needed for serving the patients of one specialty: simple (single resource) and complex (multiple resources), short and long stay, variation in the sequence of operations, etc. A difference in quality required is almost a non-issue in health care, because all patients expect to be treated with state-of-the-art quality. Differences in services required can be a useful difference, to be applied to differences in required delivery time. In emergency cases, access time should be zero; in other cases access could be postponed to some degree, and an access plan could be based on availability of resources.

However, hospitals more and more focus on patient groups that are homogeneous in term of resources needed. Thus far, this principle is applied to specific diagnostic groups that cover only a small part of the total of patient flow in a hospital. Furthermore, the principle is not applied to the whole service chain, from first visit to end of treatment, but only to a part of it. However, it can be possible to apply the principle of a focused factory for specific phases between decoupling points in the service of the patient flow (see 'Goods flow control versus production unit control' above). This needs some further explanation.

For many diagnosis groups, the process can be split into two main service phases: diagnosis and therapy. The diagnostic phase has different characteristics from the therapy phase: more uncertainty in demand, more variety in resources required, less predictability in the activities to be performed. For some patient flows the diagnostic process can be short and clear; for others, a step-by-step or sometimes iterative search process is needed.

For these reasons the principles of the focused factory tend to be more relevant to the treatment phase of patient care. The focused factory concept has shown to be successful for patient groups:

- with a predictable process, after the diagnosis, and after a treatment plan is set up
- with a low variety in the treatment processes
- with common requirements in quality and service
- that are homogeneous in resource requirements
- that do not require high flexibility.

An appealing example of a focused factory is the heart surgery clinic. This 'focused factory' is optimally designed for patients who are indicated for heart surgery. The clinic is not necessarily a separate institution or building but is generally located in a part of the hospital with its own staff and resources. The production process is highly standardised, the staff are highly skilled in their specialised work, with a high learning curve, and there are no losses due to change-over. Essential here is that the diagnostic process is decoupled from the surgery treatment process. The cardiologist is responsible for the diagnostic process, the cardio-surgeon for the surgical treatment process.

Another example is the 'cataract track', which is set up in an eye hospital, focused on the cataract patient group. This process is also characterised by high standardisation, low process variety and large volumes.

A focused factory with a more virtual character, not organised as a physical unit with its own staff and resources, is often set up for a group of cancer patients. From a medical perspective, this group is not very homogeneous and different specialties are involved. However, hospitals like to profile it as a 'cancer centre', implying that there are a lot of dedicated knowledge, expertise and resources available for this group of patients. Homogeneity can be found in the social and mental treatment that is required by this type of patient; special skills in this field are developed to meet the patient's requirements.

The conclusion is that the focused factory concept is at least partially applicable in hospitals:

- to a part of the total service chain, between well-defined decoupling points in the flow;
- to specific aspects, such as service, of the total set of requirements to be met.

The majority of processes in hospitals are not sufficiently transparent and defined in such a way that they can be analysed in terms of their homogeneity; so there is a lack of information for grouping patient flows from this point of view. However, for several reasons, such as quality assurance, efficiency, computerising and process monitoring, operational processes are being more and more explicitly defined. We expect that the principle of the focused factory will gain in applicability. Operations management will then be less complex, since the total patient flow, with a high degree of variation, will be split up into phases of care for homogeneous patient groups, resulting in reduced complexity and improved performance.

The just-in-time concept

The aim of just-in-time (JIT) production is to produce a variety of end-products with short lead-times without having to invest in stocks of end-products. The main principles are zero-defect production, set-up reduction, modular product design, process design and organisation of work (see the JIT subsection of 'OM principles and techniques' earlier in the chapter). At first sight, this approach seems to be far away from the hospital practice, because there is no equivalent for product design and stock of end-products. A hospital is a resource-oriented organisation without stocks, as all service organisations are. However, the term 'just-in-time' does appeal to the growing need to reduce and control waiting times and delivery times. And there is no doubt about the large variety in services to be produced due to a large variety in patients' demands. Meeting these demands requires both structural and operational flexibility (see 'Coordination of demand and supply' earlier in the chapter).

One way to use the JIT principle is by categorising patients according to their need for demand in terms of delivery time. Two examples will be described: care supplied by an emergency department and an outpatient clinic.

The illustration in the box describes the way the Emergency Department of the Manning Base Hospital (Australia) communicates its operations procedures to the public.

WELCOME TO THE EMERGENCY DEPARTMENT OF THE MANNING BASE HOSPITAL

The Emergency Department of the hospital is a busy area that deals with people who are suffering from a wide range of illnesses. We manage everything from children with measles to severe motor vehicle accidents. As you can imagine, every day people consult us in varying degrees of distress and with varying degrees of urgency.

OUR AIM

Our aim is to satisfy every customer's needs, either within the department, by admission and treatment as an inpatient, or by appropriate referral elsewhere outside the hospital. At times you may encounter a delay before your problem is dealt with. We endeavour to deal with everyone with a minimum of delay and overall to ensure that everyone receives the best management. This means that people with more life-threatening or painful conditions are seen before those with less urgent problems.

TRIAGE

To be fair, and to ensure that no one in real need is overlooked, we have introduced a 'triage' system. On your arrival you will be seen and assessed by a registered nurse who will prioritise your condition on a scale of 1 to 5. A >1 requires

---

immediate resuscitation, (such as an unconscious heart attack victim), A >2 is an emergency, such as someone severely short of breath, whom we aim to see within 10 minutes. Conditions assessed as >3, >4 or >5 are of decreasing urgency and are seen as appropriate once the higher grades are stabilised.

WE HAVE NOT FORGOTTEN YOU

You may, therefore, find yourself with a bit of wait. This is because the emergency staff are dealing with people who are suffering more than you. Please be patient if you have to wait; you have been seen by triage and we have not forgotten you.

YOUR LOCAL DOCTOR

The Emergency Department deals with people who often cannot be managed elsewhere and we try to be good at this. We are not as good at dealing with some types of problems, such as those involving repeat visits, general health screening, contraceptive issues and other conditions and problems far better dealt with by your own family doctor. Your doctor can provide a continuity of care that we often cannot. We will advise you on these occasions when your family doctor is a more appropriate person to consult.

http://www.midcoast.com.au/prof/medical/hosp/mbhem.html

Similarly, a system for determining access to care in an emergency department has been developed by the Manchester Triage Group (Mackway-Jones, 1996). They developed a triage standard, based upon a quick screening process, that resulted in five categories of patient with their own target times for clinical treatment. Introducing these triage standards in a Dutch hospital yielded the following results after a year of use:

- better quality, because high risk patients were selected immediately;
- reduced mean waiting time from 28 to 18 minutes;
- better informed patients who were more at ease;
- better control on services to be delivered.

In the Rotterdam Eye Hospital, referrals for the outpatient clinic are classified as A (urgent/immediate), B (semi-urgent, within three weeks) or C (no urgency, fitting remaining slots in the schedule). The underlying principles are based upon the planning principles for flight seats. The main difference is not that the price is a variable (the earlier the booking, the lower the price) but that the urgency of the patient is a variable. The release of available resources for scheduling consultations is phased over time; only 10 per cent of the slots are available for consultations over six months in advance of the date on which the appointment is booked. As time elapses more historical slots are released for scheduling patients, based upon knowledge about patterns of new arrivals. In this way, the balance between resource utilisation and service level is controlled in a dynamic way.

Production control concepts

Material Requirements Planning

The MRP-I mechanism as such is of little use for controlling hospital care processes; hospital care control is dominated by resource scarcity. However, the wider MRP-II conceptual control framework contains some elements that are also encountered in hospitals.

Two papers investigate the applicability of the MRP-II-concept to the hospital: Rhyne and Jupp (1988), and Roth and Van Dierdonck (1995). Both studies are based upon the assumptions that the diagnosis related groups (DRG) classification system can be used for product typing, and that it describes the full range of hospital products that can be delivered. We have concerns about these assumptions, but first both papers will be introduced.

The first paper introduces a health care requirements planning system (HCRPS), as an application of the MRP concept (Materials Requirements Planning) to health care, making use of the DRG classification system of products. By comparing some characteristics of demand and process between manufacturing and hospital operations, Rhyne and Jupp concluded that, although the nature of the two businesses is significantly different, many operational similarities can be detected. As MRP-I (Materials Requirements Planning) and its successor MRP-II (Manufacturing Resource Planning) were successful in manufacturing, they investigated the application of this approach to hospitals. Within the MRP concept, a bill of materials (BOM) lists all the components that go into the finished product. The DRG system can fulfil the function of the BOM in the HCRPS, as it describes the procedures, services and materials that go into a hospital product. The paper elaborates further on the components of the HCRPS, i.e. strategic planning, marketing planning, operations planning, master scheduling, capacity planning and material requirements planning.

The second paper (Roth and van Dierdonck, 1995) introduces a framework on hospital resource planning that is developed for managing hospitals but could be extended to care chains. It is a well-elaborated framework, building further on the work of Rhyne and Jupp (1988). The Hospital Resource Planning (HRP) model comprises a hospital-wide operations planning and control system. The DRGs are considered as end-item products with a bill of resources structure that simultaneously incorporates both capacity and material resources. This makes it possible to apply the concept of MRP to manage hospital activities. To apply this concept to hospitals the bill of materials (BOM) needs to be extended to a bill of resources to include equipment, supplies and especially labour. In addition, the BOM in manufacturing is unambiguously defined for each end-item, i.e. a deterministic BOM. In contrast, the variability within a DRG requires a stochastic bill of resources for health. Also, the application of the MRP concepts requires recognition that hospitals are essentially capacity oriented and not materials oriented. Therefore, the bill of resources (BOR) used for the Hospital Resource Planning model combines capacity and material resources at various treatment stages. In their elaboration of the MRP model they distinguish the following front-end components of the system: a master admissions schedule (anticipated admissions by DRG per day in a period), aggregate admissions planning, the demand management module and a rough-cut capacity planning module.

A point of criticism on both approaches is that DRGs may be an excellent tool to market and finance hospitals, but they are probably not a good basis for logistic control and for managing day-to-day hospital operations. DRGs might be useful as a decision support system at macro and institutional level but not at the operational level. In a study comparing different classification system, de Vries *et al.* (2000) came to the conclusion that for a patient classification system to be suitable for production control in hospitals the system needs to be focused on the homogeneity of the underlying process. The aspect of time has to be included (sequence and timing of operations) and in addition the different levels of decision making have to be taken into consideration, the operational as well as the tactical and the strategic level.

First of all, the iso-resource grouping of DRGs does not necessarily lead to the iso-process grouping that we need for managing patient groups as focused factories. This can be illustrated by an analysis of patient characteristics in a database of 3,603 patients with peripheral arterial vascular (PAV) diseases (Mǎruşter *et al.*, 2002). Using logistic variables (such as the number of specialists involved in care and the number of shifts per month), clustering techniques were used to group the medical cases in logistically homogeneous groups. One of the results was that PAV patients could be subdivided into two clear-cut clusters, namely 'complex' and 'moderately complex' patients. In other words, it was not the single DRG but a combination (inclusion or exclusion) of diagnoses for an individual patient that gave predictive validity for clustering. Second, the uncertainty that is inherent to processes in the short term will not allow these processes to be organised on the basis of DRGs: within a specific DRG, demand of care and length of stay may vary considerably between patients. Third, the aspect of time (sequence and timing of operations) is lacking in the DRG product characteristics (though in their planning model, Roth and Van Dierdonck include various treatment stages).

33

In industry, MRP-II was succeeded by ERP (Enterprise Resource Planning). ERP systems plan demand and capacity on an aggregate level for the long term. To plan for the short term the aggregated estimates are disaggregates to individual products and capacities. Van Merode *et al.* (2004) review the potential of ERP systems for health care delivery organisations. They mention some problems due to assumptions and requirements underlying ERP that do not fit or only for a small part with characteristics of patient care processes, such as:

- the requirement for processes to be described very precisely;
- the requirement that not only organisational data but also knowledge is stored in a structural way;
- the assumption that supply lead-times are known and do not vary with demand and flow;
- the requirement of fixed processes or routings, ignoring the possibility of alternative processes;
- the assumptions of deterministic processes, with parameters equal to the average of the corresponding distributions.

Van Merode *et al.* conclude that hospitals cannot use an ERP concept for the whole organisation. Many patient processes in hospitals differ substantially in their degree of variability and stochasticity. In their opinion, the use of ERP systems makes only sense for deterministic processes. Theoretically we agree with this, but we question the assumption that deterministic processes, strictly speaking, exist in a hospital. Deterministic or stochastic is a too simple dichotomy. Processes vary in their degree of predictability, and predictability is one of the aspects of the homogeneity we mentioned before. Homogeneity of a patient group is the basis for the application of the focused factory principle.

A logistic approach to production management of hospital processes has to be based on knowledge of the characteristics of hospital care processes and their interaction with resources. Some resources are scarce, and the allocation of resources to processes is a dominant aspect of health care. The following requirements for coordination of capacity allocations can be mentioned (De Vries *et al.*, 1999):

- coordination of the allocation of 'leading' resources to specialties sharing the same resource: capacity load levelling per 'leading' resource;
- coordination of the resource impacts for 'following' resource departments that are shared by specialties but often not allocated to specialties (e.g. X-ray);
- coordination of the allocation of different resources to one specialty: capacity load levelling per specialty;
- coordination of specialist capacity within a specialty: specialty-planning restrictions.

In chapter 4, these principles will be elaborated further.

Optimized Production Technology®

The essential assumption underlying the OPT® mechanism is that there exists a stable bottleneck resource in the production system. By definition, this is also the case for production processes in hospitals. Applying this principle is very useful in tracing the bottleneck. Given the great variation in patient flows, there is often more than one potential bottleneck for the hospital as a whole. An analysis of patient flows gives insight into the bottleneck for each of these flows; one of the production units that serves a patient in his flow is the bottleneck in this flow (unless all required resources are perfectly balanced). The relevance of tracing the bottleneck is obvious:

- to optimise the use of this resource
- to enlarge this specific resource
- to reduce the throughput time.

Symptoms of bottlenecks are a high workload level in the bottleneck unit (and, reversibly, a low workload level in other units), a backlog in order processing and the queuing up of patients (the analogue of work-in-process in manufacturing industry). For surgical patient flows, the operating phase is often the bottleneck. Further investigation is then needed to point out which kind of resource within this phase is the ultimate bottleneck on the critical path. If it is staff capacity, it must be specified to nursing staff, anaesthetic staff or surgical staff. However, for other surgical patients the intensive care unit, as the next unit in the flow of care, can turn out to be the bottleneck. Because it is not acceptable, from a medical point of view, to stock patients before they are admitted to the intensive care (IC) unit, their surgical operation will be postponed until a bed is available at the intensive care unit. This may result in a (too) low utilisation rate for the operating theatre (OT).

The existence of shared resources is a typical characteristic of hospital organisations and hospital processes. It is inevitable because of the required technical infrastructure and highly specialised staff. Principles to manage the shared resources are allocation and time sharing. An allocated part of a shared resource can be part of the 'focused factory' resource structure for a specific diagnoses group. An example of a heart surgery patients group can be mentioned here, especially those undergoing elective by-pass operations. In a 700-bed hospital, a yearly production of 1,200 by-pass operations had to be realised. The main resources for this patient group were operating theatres, the intensive care unit and the nursing unit. A special part of the OT complex was dedicated to cardiothoracic surgery. The intensive care unit, however, was a general intensive care unit for all kind of patients from different specialties, post-operative as well as others. To realise a continuous production flow it was important that operating capacity and intensive care capacity were in perfect balance. Most admitted patients had a 24-hour stay in the intensive care unit and were then transferred to a step-down facility (medium care or nursing unit). However, for a small group of patients this was not possible because of complications. If these patients 'blocked' the bed capacity of the IC unit, heart operations could not be executed at the OT, resulting in under-utilisation, underproduction and growing waiting lists. As a solution to this problem, the IC unit was split up into two parts. One part of the IC unit was dedicated exclusively to the 24-hour post-operative care of heart surgery patients; patients who still needed intensive care after 24 hours were transferred to the other, 'general', part of the IC unit. For that general part, the principle of slack resource was introduced, including the overflow of the 24-hour stay. In this way the elective flow could be continued by eliminating the bottleneck problem. This measure also illustrates the principle of decoupling patient flows that differ in variability and predictability.

Hierarchical production control

Hierarchical production control concepts are certainly applicable to hospital care. However, the various decision functions to be distinguished in the hierarchy, and their relationships, should be based on the typical characteristics of the demand and the process resources in health care. Guidelines for the design of hierarchical control systems have been given in the section 'Principles for production control system design'. In chapter 6 of this book we will use these principles for the development of a hierarchical framework for health care production control.

SUMMARY

In this chapter we have presented a number of concepts, methods and techniques for production control that have evolved over the last 50 years in manufacturing industry. We have discussed the focused factory concept, just-in-time, the production control concepts MRP and OPT®, hierarchical production control and design principles for production control systems. We have identified similarities and differences between industrial manufacturing processes and hospital health care processes and discussed the applicability of the concepts, methods and techniques to hospital health care. We have shown that, at the conceptual level, much can be learned from industrial production control. However, methods and techniques are mostly not directly applicable due to the very specific characteristics of certain hospital health care processes. These include the high variability and high uncertainty in the processing steps required, the use of a specialist resource in many processing steps, and the different levels of urgency in providing health care.

QUESTIONS AND EXERCISES

1   Discuss the possible role of the MRP-I mechanism for controlling hospital health care processes.
2   Discuss the role of the medical specialist in different operational processes.
3   Give examples of the focused factory concept, different from the ones mentioned in this chapter.

REFERENCES AND FURTHER READING

Argote L., S.L. Beckmann and D. Epple. The persistence and transfer of learning in industrial settings. *Management Science*, 36(2), 1990, 140–154.

Bailey C.D. Forgetting and the learning curve: a laboratory study. *Management Science*, 35, 1989, 340–352.

Bertrand J.W.M., J.C. Wortmann and J. Wijngaard. *Production Control. A Structural and Design Oriented Approach.* Elsevier, Amsterdam, 1990.

Bitran G.R. and A.C.Hax. On the design of hierarchical production planning systems. *Decision Sciences*, 8, 1977, 28–35.

Delesie L. Bridging the gap between clinicians and health managers. *European Journal of Operational Research,* 105, 1998, 248–256.

Globerson S., N. Levin and A. Shtub. The impact of breaks on forgetting when performing a repetitive task. *I.I.E Transactions*, 21, 1989, 376–381.

Goldratt E.M. Computerized Shop Floor Scheduling. *International Journal of Production Research*, 26 (3), 1988, 443–450.

Hax A.C. and J.J. Golovin. Hierarchical Production Planning Systems. In A.C. Hax (ed.) *Studies in Operations Management.* Elsevier, Amsterdam, 1978, 429–461.

Kelsey S.F., S.M. Mullin, K.M. Detre, H. Mitchel, M.J. Cowley, A.R. Gruentzig and K.M. Kent. Effect of investigator experience on percutaneous transluminal coronary angioplasty. *Amer. J. Cardiology*, 53, 1984, 56c–64c.

Mackway-Jones K. (ed.) *Emergency triage.* Manchester Triage Group, Manchester, 1996.

Mărușter Laura, Ton Weijters, Geerhard de Vries, Antal van den Bosch and Walter Daelemans. Logistic-based patient grouping for multi-disciplinary treatment. *Artificial Intelligence in Medicine* 26, 2002, 87–107.

Merode G.G. van, S. Groothuis and A. Hasman. Enterprise resource planning for hospitals. *International Journal of Medical Informatics*, 73, 2004, 493–501.

Monden Y. *Toyota Production System.* Industrial Engineering Press, Atlanta, GA, 1993.

Orlicky J.A. *Material Requirements Planning.* McGraw-Hill, New York, 1975.

Rhyne D.M. and D. Jupp. Health care requirements planning: a conceptual framework. *Health Care Management Review*, 13 (1), 1988, 17–27.

Roth A. and R. Van Dierdonck. Hospital resource planning: concepts, feasibility, and framework. *Production and Operations Management*, 4 (1), 1995, 2–29.

Royston G. Shifting the balance of care into the 21st century. *European Journal of Operational Research*, 105, 1998, 267–276.

Schneeweiß Ch. and H. Schröder. Planning and scheduling the repair shop of the Deutsche Lufthansa AG: a hierarchical approach. *Production and Operation Management*, 1(1), 1992, 22–23.

Schönberger R.J. Just-in-time production systems: replacing complexity with simplicity in manufacturing. *Management of Industrial Engineering*, 16 (10), 1984, 52–63.

Shingo S. *A Revolution in Manufacturing: The SMED-System*. Productivity Press, Cambridge, MA, 1985.

Shtub A., N. Levin and S. Globerson. Production breaks and the learning curve: the forgetting phenomenon. *International Journal of Human Factors*, 3, 1996, 293–305.

Skinner W. *Manufacturing: The Formidable Competitive Weapon*. Wiley & Sons, New York, 1995.

Stalk G. and T.M. Hout. *Competing Against Time*. The Free Press, New York, 1990.

Vissers J.M.H. *Patient Flow based Allocation of Hospital Resources*. Doctoral thesis, University of Technology, Eindhoven, 1994.

Vries G. de, J.W.M. Bertrand and J.M.H. Vissers. Design requirements for health care production control systems. *Production Planning and Control*, 10(6), 1999, 559–569.

Vries G.G. de, J.M.H. Vissers and G. de Vries. The use of patient classification systems for production control of hospitals. *Casemix*, 2(2), 2000, 65–70.

Yelle L.E. The learning curve: historical review and comprehensive survey. *Decision Sciences*, 10, 1977, 302–328.

Chapter 3

Health operations management
Basic concepts and approaches
Jan Vissers and Roger Beech

INTRODUCTION: PRODUCTS/SERVICES AND CLIENTS

In chapter 1, health OM was defined as 'the analysis, design, planning and control of all of the steps necessary to provide a service for a client'. Hence, health OM transforming processes are driven by a desire to produce a service or product for a client. For many health OM processes the most important client is the patient and the product produced might be their diagnosis and/or treatment.

As a minimum, such products are usually defined according to the specialty classification of patients: for example, orthopaedic patients. However, products might be further subdivided according to the diagnostic grouping of patients (for example, patients with diabetes), their ages (for example, services for older people), or according to the type of health care procedure that they require (for example, patients requiring hernia surgery). Methods of grouping patients have also been based upon their likely consumption of health care resources (diagnosis related groups and health resources groups) or their expected benefit from treatment (health benefit groups).

In practice, the most appropriate way of classifying patients or patient products will depend upon the purpose for which such information is required (Ploman, 1985). Within this and subsequent chapters discussion will focus on groupings that facilitate the design, planning and control of health OM processes. As will be seen, no single patient or product classification system is sufficient.

In addition to patients, the clients of most health OM processes are health and/or social care professionals. For example, a client of an X-ray department is a doctor and the product provided is information (in the form of a diagnostic image and a report) to inform the doctor on the diagnosis or effect of treatment in the ongoing process of treating a patient. Similarly, the client of a finance department might be a ward manager and the product provided is budgetary information to help plan ward staffing levels. Finally, the clients of a wages department are health care staff and the product provided is the timely and accurate payment of salaries.

Hence, within the health and social care environment there are a variety of clients, transforming processes and products. The remainder of this chapter discusses key stages in analysing, designing, planning and controlling health OM processes. Illustrations tend to focus on processes to support patient care. However, the principles outlined can be applied to other health OM processes.

OPERATIONS

Operations are at the heart of an organisation. Organisations exist to create value and operations involve activities to create value. An operation can be defined as an activity that transforms inputs into outputs, and thereby adding value.

Consider a patient requiring a hip replacement. Key operations involved in delivering this service for the patient include: X-ray procedures to diagnose the problem; surgical procedures to replace the hip; and physiotherapy sessions to facilitate the rehabilitation of the patient. Each of these operations adds value and each generates an individual product. However, the cumulative effect of these individual products is a patient 'successfully' treated with a hip replacement. Hence, the first stage in 'the analysis, design, planning and control of all of the steps necessary to provide a service for a client' is to identify the key operations that are required to deliver that service.

Note that an operation can also imply a group of activities that constitute together the operation. A surgical procedure, for instance, consists of activities by the surgeon, the anaesthetist and the supporting personnel. An activity in itself, again, involves different tasks. For instance, the 'surgical procedure' activity implies for the surgeon the following tasks: preparing for the procedure, starting the procedure, performing the procedure, ending the procedure and cleaning. From this example we can see that tasks constitute an activity, and activities constitute an operation. We regard the surgical procedure as an operation, because at this level of activity the added value (patient after surgical procedure) becomes obvious. Note also that there is little or no freedom in the relative timing of tasks or activities, as they all contribute to the operation. Operations are, therefore, the basic elements in a logistic approach.

Operations can be grouped into operation types. An operation type is a group of operations using the same resources, though the amount of resources used may differ. A resource is an input for an operation that is used for the transformation into outputs, but can be used again for another operation – as opposed to material inputs that become part of the output. So, operating theatres, operating theatre personnel and operating theatre equipment are resources, but the prosthesis that is placed in a patient during an orthopaedic surgical procedure is a material input for the process that becomes part of the product.

A unit is a department in a health system that performs operations of the same operation type: for example, imaging departments undertake X-ray procedures. A unit also has access to the key resources (staff, capital equipment, and materials) required to undertake operations of the same type.

For example, an imaging department contains the specialist staff and equipment required (resources) to carry out X-ray procedures, but the films are materials that become part of the output of the process (patient with diagnostic information). Table 3.1 gives an example overview of units, resources and operation types in a hospital setting.

In the general OM literature, operations are classified under the following types: alteration, transportation, storage and inspection. In health OM we tend to include alteration (e.g. a surgical procedure in an operating theatre), transportation (e.g. the transport of the patient from the ward and vice versa) and inspection (e.g. inspection of the wound) in one operation (e.g. the surgical procedure). Storage of intermediate products in OM compares to waiting for operations in health OM. Not all waiting in health care systems is unproductive. Waiting for a drug to become effective or for recovery in a ward after an operation are examples of productive waits. This is also the reason to include them in the operation definition. The non-productive waits are important indicators for the malfunctioning of the system.

Table 3.1 *Units, resources and operation types in a hospital setting*

Unit	Resources	Operation types
Emergency Department	Treatment rooms, nursing staff, physicians.	First aid (small injuries). Acute admissions. Trauma.
Outpatient Department	Diagnostic and treatment rooms, administrative and nursing staff, physicians.	First and follow-up visits. Small treatments.
Diagnostic and Therapy Departments (e.g. Radiology, Pathology, Physiotherapy)	Diagnostic and therapy rooms, equipment, paramedical staff, physicians.	Diagnostic tests. Therapies.
Operating Theatres Department	Operating rooms, assisting operating personnel, physicians.	Surgical procedures.
Intensive Care	Beds, equipment, nursing staff, physicians.	Monitoring. Acute interventions.
Wards	Beds, nursing staff, physicians.	Recovery. Cure and care. Monitoring.

RESOURCES

If the identification of key operations represents the first stage in 'the analysis, design, planning and control of all of the steps necessary to provide a service for a client', the second stage is to understand the ways in which operations use and consume resources. Operations can be characterised by duration (i.e. time to undertake the operation) and by the workload placed on the resources that are required for the operation (e.g. number and types of staff required for the operation). A basic philosophy of OM is that these duration and workload characteristics of operations (and of processes as the constellation of operations to produce a service) determine the way operations (and processes) can be planned and controlled.

Figure 3.1 shows a distribution of the length of stay for admissions to general surgery. Such data inform decisions about the amount of beds (resources) that are required while patients receive those operations delivered to provide care on wards. As can be seen, the distribution of the length of stay has a peak in the beginning and a long tail to the right. The average length of stay is 5.4 days, while the standard deviation is very large (70 days) due to the long tail. This is typical for many service distributions in health care. The Erlang or Gamma distribution (a skew distribution characterised by an early peak and a long tail to the right) is often used to arrive at a good fit with this type of distributions.

It is important that an OM practitioner questions the data and asks him/herself whether the data shown can be used for taking decisions. For instance:

- Is the aggregation level correct (all surgical patients) or should the analysis apply to different patient groups within general surgery?

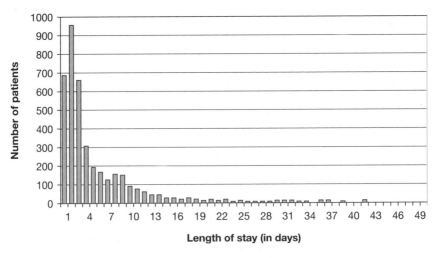

Figure 3.1 Distribution of length of stay for general surgery (n = 3,960 patients).

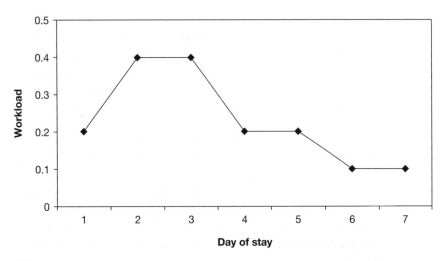

Figure 3.2 *Workload of general surgery admission for nursing staff (expressed in the number of FTE nurses needed to perform the nursing requirements on that day).*

■ Does the small hub around 8/9 days indicate that at least one group needs to be taken apart, for instance oncology patients, having an average longer length of stay?

■ Are the patients with a very long length of stay to be accepted as statistical variation or are there explanations of another kind (e.g. patients are waiting for an empty bed in a nursing home)?

The first two concerns are relevant to the earlier discussion of product definitions. Here, any decision to re-classify products would be driven by a need to identify a level of aggregation that usefully supports the health OM task.

Figure 3.2 shows the average daily demands for nursing care by general surgery patients, expressed as full time equivalent (FTE) nursing inputs per day. In this illustration, the average length of stay of general surgery patients is seven days and they have a surgical procedure on their second day. As can be seen the nursing workload is less on the day of admission, rises on the day of the surgical procedure and the day after, returns at the starting level in the following days and is low at the days before the discharge. The operations manager therefore needs to be aware of such fluctuation in demand when scheduling nursing resources to support ward-based operations.

PROCESS OR CHAIN

As indicated earlier, operations represent the building blocks that, when added together, generate the overall set of transforming processes required to deliver a product for a client. Having identified these individual building blocks, and the resources that they use, an operations manager needs to identify the ways in which they should be linked to produce a particular service. This chain of operations (or overall delivery process) may include both productive activities and productive periods of waiting (e.g. waiting for a drug to become effective). A process or chain can therefore be defined as the chain of operations that need to be performed to produce a particular service.

Often the label 'process' is used to identify the delivery of a service that is delivered by a single provider, and the label 'chain' or 'supply chain' is used for the process of a service that is produced in collaboration between different providers. Note that health care does not yet have an established term to parallel supply chain (care chain, perhaps?). Supply chain refers to the flow of goods while in health care we would like to refer to the flow of patients. Complex processes in hospitals that include many departments in the patient journey could also be labelled as a care chain.

Each process has a customer, whether it is an internal customer for a process that focuses on a part of a chain (for instance a specialist who orders a test from pathology) or an ultimate consumer of the service, i.e. a patient. Each process should also have a process owner, who is responsible for managing the process. This is, of course, a weak point in many health care organisations, as processes are not well managed because of lack of process ownership.

An analysis of existing chains may also reveal non-productive operations and periods of waiting. A knowledge of these non-productive operations helps to expose areas where the performance of health processes might be improved.

In addition to having awareness about the 'links' in the chain of operations that generate health care processes, an OM approach also requires reflection on other key characteristics of processes. This additional understanding helps the OM manager to establish appropriate control systems and it informs decisions about the allocation of resources.

Table 3.2 presents an overview of the most important characteristics of processes from an OM point of view. These characteristics are illustrated by considering those processes required to deliver services for different patient groups within the specialty of general surgery.

An important distinction in health care processes is whether or not access to resources can be scheduled. Emergency processes, such as many aspects of care for trauma patients, cannot be scheduled, so the resources to undertake operations need to be readily available. This reduces flexibility in resource allocation decisions and potentially means that 'spare' capacity might need to be available. For elective patients, access to resources can be scheduled (and delayed) in an attempt to maximise efficiency.

Regardless of whether or not the chain of operations is classified as emergency or elective, judgements are required along the chain about the level of

Table 3.2 *Characteristics of processes, illustrated for key patient groups within general surgery*

Characteristic of process/Chain	Trauma patients	Oncology patients	Veins and arterial patients	Remaining patients
Emergency or elective	emergency	elective	elective	elective
Low, medium or high urgency	high	high	medium	low
Short, long or chronic	short	chronic	long	various
Complexity				
Diagnostics	X			X
Consultation		X	X	
Multi-specialty		X		
Cyclic				
Predictability				
Number of operations	X			X
Durations			X	
Routing	X			
Other aspects to take into account				
Volume	high	medium	high	medium
Decoupling point		diagnosis	diagnosis	diagnosis
Shared resources	X-ray OT ward	X-ray OT ward	X-ray OT ward	X-ray OT ward
Bottleneck resource	OT	OT	OT	OT

Note: X means that the characteristic is relevant

urgency attached to its operations. The urgency of individual operations affects prioritisation decisions, i.e. resource allocation decisions within units, when different patient groups compete for the same type of resources. For example, in comparison to 'veins and arterial' elective admissions, trauma patients will have a higher priority in terms of access to hospital beds and operating theatres. However, the urgency attached to operations can change, and initiatives such as 'booked' admission systems and 'minimum' waiting time standards might increase the priority attached to elective patients.

The length of a process, in terms of the number of operations that constitute the chain, is another important characteristic. A short process, for instance a diagnostic consultation following a request by a general practitioner (GP), offers different challenges when scheduling the allocation of resources compared with a long process, involving many operations, or a chronic process, which may not have a clearly defined ending.

The complexity of a process also influences the ease with which it can be designed and planned. A process can be complex due to: the number of diagnostic and therapeutic procedures required for patient care; the necessity to consult another specialist for further treatment; the involvement of another specialty in the treatment; or the cyclic character of parts of the process. An example of the last reason is the annual check of a diabetic patient who is under the care of an internal medicine consultant but who needs to see an ophthalmologist.

Similarly, the design and planning of a process is influenced by its predictability. We distinguish this further into predictability of the number of operations in the chain, predictability of the durations of the operations and predictability of the routing of patients through the chain of operations. When there is much variation in these characteristics and therefore less predictability, planning these operations requires more flexibility than in the case of small variations. Predictability is one of the most important characteristics to take into account when designing a process.

The volume of patient flow is not as such a characteristic of a process, but it is another important aspect to take into account. Higher volume means that potentially more data are available to investigate the characteristics of the process in terms of, for example, its complexity and predictability. The volume of patient flow also supports decisions about whether or not it makes sense to develop a dedicated service for a patient group. A short process, combined with high predictability on all aspects and a high volume, is an indicator for a dedicated organisation (for instance a 'cataract track').

Processes might also include decoupling points. This is a point in the process where operations before and after are decoupled by a 'waiting list' or a 'productive period of waiting'. 'Waiting list' decoupling points are often used before a bottleneck resource to ensure a maximum use of this resource: for example, waiting for a general surgical outpatient appointment to ensure that the time of the consultant is fully utilised. A 'productive period of waiting' might be a point in the process where there is a large change in the predictability of operations. For instance, until a diagnosis is reached the nature of subsequent operations in the chain might be unpredictable. Once a diagnosis is achieved the treatment path might become predictable.

The last aspect mentioned refers to the use of shared resources (resources that are shared by different patient groups or different specialties) in the process considered, or the use of a bottleneck resource. In the general surgical illustration, all patient groups share X-ray, ward, and operating theatre resources. A process that uses many shared resources, including a bottleneck resource, is more difficult to organise than a process with no shared resources. This is because patient groups must compete for resources.

LOGISTIC APPROACHES

This chapter has introduced the health OM terms 'products', 'operations', 'units', 'resources' and 'processes/chains'. Units carry out the same types of operation for different types of product whereas processes/chains represent a series of different operations (undertaken in different units) for the same type of product. Resources are used both within units and along chains, but the requirements and incentives in term of the planning and control of these resources differs according to whether a unit or chain perspective is adopted. This final section illustrates the key differences between unit and chain logistics approaches when planning and managing resources. Unit logistics concentrates on the logistics of a single unit. Chain logistics considers the logistics of a single chain. Network logistics combines both perspectives. Each of these logistical areas and approaches is discussed further in chapters 4–6.

Figure 3.3 illustrates these different logistical perspectives for a hospital setting. It describes a hospital as a representation of units and chains. As can be seen from the example, general surgery has its own outpatient department (OPD) that is not shared with, for instance, general medicine. Diagnostic departments, such as radiology and pathology, are shared by all patient groups and specialties. Wards are

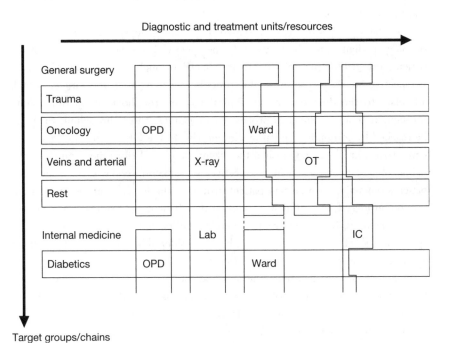

Figure 3.3 *Unit, chain and network perspectives.*

shared by the different patient groups within a specialty, with sharing of beds between specialties limited to overflow. In addition, not all patient groups use the ward at a similar level. All surgical patient groups share the OT department, though some groups are treated without an intervention. The IC unit is again shared by all specialties, though the use of the IC unit differs much between patient groups.

The unit perspective is represented by the units 'OPD', 'X-ray/lab', 'ward', 'OT' and 'IC'. Managers of these units are responsible for the running of the unit, for the level of service the unit offers to physicians requiring a service on behalf of their patients, and for the efficient use of the resources available. This is regarded as a total responsibility. The unit's concern is the total flow of all patients requiring a service of the unit, as this determines the prime objective of the unit, i.e. reaching a high but balanced use of resources without peaks and troughs in the workload during the hours of the day and days of the week. High occupancy level or use is seen as an important indicator of the 'efficiency' of the unit while balanced use is important not only for efficiency but also for the working climate of the personnel in the unit. Additional aims from the perspective of the unit are to produce the amount of output required with as few resources as possible or to produce as much output as possible with the amount of resources available (capacity management). The focus of unit logistics is therefore on the total flow of the patients using the unit, and on the effect of this flow on the use of resources and the workload of personnel.

The chain perspective is represented by patient groups, i.e. trauma patients, oncology patients, etc. The focus of this perspective is on the total process of the patient, using different units on their journey through the hospital. The chain perspective strives to optimise this process according to some targets, which all relate to the time dimension. Typical targets are: short access time, short throughput time and short in-process waiting times. Short throughput time can be reached by combining operations in one visit to the OPD, instead of having to come twice, or by having finished the diagnostic phase before the admission. The prime objective of the chain perspective is to maximise the service level for patients belonging to a certain patient group. As the focus is on the one patient group considered, it is difficult to look at the efficiency of the chain in terms of use of resources. Resources are, in general, not allocated to patient groups, but to specialties, so efficiency issues can only be considered at the level of flows from all patient groups belonging to the specialty.

Network logistics combines the unit and the chain perspectives. It draws on the notion that optimisation of the service in the chains needs to be balanced with efficiency in the use of resources in the units. A network logistics approach will make explicit any trade-off to be made between the service level provided in the chains and the utilisation of resources in the units: for example, a desire to improve patient access to diagnostic services by making these services available for

24 hours per day might have a negative impact on the performance of diagnostic departments.

For a network logistics approach, ideally all chains and all units, i.e. the whole hospital, need to be included. However, this might be regarded as too complex, especially for a change to improve the performance of the process for a single patient group. There might be a desire to address such a change via a chain logistics approach. However, one should also strive for a network logistics approach by, for example, including all patient groups of the relevant specialty in the analysis. This would make it possible to look at the impact of the change on the use of resources available for both the specialty as a whole and for the other patient groups within it.

Consider a change that aims to improve patient access to physiotherapy by stroke patients. If there is a limited supply of physiotherapy services, improvements in the process of care for stroke patients might result in a reduced level of service for other patient groups both within neurology (the specialty that treats stroke patients) and within other specialties containing patient groups that require physiotherapy. These adverse consequences would go unnoticed if only a chain logistics approach is adopted. A network logistics approach therefore helps to avoid a situation where an improvement in one process goes unnoticed at the expense of a drawback for other processes.

The OM approach implies making explicit the choices to be made in a systems perspective. This serves also as a warrant for sub-optimisation, i.e. an improvement in one part of the system goes at the expense of the functioning of the system as a whole.

Table 3.3 summarises the main differences between the unit, chain and network logistics approach.

Table 3.3 Differences between the unit, chain and network logistics approaches

Perspective Item	Unit logistics approach	Chain logistics approach	Network logistics approach
Focus points	Resource utilisation; workload control	Service level	Trade off between service level and resource utilisation
Strong point	Capacity management	Process management	Combination
Weak point	Not process oriented	Not related to the use of resources	More effort
Suitable for	Efficiency analysis of OTs, OPDs, etc.	(Re)design of a process	Redesign and efficiency

QUESTIONS AND EXERCISES

1   Describe the practice of a general practitioner in terms of units, resources and operations.
2   How can you improve the quality of the presentation of the distribution of the length of stay in Figure 3.1?
3   Who is the owner of a process for a patient group in a hospital setting? Who should be the best choice for being the owner of the process and why?
4   In what way does working with service contracts make a difference for unit logistics?
5   Orthopaedics wants to redesign the process for patients who come for hip replacement. What approach would you suggest? What are the pros and cons of your approach?
6   There are complaints by surgeons on the long change-over times between different operations in the OT. What approach would you suggest? What are the pros and cons of your approach?

REFERENCES AND FURTHER READING

Lillrank P. and M. Liukko Standard, routine and non-routine processes in health care. *International Journal of Quality Assurance,* 17(1), 2004, 39–46.

Meredith J.R. and S.M. Shafer. *Operations Management for MBAs.* New York and elsewhere: John Wiley & Sons, Inc. Second edition, 2002.

NHS Modernisation Agency. *Improvement Leaders' Guides* (series 1, guide 1). Process mapping, analysis and redesign, 2002. Ipswich: Ancient House Printing Group.

NHS Modernisation Agency. *Improvement Leaders' Guides* (series 1, guide 2). Matching capacity and demand, 2002. Ipswich: Ancient House Printing Group.

NHS Modernisation Agency. *Improvement Leaders' Guides* (series 1, guide 3). Measurement for improvement, 2002. Ipswich: Ancient House Printing Group.

Ploman M.P. Choosing a patient classification system to describe the hospital product. *Hospital and Health Services Administration,* 30, 1985, 106–117.

Plsek P.E. Systematic design of health care processes. *Quality in Health Care,* 6, 1997, 40–48.

Vissers J.M.H. Health care management modeling: a process perspective. *Health Care Management Science* 1(2), 1998, 77–85.

Chapter 4

Unit logistics

Allocation and utilisation of resources

Jan Vissers

INTRODUCTION

Chapter 3 introduced the health OM terms 'products', 'operations', 'resources', 'units', 'processes' and 'chains'. Units carry out the same types of operation for different types of product whereas processes and chains represent a series of different operations (undertaken in different units) for the same type of product. Resources are used both within units and along chains, but the requirements and incentives in terms of the planning and control of these resources differ according to whether a unit or chain perspective is adopted.

This chapter focuses on the unit perspective and discusses key issues surrounding the allocation and control of resources within units. The unit's concern is the total flow of all patients or clients requiring a service of the unit. High occupancy level or use is seen as an important indicator of the 'efficiency' of the unit while balanced use is important not only for efficiency but also for the working climate of the personnel in the unit. Additional aims from the perspective of the unit are to produce the amount of output required with as less resources as possible or to produce as much output as possible with the amount of resources available.

The following section of this chapter identifies important issues to consider when analysing and planning the allocation of resources, the initial stages of the health OM function. Issues to consider when monitoring the impacts of different allocation decisions on resource performance are discussed in the subsequent section. The remaining sections of the chapter illustrate the points raised with reference to specific departments, types of resources and areas of resource control.

RESOURCE TYPES AND CHARACTERISTICS

Resources can be defined as objects that are used in the production process, but not transformed or consumed by production (such as materials). Examples of resources are personnel, buildings, materials and equipment. A resource has a capacity, which refers to the ability of a resource to generate production, measured in the amount of products per unit of time. A second interpretation of capacity is the amount of resource that is allocated for production. Listed below are different ways of classifying resources. They represent key issues to consider when allocating resources for production. Key goals are to achieve high occupancy and high productivity in terms of the use of resources. The analysis of the use of resources is discussed in the following section.

Dedicated and shared resources

Within units most resources are shared, being used by different product lines. For example, X-ray machines will be used by a number of patient groups. However, some resources might be dedicated and be only for use by a single patient group or specialty. An example is a diabetics nurse who is allocated to general medicine as a specialty (or unit) but who focuses on the care of diabetic patients only.

The decision to consider a resource as shared at hospital level is part of the hospital strategic policy making. Reasons for sharing resources can be costs, quality and the control of resource use. The sharing of resources will facilitate the goals of high occupancy and productivity. Sharing of resources might also be seen as a means of improving the quality of health care processes. For example, access to a range of patient groups and needs might help to improve the skills of ward nurses.

Regarding shared resources, we make a further distinction between time-shared resources and other shared resources. Time-shared resources are resources that are allocated to a user, i.e. a specialist, for specified periods, i.e. time-phased allocation. Operating theatres and outpatient facilities are examples of time-shared resources. A patient group or specialty can indicate preferred periods for time-shared resources, but its final allocation depends on the total of allocations to be made to all specialties. Specialist capacity is the main resource in these allocations and its availability needs to be checked at the level of the specialty. Allocation of time-shared resources will therefore first be realised at the level of a specialty; the specialty can then allocate these resources further to the patient groups or use them as a shared resource.

Other shared resources are resources that are generally available for all specialties and do not have special allocation arrangements. Examples are intensive care units and diagnostic departments such as X-ray. There is a development to define service-level agreements between specialties and supporting services about the number of services required at annual level; sometimes it is even possible to make arrangements for reserving capacity at service departments for an average number of patients that can be expected from outpatient clinics; this is an example of decoupling the patient flows between units.

Leading and following resources

We call a resource 'leading' if it is the trigger for generating production on other resources that 'follow'. Allocation of capacity to leading resources generates capacity requirements on following resources. If insufficient capacity is allocated to following resources, the overall efficiency of the health care process will be jeopardised. Hence, knowledge of leading and following resources is crucial when allocating resources for production.

Within units some resources will be leading and some following. For example, within a medical assessment unit, resources for admission trigger the need for resources for investigation and diagnosis. However, products, in terms of patient groups, flow along health care chains and use resources provided by a number of units. Those responsible for allocating resources within units therefore need to be aware of the nature of these chains, as key leading and following resources may lie beyond the boundaries of the unit.

For example, for surgical specialties, the allocation of operating theatre time acts as a trigger for the requirement of bed capacity and nursing staff; the allocation of operating theatre time to a specialist at a specific period within a week will lead to the admission of patients on the day before or on the same day and the occupation of beds and nursing workload during the patients' stay. Operating theatres are, therefore, leading resources, and beds and nursing staff are following resources.

Analogously, clinics are leading resources because their allocations generate work at the diagnostic departments, which can be labelled as following resources. Part of the workload of these departments is directly related to clinic session allocations, as patients are referred from these clinics to diagnostic departments, to be examined without having to make an advance booking. This creates a further dependency in terms of specialist time as a resource, as specialists need to be available in diagnostic departments so that they can provide timely feedback to specialists in clinics.

Bottleneck resources

A bottleneck resource is the resource that is most scarce and therefore determining for the overall volume of production. In general, one tries to maximise the use of the bottleneck resource. For example, bed capacity or nursing staff capacity might be seen as the bottleneck for the overall volume of inpatient production, hence the focus on bed occupancy as a measure of efficiency.

The labels 'bottleneck' or 'non-bottleneck' should not be confused with qualifying resources as 'leading' and 'following'. For example, although access to surgical beds might be the bottleneck, operating theatre capacity is 'leading' in terms of generating production and bed capacity needs. Hence controlling access to leading and following resources represents key ways of ensuring that bottleneck resources are used efficiently. Bottleneck resources therefore represent constraints and are capacity-oriented terms, while 'leading' and 'following' resources refer to the resource requirements of patients and are therefore patient flow based terms.

Continuous or intermittently available resources

A fourth characteristic of resources is whether or not they are continuously or intermittently available. Some resources, such as beds and the emergency department, are available on a continuous basis. Others are, in principle, only available during specified hours; examples are regular clinics in the outpatient department, operating theatre sessions and regular opening hours at diagnostic departments.

The goals of high occupancy and high productivity will influence decisions about whether or not resources should be continuously or intermittently available. The focus will not only be on the resources themselves but on other areas of the hospitals that use those resources. For example, in the NHS of the UK limited access to 'out of hours' diagnostic resources has been seen as a cause of inefficiencies in the use of A&E (accident and emergency) resources (delays) and hospital beds (avoidable admissions). Here, decisions about extended opening hours will need to balance the efficiency goals of diagnostic departments, A&E departments and hospital wards.

Specialist-time as a shared resource

The time of specialists within a specialty is regarded as a resource that is shared between the patient groups served by the specialty. Yet its sharing is of a different kind to the sharing of other resources such as operating theatres. This is due to the multi-functional character of the specialist as a resource. By allocating their time to patient care activities, such as surgery sessions or clinic sessions, they participate in different phases of the production process. Each of the types of activities is separately covered by the shared resources involved, as discussed before. However, the allocation of specialist-time over the different patient care activities is not addressed. Specialist-time as a resource needs to be approached as a separate dimension of sharing, apart from the allocations in time of shared resources to patient groups.

Summary

The characteristics of the resources used for hospital production are (see also Vissers, 1994):

- Availability and utilisation level are pre-determined and reasonably fixed.
- There are many dependencies between the use of resources, concurrently (shared resources) as well as consecutively (knock-on effects).

- It is difficult to isolate resources in time for dedicated use by a specified product group, as those resources are also used for other product groups.
- The multi-functional character of specialists (operations, clinics, examinations, ward rounds) in combination with their dominant position makes specialists the leading resources in the process of allocating resources.

RESOURCE NEED AND USE: ASSESSING PERFORMANCE

To consider the impacts of different allocation decisions on resource requirements and resource use, we need to define some criteria. In the case of allocation decisions, the impacts relate to resource requirements. Resource requirements also represent estimates of the expected use of resources. However, the impacts of the actual use of resources also need to be monitored.

We will use three types of criteria for evaluating resource impacts:

1 level of resource need/use
2 fluctuations in resource need/use
3 violations of resource restrictions.

Before these criteria for evaluating resource impacts can be used, we also need to distinguish between different types of capacity:

- *Potential capacity* This is the total amount of resources available of one resource type when all resources are used for production. If we take an operating theatre department with ten operating theatres as an example, the hospital's *potential* operating theatre capacity is said to be ten. Part of the potential capacity is not available for production if it is put out of use. This can then be labelled as 'non-available' capacity. In the case of the operating theatre department, two theatres could have been put out of use, and these would be termed non-available capacity.
- *Available capacity* This is the total amount of capacity that is, in principle, available for production. In the operating theatre example it would be eight theatres. However, part of the available capacity might have restrictions on its use: this can be labelled as *non-usable* capacity. In the operating theatre example restrictions in use could be that only one theatre is available for emergency operations outside office hours and that each theatre is unavailable for one afternoon per month because of scheduled maintenance.
- *Usable capacity* This is the capacity that is normally available for production and that is taken as the reference point for calculation of utilisation figures. Part of the usable capacity might not be used for production because there is no work available. This we can call *idle* capacity. This loss of capacity for an

operating theatre department can arise when a scheduled session is cancelled by a specialist or when a session takes less time than scheduled.

- *Utilised capacity* This is the part of the available capacity that is actually used for production, i.e. the difference between the usable capacity and the idle capacity. Part of the utilised capacity may be used for non-productive purposes such as set-up activities. This will be labelled as *set-up* capacity. In the example of the operating theatre department, set-up capacity will be needed to prepare theatres and to change over from one patient to another patient within a session.

The remaining capacity will be called the *productive capacity*. In Figure 4.1 these capacity concepts are illustrated. For defining the utilisation we focus on the utilised capacity in relation to the usable capacity, whereby the usable capacity represents the allocated capacity. The utilisation rate of a resource is the ratio between these two capacity measures.

Returning to the three types of criteria for evaluating impacts, and continuing to use operating theatres for the purposes of illustration, the level of resource need/use will be calculated by averaging the utilisation rates of the sessions or days over a period of time. For example, this period might range from a few months to a year.

Fluctuations in the need/use of resources will be determined by calculating the deviations of the (half) daily utilisation rates from the average utilisation rate. See

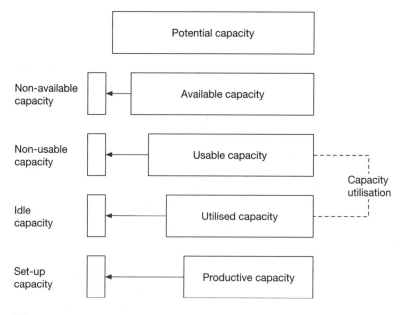

Figure 4.1 *Capacity concepts for resources.*

Figure 4.2 for an illustration of a one-week pattern of resource use for an operating theatre department. The average level of utilisation is 65 per cent, but there are considerable differences in the utilisation rates between morning and afternoon. In practice one will often use a target for the average utilisation level of, for example, 85 per cent.

Particular areas of interest are the fluctuations in the need/use of resources over the days of the week. To get enough statistical support for the existence of these weekly patterns of variations in capacity need/use it is necessary to analyse data for a number of weeks. The coefficient of variation can be used as a standardised measure to enable comparison of fluctuations in capacity need/use of different resources or different allocation schemes for resources. The coefficient of variation is defined as the standard deviation divided by the average (mean value) and will be expressed as a percentage.

There are many restrictions in the allocation and use of shared resources that need to be taken into account. *Violations of restrictions* is the third category of performance criteria when considering different allocation-schemes. The following are examples of restrictions:

- The totalled sum of specialty resource allocation figures cannot exceed the total hospital capacity for each type of resource.
- The totalled sum of allocations for all types of resources to one specialty cannot exceed the capacity of the specialty; the same applies also to the individual specialist level.

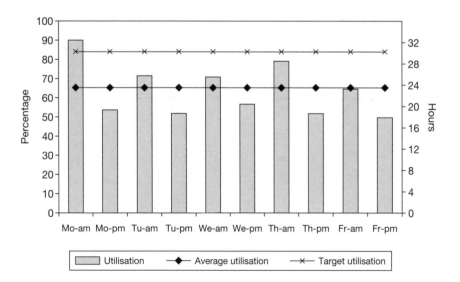

Figure 4.2 *Average resource utilisation and deviations from the average in an operating theatre department (one week).*

57

- The allocations of specialists within a specialty to different activities for each day of the week should accord with the task structure agreed for the specialty; an example of this type of restriction would be that, to allow for emergency attendance, not more than two out of four surgeons should be allocated simultaneously to operating theatre sessions.
- Allocations should take into account opening hours of facilities or periods of restricted use of a department; an example of the latter type of restriction is the agreement between a nursing ward and specialists not to make a ward round to see patients during patients' lunch hours or relatives' visiting hours.

These different restrictions imposed on hospital resource allocation make it difficult to optimise the need/use of resources in a hospital setting.

THE HOSPITAL RESOURCE STRUCTURE: EXISTING RESOURCE ALLOCATION METHODS AND THEIR IMPLICATIONS

Previous sections have discussed key concepts surrounding the allocation and efficient performance of resources for production. These concepts are now illustrated by analysing the ways in which different types of hospital capacity are organised. We will first describe the different resources considered and then the way these resources are used for hospital production.

Resources considered

In this book we will take a workstation as the basic unit for allocating resources. This is a processing point in the production chain that requires a mix of resources

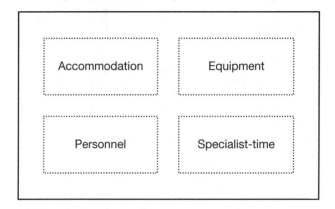

Figure 4.3 Workstation and resources.

to contribute to production. One of the resources takes the lead and will often be used as a basis for allocation; the amount of other resources needed is determined by a fixed relationship between capacities in the workstation. A workstation in a hospital usually consists of a combination of personnel, accommodation, equipment and specialist-time (see Figure 4.3).

As indicated earlier, the scheduled specialist-time available in the workstation is a capacity that is not within control of the workstation, despite the fact that workstations are of course controlled within the management structure. The specialist decides where to allocate his or her time although specialist capacity is essential to production. This makes the specialist capacity a critical resource for the workstation. Using this workstation definition, we list a number of hospital workstations and their characteristics.

Operating theatres

The operating theatres department (OT) is an important resource in the hospital. This is because the work performed in this station is very labour-intensive and involves expensive equipment and materials. Moreover, it is a shared resource and a 'leading' resource for the inpatient production of surgical specialties. The configuration of resources in this workstation consists of theatres, equipment, nursing staff who assist during the operation, the specialist (sometimes assisted by a trainee) and the anaesthetist. The allocation of operating theatre capacity to specialties is based on operating theatre hours and is regulated by the operating theatre timetable.

An average of 85–90 per cent is often used as the target level for the capacity utilisation of regular sessions in the operating theatre department. Above this level it becomes difficult to handle semi-urgent and urgent operations that are added to the session. If the target capacity is too high, it might be possible to undertake urgent operations only by using the theatre outside scheduled hours.

Nursing wards

These comprise beds as well as nursing staff. Nursing wards can act as 'leading' capacity or as 'following' capacity. This depends on the type of specialty (surgical versus medical) and on the identification of the bottleneck resource. Most hospitals use a bed-allocation scheme to allocate beds to specialties. Many have a centralised ward for day cases (one day admissions) or for short-stay patients (with a length of stay up to five days). These beds tend not to be allocated to specialties. Most wards accommodate different specialties. Nursing staff in general are allocated to wards instead of specialties. The unit of allocation is beds (per specialty) and full-time equivalent (FTE) nurses (per ward).

As a target level for the utilisation of beds during the week, in hospital practice one often uses an average of 85–90 per cent. The UK Department of Health recommends 85 per cent. Above this level it becomes difficult on busy days to find an empty bed in case of an urgent admission. As a target level for the patient-related workload for the nursing staff, one uses 100 per cent, reflecting the flexibility of this resource to adapt to circumstances.

Outpatient department

The outpatient department (OPD) accommodates different clinics where specialists can be consulted by ambulant patients referred by general practitioners. The OPD is the 'leading' resource that generates resource requirements at diagnostic departments. The clinic as workstation combines as resources accommodation (consulting and examination rooms), nursing and administrative staff, and specialist-time. Sharing of resources between specialties may occur for rooms and staff. The larger the hospital or the specialty, the more sharing of rooms and staff is restricted to the clinics held by specialists belonging to the same specialty. When the hospital's spatial capacity allows for it, most specialists prefer to have their own consulting room, which also serves as an office outside clinic hours.

Clinic hours are used as a unit for OPD capacity allocation. For each type of clinic there is a fixed relationship with room needs and staff requirements. The OPD allocation is regulated by a clinic timetable.

Diagnostic departments

These include X-ray departments, laboratories and organ examination departments (electrocardiograms, lung functions, endoscopies, etc.). In the X-ray department most rooms are only suitable for specific categories of examinations linked to the equipment that is located in the room. X-ray technicians can handle most categories of examinations. The intake capacity of laboratories is determined by the specimen collection unit, where blood and other specimens are collected. The capacity of organ examination departments (e.g. ECG (electrocardiogram), EEG (electroencephalogram), etc.) is determined by the available rooms, which often have a dedicated purpose, as well as by the often specialised paramedical staff. Some diagnostic investigations are performed by a specialist, requiring specialist-time as resource.

The diagnostic departments are often centralised general-purpose departments, being used by inpatients as well as outpatients from a range of specialties. When a department is almost exclusively used by one specialty, the department is often integrated into the clinic of that specialty. The X-ray department often has a few rooms that handle the walk-in patients flow referred by specialists or general practitioners, so that those patients can be examined immediately.

The capacity of diagnostic departments is not allocated to specialties, apart from examinations that are performed by the specialist. Requests for examinations are handled as they arrive, with some examinations requiring preparation and an appointment to be made in advance.

Treatment departments

As well as the operating theatres discussed above these are departments such as physiotherapy, radiotherapy and occupational therapy. These departments can be described in a similar way to the general-purpose diagnostic departments. Most of them are able to control their workload by an appointment system. This does not apply to the emergency department or the intensive care department, which have to deal with an unscheduled flow, and therefore require over-capacity to deal with peaks.

Specialist-time as a resource

Apart from the resources discussed before, which are allocated to specialties or used by specialties, there is the capacity of the specialist or specialty itself to consider as resource. This requires some explanation as this resource is quite different from the other resources considered up until now. When holding a clinic in the outpatient department, a specialist may decide to refer the patient for examinations to diagnostic departments, to admit the patient as an inpatient or to ask the patient to return for continued outpatient treatment. These actions generate resource requirements that often include specialist-time, also from other specialists.

Specialist-time is the label we use when addressing the specialist as a resource. This is the amount of time available for a specialist to allocate to different categories of activities in the hospital. A general surgeon, for example, needs to allocate time to the following activity types:

- clinic: to see or treat outpatients in the outpatient department;
- diagnostic examinations: to examine patients using equipment requiring the attendance of the specialist, mostly taking place in a special organ examination department (for example gastroenterology);
- operations: to operate on patients in the operating theatre department;
- minor surgery: to perform minor operations on patients in, for example, a treatment room located in the outpatient department;
- ward round: to see inpatients in wards, for example before or after an operation;
- other activities not in direct contact with patients, such as administration, committees or external activities.

The specialist-time is distributed over different workstations in the hospital. From this point of view specialist-time can be labelled as a shared resource. It is possible to define for every hour of each of the activity types the amount of other resources needed. However, unlike other shared resources it is more difficult to allocate specialist-time as a resource, which makes it an important aspect of the analysis of hospital capacity. For this reason, presented below is a more detailed consideration of specialist-time as a shared resource.

Specialist-time as a shared resource

As we have seen when discussing the resources of workstations, most involve some specialist-time. Specialist-time is a bottleneck capacity for the workstation, because specialists want their time, rather than the capacity of the workstation, to be fully utilised. Moreover, they are required to enable production in the workstation by using its other resources. This makes specialist-time a critical resource for the resource use performance of all workstations.

Specialist-time at the 'aggregate level of a specialist' is, however, a very flexible human resource. The length of the working week of a specialist is not defined. But also when restricted to office hours the specialist needs much flexibility in hospital practice. This is because 100 per cent of 'office hours' of specialist-time is allocated. If the first scheduled activity of a specialist during a day overruns the scheduled time, it results in start delays for subsequent scheduled activities. During a working day the available specialist-time draws a critical path through a number of workstations.

There is no equivalent to the specialist as a resource in production control applications in industrial settings. Considered at the level of a product line (for example diabetic patients) the specialist acts as an operator at different stages of the product line (seeing patients in the outpatient department, referring patients for further examination, deciding to admit a patient, treating patients during their stay in the ward, etc). The specialist is also the 'product line key operator' as no one else is able to take over the specialist's tasks, and other categories of personnel assist the specialist in the different workstations. Considered at the level of a specialty, with a number of specialists available within the specialty, the specialist can be considered as a 'multi-functional operator' going from one station to another station, each time being the critical resource for generating production.

From a specialty point of view, supposing that each specialist can perform all tasks within a specialty, specialists can be allocated to different functions. Figure 4.4 illustrates this and shows how the hospital's capacity structure on the level of an individual specialist can be represented as a match between specialist-time and workstations.

The four workstations indicated are dependent on the availability of the operator specialist for the different activities scheduled subsequently during a

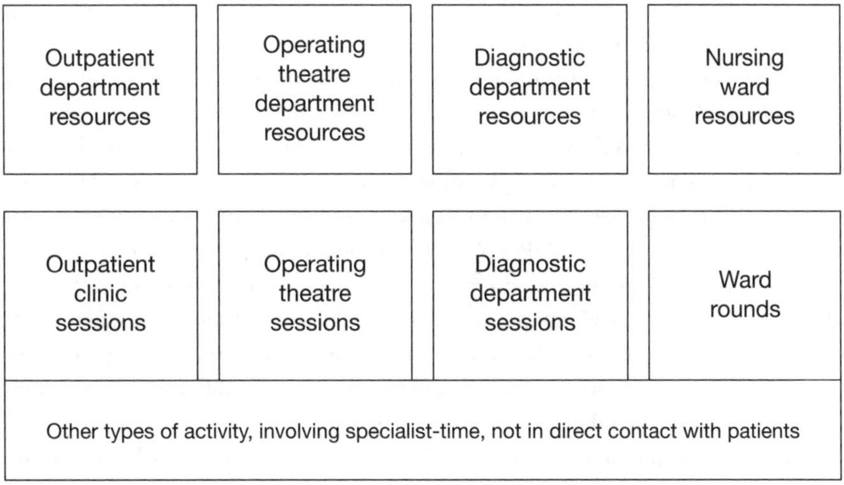

Outpatient department resources	Operating theatre department resources	Diagnostic department resources	Nursing ward resources

Outpatient clinic sessions	Operating theatre sessions	Diagnostic department sessions	Ward rounds

Other types of activity, involving specialist-time, not in direct contact with patients

Figure 4.4 *The hospital's supply structure as an interaction between specialist-time and workstations.*

day. The degree of dependency of departments on the availability of the specialist differs for the departments considered. The outpatient department and operating theatre department are fully dependent on the availability of specialist-time, while diagnostic departments and nursing departments are only dependent for their production when they need to consult a specialist. For example, the ward round that requires the attendance of the specialist represents an important but nevertheless a small part of the activities on a nursing ward.

One way of looking at the hospital supply structure would be to consider its capacity as a combination of a number of these individual specialist-related capacity structures. This picture can be further complicated by the interactions of these individual structures in workstations that are shared between specialists. Hospitals use sessions to regulate these shared resource interactions in practice.

Sessions as a batch-processing mechanism

A session is the period of time allotted to a specialist in a workstation (for instance a clinic) to treat a number of patients (a batch) requiring the same type of activity and resources. It is usual for a session to take a few hours, half a day, or a day, on a regular weekly basis. However, sometimes the frequency of sessions differs from this one-week production cycle. Sometimes sessions are allotted to the specialty instead of a specialist, which gives the opportunity to decide the individual allotment at a later stage. Examples of sessions for a general surgeon are: a general type of clinic session on Monday morning, a session with vascular operations on

Monday afternoon, a general type of operating theatre session on Tuesday morning, a fracture clinic on Tuesday afternoon, and so on.

Patients are scheduled for these sessions from an elective waiting list (in the case of inpatients) or at the moment the need for this service arises (in the case of outpatients referred by a general practitioner). Timetables regulate the allotment of sessions within a workstation to specialists or specialties. The most important timetables are the OT timetable, which regulates the operating theatre sessions allotment, and the OPD timetable, which regulates the allotment of clinic sessions in the outpatient department. These timetables tend to perform the same function as master production schedules in industrial settings (Vollmann *et al.*, 1988). Instead of defining the number of patients to be treated per production period as the master production schedule does, the timetable can be considered as a production schedule for each week of the year.

Regular production in hospitals is organised in sessions primarily because of the costs of some of the resources. Operating theatre hours, for example, are very expensive, involving a room, equipment and various types of surgical personnel. To use these resources efficiently one has to define exactly when specialist and resources are to 'meet' to realise production, not for one patient but for a series of patients. In this way change-over times are minimised, going from one type of operation to another type of operation. The aim is to optimise both the time of the doctor and the use of other expensive resources within the theatre. In doing so, specialist-time can be regarded as a flexible resource unlike other operating theatres resources.

Another reason for using sessions as combinations of specialist-time and other resources during a defined time interval is the fact that the same resources need to be shared between different specialists and different specialties. This is again because of the costs of the resources involved. On the other hand, resources are not easily exchangeable, so an operating theatre session prepared for a general surgeon can not be exchanged with a session for a gynaecologist without changing the configuration of resources needed.

This way of organising production in hospitals using the session mechanism optimises the use of session hours but has a number of negative effects, such as:

- It introduces an extra waiting time because sessions are only organised once or twice a week.
- It introduces patterns of workload for other resources required for patients before or after this stage of the process.
- It creates a rigid planning of specialists and resources. Because of the dependency in the system, one change of sessions may cause a number of changes elsewhere. Fixing the schedule for one specialist is usually regarded as the maximum attainable. This makes it difficult to rearrange master schedules, once fixed, even if such a rearrangement would benefit the total use of resources at the level of the hospital.

The length of the session or size of the batch is one of the decisions to be made. One alternative would be to use only whole-day sessions (maximal batch size) to avoid change-over times between sessions during the day and to optimise the use of a resource. This system of allocation is often used for operating theatres, because of the expensive character of this resource type. This will require larger 'buffers' of patients for these sessions and it introduces waiting times for patients because sessions are less frequently organised. This is also a reason for some specialties to prefer a balanced distribution of sessions over weekdays. Another consequence of long sessions can be that this requires larger numbers of patients to be admitted on the same day, which can cause peaks and troughs in the requirements for beds and nursing staff at wards.

The use of the session mechanism as a guarantee for optimal use of specialist-time and expensive resources creates the typical pattern of peaks and troughs in the use of resources at the hospital level. This is because the present way of allocating 'leading' resources that use this session mechanism does not take into account the overall impact on 'following' resources for the hospital as a whole. The remainder of this chapter discusses approaches that can be used to create resource allocation mechanisms that help to smooth such variations in the efficient use of resources.

MULTIPLE RESOURCE CONSTRAINTS: DEVELOPING IMPROVED APPROACHES TO RESOURCE ALLOCATION

Vissers (1994) has developed a method to analyse the consequences of capacity allocation strategies and to address capacity coordination requirements when allocating resources to specialties. The list below identifies the key coordination requirements to be addressed and their interdependencies:

- coordination of the allocations of 'leading' resources to specialties sharing the same resource; by capacity load levelling per 'leading' resource department, one can prevent capacity loss due to peaks and troughs in the workload of these departments (for instance an operating theatre department);
- coordination of the resource impacts for 'following' resource departments that are shared by specialties but not allocated to specialties: capacity load levelling per 'following' resource department (for instance an X-ray department);
- coordination of the allocations of different resources to one specialty; by capacity load levelling of the different resources per specialty one can avoid capacity loss due to relative over-capacity of a resource (for instance too much outpatient capacity compared with inpatient capacity);
- coordination of specialist capacity within a specialty; by considering the allocations of specialist-time of the different specialists within a specialty in

relation to planning restrictions, one can avoid violations of the planning policy of the specialty (for instance, identifying the maximum number of specialists that can be scheduled simultaneously during a period for the same activity).

Ignoring these coordination requirements may result in avoidable capacity losses, i.e. a poor performance in handling the aggregate patient flow. Each coordination requirement is discussed in turn below.

Load levelling of allocated capacities per 'leading' resource department

Each resource department whose resources are allocated to specialties requires coordination of allocations over specialties per period to avoid peaks and troughs in the need of this resource during the weekly production cycle. This procedure is called capacity load levelling and applies to departments such as operating theatres, outpatients and wards (in the case of a medical specialty).

Data previously presented in Figure 4.2 showed daily variation in the utilisation of an operating theatre department. In this scenario, this variation could be considerably reduced if a number of sessions were shifted from morning to afternoon. See Figure 4.5 for a levelled resource requirement scenario.

If one succeeds in shifting a number of operating theatre sessions to the afternoon, thereby levelling the need for operating theatre resources, the maximum of

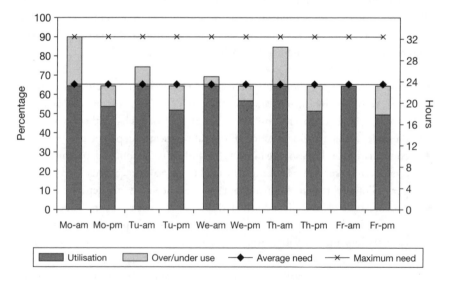

Figure 4.5 *Capacity load levelling per 'leading' resource department.*

32 OT hours could be reduced to 24 OT hours. Alternatively expressed in number of OT crews needed per half day, this would reduce the number of teams to staff all sessions from eight to six.

Capacity load levelling for 'following' resource departments

One also needs to ensure that the allocations of 'leading' resources to specialties do not result in peaks and troughs in the requirements of those 'following' resources that do not allocate capacity to specialties. This applies to diagnostic departments like X-ray, laboratories and organ examination departments. For example, peaks and troughs in the workload of the X-ray department would be generated if general surgery and orthopaedic clinics were organised concurrently, as these specialties refer many patients for direct examination to the X-ray department. This lack of coordination for resource requirements at 'following' workstations can also arise in surgical wards where the peak hours for the ward coincide with the weekly variations in OT time. To prevent these peaks and troughs – implying the occurrence of capacity losses – requires levelling of capacity needs at 'following' workstations due to allocation of capacity at 'leading' workstations.

Load levelling of different resources per specialty

When allocated capacities to specialties are not in balance for each specialty, the result may be that one capacity is always overloaded – thus becoming the bottleneck for this specialty – with other resources under-used. In Figure 4.6 this is illustrated for the workstations in the inpatient process of a surgical specialty.

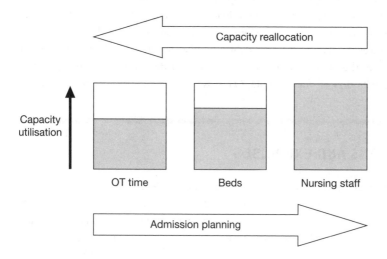

Figure 4.6 Capacity load levelling per specialty (inpatient process).

The figure shows imbalances between the allocated OT hours, beds and nursing staff. In this case one can expect a considerable under-use of allocated OT time because the bottleneck capacity, nursing staff, is already fully used. Alternatively, one might reduce the OT time allocated and the amount of beds – thereby levelling the successive capacities in the inpatient process per specialty – and still realise the same level of production as before. Of course, if the bottleneck capacity is beds or operating theatres, the procedure for levelling needs to be adapted accordingly.

Coordination of allocated capacities per specialist within a specialty

The last category of capacity coordination requirements refers to the intra-specialty organisation of activities. As we have seen that sessions involve some specialist-time, every reallocation at a leading workstation influences the internal specialty organisation. Reorganisation of timetables therefore requires coordination of the allocations of specialty time from the point of view of a single specialty or even a single specialist. This coordination at the level of a specialty prevents violation of arrangements that are agreed upon as important for optimising the intra-specialty organisation.

Examples of such arrangements were given earlier when discussing restrictions in the allocation and use of resources. One example was limiting the number of specialists that are simultaneously scheduled for the same type of activity or, expressed differently, levelling the specialist-time allocations of one type of activity throughout the week over the different specialists belonging to the specialty considered. The coordination at the level of an individual specialist within a specialty prevents development of a weekly plan that is contra-productive from the point of view of good practice for an individual specialist. An example of this would be the concentration of all OT sessions in the first half of the week. To prevent this requires a weekly plan for an individual specialist that shows well-distributed time allocations to the same type of activity throughout the week, thus taking care for a good distribution of, for example, OT sessions over the days of the week.

QUESTIONS AND EXERCISES

1   The workstation concept in Figure 4.3 combines different resources: accommodation, equipment, personnel and specialist-time. Consider an operating theatre setting and discuss the characteristics of these resources in this setting.

2   Suppose you are going to optimise the use of these different resources. Propose a weight function by providing each resource with a weight between 1 and 10 (10 being the highest weight) that reflects their relative importance.

3   Suppose an X-ray department has four rooms that do not require preparation and where examinations can be performed. Patients can be referred from clinics in the outpatient department and examined without appointment. The workload of these rooms varies with the number of clinics held in the outpatient department and the number of patients seen in clinics. Suppose the number of units in use on each hour on Monday is given as below.

Hour	8–9	9–10	10–11	11–12	12–13	13–14	14–15	15–16	16–17	17–18
Number of units in use	1	3	4	4	1	2	3	4	2	1

Prepare a graphical presentation of the use (in absolute numbers) of rooms over the hours on Monday. What is the occupancy percentage of the rooms per hour? Visualise the occupancy per hour on a secondary axis.

4   What would be the maximum gain to be made by a better spreading of examinations? What would be necessary to realise this optimal use of X-ray rooms? Why is this not realistic? What would be a realistic level of improvement?

REFERENCES AND FURTHER READING

Kusters R.J. and P.M.A. Groot. Modelling resource availability in general hospitals. Design and implementation of a decision support model. *European Journal of Operational Research*, 88 (1996) 428–445.

Luck G.M., J. Luckman, B.W. Smith and J. Stringer. *Patients, Hospitals and Operational Research.* Tavistock Publications, London, 1971.

Nelson C.W. *Operations Management in the Health Services.* North Holland Publishing Company, New York-Amsterdam-Oxford, 1982.

NHS Modernisation Agency. *Improvement Leaders' Guides* (series 1, guide 2). Matching capacity and demand, 2002. Ipswich: Ancient House Printing Group.

Roth A. and R. Van Dierdonck. Hospital resource planning: concepts, feasibility, and framework. *Production and Operations Management,* 4(1), 1995, 2–29.

Vissers J.M.H. *Patient Flow based Allocation of Hospital Resources.* Doctoral thesis, University of Technology, Eindhoven, 1994.

Vollmann T.E., W.L. Berry and D.C. Whybark. *Manufacturing Planning and Control Systems.* Second edition. Dow Jones-Irwin, Homewood IL, 1988.

Vries G. de (ed.) *Patiëntenlogistiek in ontwikkeling. Inzichten en toepassingen* (in Dutch). De Tijdstroom, Utrecht, 1993.

Vries G. de. Nursing workload measurement as management information. *European Journal of Operational Research,* 29, 1987, 199–208.

Chapter 5

Chain logistics

Analysis of care chains

Jan Vissers and Roger Beech

INTRODUCTION

In chapter 3 we defined processes and chains as a series of operations (often performed in different units) that need to be performed to produce a particular service or product. Although we distinguished in that chapter between process (delivery of a service by a single provider) and chain (delivery of a service produced in collaboration between different providers) we will use chains in this chapter as a common denominator.

In chapter 4 the unit logistics perspective was elaborated: the focus was on the total flow of patients served by the unit with the key aim being to maximise the efficient use of the resources available to the unit. For example, a key goal of the ward manager is to ensure that the casemix and volume of patients treated on a ward generates 'acceptable' levels of bed occupancy. This chapter focuses on the chain perspective and discusses key issues surrounding the description and analysis of care chains. This involves: the definition of the product to be delivered by the chain; the description of the operations in the chain and the duration of these operations; and the coordination and planning of the different operations.

CLASSIFICATION OF PRODUCTS/CHAINS

In chapter 3 we demonstrated that there are different ways to classify hospital products, depending on the focus of the classification. Given that chains generate a service for a client, the focus for product classifications is driven by the requirements of the client. In particular, clients want a service that is efficient (for example, unnecessary delays in treatment are avoided) and effective (for example, evidenced-based practices are used). In turn, the achievement of these goals is likely to increase levels of client satisfaction. Hence, in chains, operations managers want a product classification that allows them to plan and monitor the efficient and effective delivery of products.

This means that an iso-process perspective is required. A patient group in an operations management perspective can include different products/subgroups that are homogeneous in terms of market performance and process.

Homogeneity in terms of market performance implies similar criteria for urgency, acceptable waiting times, etc. An example of such a subgrouping based on market performance could be that a product needs to be delivered on an emergency basis (e.g. process chain: attendance at emergency department, ward admission, outpatient follow-up) or on a scheduled basis (e.g. process chain: referral to outpatient department, elective admission, outpatient follow-up). The first subgroup will require a different planning approach to the second subgroup.

Homogeneity in terms of process implies that the patients within the product group use the same constellation of resources. Patients requiring routine diabetes care (such as a one-off consultation) might be grouped with more complex patients who require more follow-up visits. This is because they are essentially using the same constellation of resources, for example, access to a clinician and a diabetic nurse. However, the overall amount of resources used by patients within the group may vary considerably, a fact that would need to be allowed for when planning capacity requirements. This iso-process grouping makes a logistics approach different from an economics approach (iso-resource grouping) and a medical approach (iso-diagnosis grouping).

Below we discuss some alternative ways of classifying health care products. We will focus on their suitability for analysing health care chains from an operations management point of view. Again, this review of alternatives will demonstrate that no single way of defining products from an operations management perspective exists. Instead, we aim to offer a framework that allows the reader to judge the merits and relevance of alternative product classifications for their application and setting.

The traditional way of classifying 'individual' patient products in the acute hospital is according to their complaint or diagnosis. Iso-diagnosis groupings of patients, for instance, are based on well-accepted international classification schemes such as the ICD (International Classification of Diseases). These classification systems can be very extensive: for example, the ICD-9-CM version of 1979 counts 398 main groups and 7,960 subgroups. However, such product classifications are mainly used for medical purposes. The number of patient groups that they generate, and the fact that some may generate very few admissions during a planning period, mean that it is difficult and usually undesirable to use them to plan and schedule care from an operations management perspective.

Acute hospitals traditionally group patients by specialty, for example, general medicine patients, orthopaedic patients etc. However, these groupings are too aggregated from an operations management perspective, as the constellation of resources used by patient types within specialties is likely to be very different. For example, patients diagnosed with asthma or stroke might both be grouped under the specialty general medicine but the care that they receive will be very different.

Hence, from an operations management perspective, a product classification somewhere between these two 'traditional' approaches seems to be required. The first attempt to define hospital products from a managerial perspective can be credited to Fetter and his colleagues (Fetter, 1983). They developed the DRG system (diagnosis related groups) to classify all diagnoses into groups of diagnoses that are recognisable for physicians and homogeneous in terms of use of resources. Up to then, X-rays, lab tests, medication, surgical procedures – in the DRG system seen as intermediate outputs – were considered as hospital outputs. Fetter developed 467 DRGs to describe the hospital's inpatient output.

Continuing lines of development have included ambulatory visit groups (AVGs) for classifying ambulatory care products (Fetter and Averill, 1984), and a refinement of DRGs that takes into account the stage of development of the disease with the patient (Fetter and Freeman, 1986). Another line of development in the Netherlands – with many parallels to the DRG approach – is to define hospital products as combinations of diagnosis and treatment (Baas, 1996). Similarly, in the United Kingdom, and again based on the DRG approach, health related groupings (HRGs) have been developed.

Product groupings such as DRGs were primarily developed to support the financial reimbursement of hospitals rather than to support the planning and management of health care chains. However, they have relevance to operations management as there will be a direct relationship between, for example, a hospital's DRG cost and the efficiency with which resources are used within a DRG. Hence, there are parallels between the analysis of DRG costs and the efficient planning of care within process chains.

However, although specific groupings within, for example, the DRG system may be useful for operations management purposes, the overall number of groupings generated by such systems is again likely to be too large. In addition, products that use a similar amount of resources (iso-resource) will not necessarily use a similar constellation of resources (iso-process). For instance, a patient with a DRG/AVG profile of an admission of five days, five lab tests and three outpatient visits may represent a patient admitted on an emergency basis (with five tests during admission, and three outpatient visits to a specialist), as well as a patient admitted on a scheduled basis (with three preceding outpatient visits always using the same constellation of resources, i.e. the specialist, a specialised nurse and the lab). Finally, the boundaries of health care chains may stretch beyond, for example, DRG boundaries. For example, the care chain for a patient who has suffered a stroke will include follow-up care in the community. However, the DRG(s) to which such patients are assigned will only embrace their care within the acute hospital.

Alternatively, it might be possible to generate product groups because the care of the patients covered can be regarded as being delivered in a 'focused factory', a business unit concept. De Vries *et al.* (1999b) specified the requirements for a 'focused factory'. These were: that there is a clear relationship between the product group and the resources required; that the volume of activity is large enough to allow the allocation of dedicated resources; and that it is possible in advance to identify the level of specialisation required.

Some 'focused factory' product groups might contain the same types of patient. For example, dedicated facilities and units for patients requiring treatment for cataracts have been established. In other 'focused factory' product groups, different types of patient might be clustered so that the volume of activity justifies the provision of dedicated resources. An example might be patients requiring day surgery. In the UK, the development of dedicated diagnostic and treatment centres will further increase the relevance of patient groups based upon the principles of a focused factory.

Finally, regardless of concerns about the volume of activity and clarity of resource requirements, client concerns about the continuity and coordination of existing services within a care chain might be the main driver for the creation of product groups. Such client concerns tend to be most evident for illnesses with a relatively long duration and/or those that require contact with a range of professionals or agencies. Hence, in the UK, National Service Frameworks have been developed that map out the desirable care pathways and services required for patients receiving treatment for conditions such as diabetes and stroke. To some extent, product groupings driven by a desire to promote continuity and coordination mirror developments in clinical protocols and pathways. However, the variety of processes and agencies involved means that planning and controlling the care of patients within such multidisciplinary patient groupings is extremely complicated.

Although the above discussion has outlined a range of product classifications and groupings, it should be noted that there are some process characteristics that have a strong impact on the predictability of resource use by patients within product groups. An awareness of these characteristics is therefore helpful when developing product groups. They are as follows:

- Treatments for well-defined complaints with almost 100 per cent certainty about the processes required and the outcome (e.g. a bone fracture) should be distinguished from treatments for ill-defined complaints with no routine treatment path available and no certainty about results. We call these the routine and non-routine processes (see also Lillrank and Liukko, 2004).
- For routine processes it is possible to define a treatment path, often based on a clinical guideline or protocol, which defines the different operations in the process and their timing. The variability in resource use for these routine processes can still be quite high due, for example, to practice variations,

different modes of treatment and the consequences of the interaction between doctor and patient. Nevertheless, process patterns can be recognised.

■ For non-routine processes, the specialist will proceed in a step-by-step way, checking the patient's reaction on a treatment and deciding on the next step from there. There is no guarantee on the outcome, and there is no in advance lay-out of the process the patient will follow. Naturally, the predictability of resource use is much lower here than with routine processes.

Of course, these are the extremes on a continuous scale; there is much variation between specialties and within a specialty. However, the variation between specialties is dominant. For a surgical specialty with many protocol patients, such as orthopaedics, the number of routine processes may be very high but for a non-surgical specialty, such as internal medicine, it may be much less.

To conclude, whatever system for classifying products or product groups is chosen (diagnosis, DRG and its refinement, AVGs or diagnosis-treatment combinations; see also Ploman, 1985), some variation is likely to remain in the homogeneity of the mix of individual patients that forms the product and in the range of services and resources that are used to produce the product. The reasons for a lack of homogeneity include inter-doctor variation within a product group and inter-practice variation between hospitals. For example, within a product 'treatment for arthritic hip', surgeons may differ in the proportion of patients considered eligible for surgery and/or the type of surgical procedure used. Such variations will, of themselves, affect the requirement for resources and services. In addition, variation will exist because of the fact that the eventual service delivered is always the outcome of the interaction between the patient and the doctor.

Therefore the main characteristics of any hospital products that are generated and used are that:

■ there is no single way of classifying hospital products, and even the concept of hospital product is not yet fully developed;
■ whatever classification system is used, the number of different hospital products is considerable;
■ within product groups the process variability is high and the homogeneity low due to inter-doctor and inter-practice variation and inter-patient variation at the level of a single specialist's practice.

PROCESS MAPPING OF A CHAIN

There are many ways to describe a process or a chain, but we concentrate here on ways to map a process from an operations perspective. The techniques for mapping processes can vary from standardised software tools (for instance FlowCharter) to tailor-made personal ways of describing a process. We will illustrate the mapping of a process in this section, using a mix of techniques, from the personal domain of the author.

We start with a simple description of a process of patients that need to undergo a protocol-based hip replacement, and return home after the hospital admission. Note the phrase 'protocol-driven' as it is here that the operations manager will want to check that there is not a discrepancy between 'effective' and 'existing' practice. This process is likely to involve the following steps:

- a referral by a general practitioner and the wait for the appointment with an orthopaedic surgeon;
- a first visit to an orthopaedic surgeon in the outpatient department of a hospital;
- a referral and X-ray examination at the radiology department;
- a second visit to the orthopaedic surgeon to discuss the results of the examination and the need for an operation and a hospital admission;
- the placement of the patient on the waiting list and the wait before the admission;
- the admission to the ward and the pre-operative stay;
- the operation;
- the post-operative stay at the ward;
- the discharge;
- a follow-up visit to the orthopaedic surgeon in the outpatient department;
- the referral back to the general practitioner.

Figure 5.1 describes this process, leaving aside the administrative steps (referral, placement on the waiting list) and concentrating on the process within the hospital. The figure illustrates that the process can be described in operations management terms as a series of operations connected by the flow of patients and that there are two buffers in the form of waiting lines or queues. For reasons of simplicity, we have left out the pre-operative screening and follow-up processes outside the hospital, for instance home care, physiotherapy services or nursing home care.

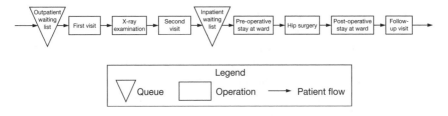

Figure 5.1 *A graphical presentation of a process for a patient for hip replacement.*

Whatever system of representation for mapping the process is chosen, it is important to define the symbols used in a legend.

Some remarks can be made about the choices made in describing the process:

- It often depends on the issue under discussion as to what to emphasise in the description. In this case we chose to leave out the administrative operations and to focus on the contacts between the patient and the providers of medical services. We also left out the 'in-process' waiting times, for instance the waiting in the waiting room before seeing the surgeon or the waiting in the X-ray department before being served.
- The process shown is based upon the protocol for a hip replacement. If real data covering the actual routings followed by patients for hip replacement had been used, we would have seen that some patients deviate from this routing. Some patients would, for instance, have visited the orthopaedic surgeon three times before the decision of admission was taken (in the case of a requirement for an extra pathology test), and some patients would have needed two follow-up visits before they were referred back to the general practitioner. Some variation will be due to differences in the clinical characteristics of patients. However, some may be due to 'out-dated' practices and hence represent an area for service improvement.
- Often there are decision points in a process that lead to a split into subgroupings of patients. For instance, the decision to choose a surgical intervention or a conservative treatment for the care of a patient with a broken ankle can lead to two subgroups. The preference of the author would be to define two processes, illustrating that there are two products (patient that undergoes surgical procedure and patient treated in a conservative way) with different resource requirements, instead of one process with a decision point. This illustrates also the difference between the medical decision process and the process of how to organise a service.

The picture can also become more complicated where a patient is treated in a multidisciplinary setting. When mapping such a process, parts of the process might be identified as serial processing or parallel processing, joint treatment (team processing) or cyclical treatment/processing (see Figure 5.2).

In *serial processing* the patient is transferred from one specialty to another. For instance, a patient is admitted to internal medicine for treatment of gastro-intestinal problems. Later on, when the treatment with drugs does not have the anticipated effect, it is decided that the patient will be transferred to general surgery for a surgical intervention. In *parallel processing* the patient is processed by two specialties during the same period for medically related problems. Often one specialty has the lead in responsibility for the treatment of the patient, and the other specialty is supportive. This happens, for instance, when during the treat-

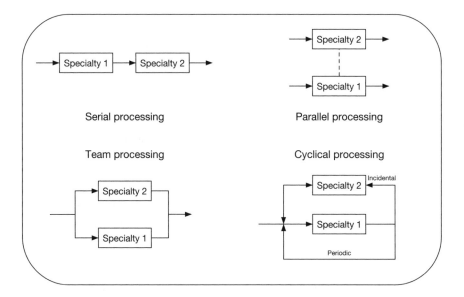

Figure 5.2 *Forms of multidisciplinary processing.*

ment of a patient a doctor from a second specialty is asked to give an expert opinion. Another example is a patient with claudicatio intermittens where the endocrinologist treats the diabetes and the vascular surgeon performs the vascular procedure.

In the case of *team processing*, the patient's problem is being jointly treated by two or more specialists from different specialties. This could, for instance, be the treatment of oncology, requiring involvement of internal medicine and oncology surgery. *Cyclical processing* refers to the treatment process of a patient that shows cyclic patterns. This often happens with patients with chronic conditions. A diabetes type 1 patient, for instance, might visit the clinic of a general medicine physician specialised in diabetics 10 times a year but only once a year visit an ophthalmologist for possible eyesight effects caused by diabetes.

ANALYSIS OF THE PERFORMANCE OF A CHAIN

We will first analyse the resource use of a chain and then analyse the performance of the chain in terms of the throughput time and waiting times.

For a description of a process in an OM perspective, there should always be an explicit relationship with the use of resources in each step of the process. To illustrate this feature of an OM analysis of a process, we return to the example of the process of the patient requiring a hip replacement, and provide more information on each step in the process in Table 5.1.

Notice that we have recorded only the use of resources and not the use of materials such as disposables at the ward or the use of the prosthesis for the surgery. Also, the description is limited to the use of resources for the clinical process and does not include the use of ancillary processes such as housing and cleaning. Having defined each step in the clinical process, and the use of resources in each step, it is possible to look at the total use of resources by the chain (see Table 5.2).

Although we have now quantified the resources used by the chain, we are still to develop an insight into the overall duration of the chain in terms of time and its performance in terms of waiting times and throughput time. Figure 5.1 indicated that there are waiting times at two positions (at least) in the chain. Further, the process map does not say anything about the time between the first and the second visit to the orthopaedic surgeon, or the time between the discharge from the hospital and the follow-up visit. Therefore, to get a better insight into the performance of the chain in terms of waiting times and throughput time, we need

Table 5.1 *Analysis of resource use of the chain for patients with hip replacement*

Step	Description of the content	Duration of the step	Resources	Resource use
1	First visit to orthopaedic surgeon	10 minutes	Specialist-time Outpatient facility Clerical staff	10 minutes 15 minutes 5 minutes
2	X-ray examination	15 minutes	Radiographer Radiologist X-ray room and equipment	15 minutes 2 minutes 20 minutes
3	Second visit	15 minutes	Specialist-time Outpatient facility Clerical staff Admission officer	15 minutes 20 minutes 5 minutes 15 minutes
4	Admission and pre-operative stay at ward	1 day	Bed at ward Nursing staff Anaesthetist	1 day 60 minutes 5 minutes
5	Operation	90 minutes	Operating theatre Anaesthetist Anaesthetic nurse Operating assistant Specialist-time	120 minutes 10 minutes 45 minutes 120 minutes 75 minutes
6	Post-operative stay at ward	7 days	Bed at ward Nursing staff Specialist-time	7 days 300 minutes 10 minutes
7	Follow-up visit to orthopaedic surgeon	10 minutes	Specialist-time Outpatient facility Clerical staff	10 minutes 15 minutes 5 minutes

Table 5.2 Summary of resource use of the chain for patients with hip replacement

Department	Resource	Amount of resources used
Outpatient department	Facilities	40 minutes
	Clerical staff	15 minutes
Admission office	Admission officer	15 minutes
X-ray department	X-ray room and equipment	20 minutes
	Radiographer	15 minutes
	Radiologist	2 minutes
Ward	Bed	8 days
	Nursing staff	360 minutes
Operating theatres	Operating theatre	120 minutes
	Anaesthetic nurse	45 minutes
	Operating assistant	120 minutes
Anaesthetist	Specialist time	15 minutes
Orthopaedic surgeon	Specialist time	120 minutes

also to consider the time dimension. Table 5.3 suggests the waiting times and lead-times that we might have to deal with.

From this information it now becomes clear that the second visit to the orthopaedic surgeon can take place on the same day, and that the patient returns after 20 days to the orthopaedic surgeon for a follow-up visit of the admission. We now also see that the time between the first and second visit is not a waiting time but a lead-time required to perform the X-ray examination. Also, the time between the discharge and the follow-up visit is not a waiting time but a time for recovery of the patient before it makes sense to evaluate the medical outcome. In Figure 5.3 the process, the waiting times and the lead-times are placed on a time axis.

We now can see that the total time for the throughput of a patient counts 101 days from the moment of referral to the moment of back referral to the general

Table 5.3 Waiting times and lead-times in the chain for patients with hip replacement

Period	Description of period	Term	Duration
1	Time between the referral and the first visit	Access time	10 days
2	Time between first visit and second visit	Response time	60 minutes
3	Time between second visit and day of admission	Waiting time (on waiting list)	2 months
4	Time between discharge and follow-up visit	Follow-up time	20 days

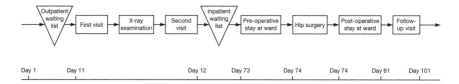

Figure 5.3 *Waiting times, lead-times and operations on a time dimension.*

practitioner. The 101 days consist of 71 days of waiting, 10 days of processing and 20 days of recovery time.

In general we can distinguish different types of waiting time according to the source of origin. The most common type of waiting time is the time waiting in the queue before one is being served. We can call this *access time* or just *waiting time* (on the waiting list). The term access time refers to the time one has to wait before one gets access to a service. Once one has got access to a service the next time one has to wait is called waiting time. If one wants to refer to the time in the process at a more detailed level of an operation, one often uses the label *in-process waiting time*. This can, for instance, be the waiting time in the waiting room before one sees the doctor, or the waiting time in the waiting room before the X-ray examination.

Another type of waiting time is the *batch waiting time*. This refers to the time a patient has to wait before there are enough patients available (the batch number) to fill a clinic session or an operating theatre session.

The third type of waiting time can be labelled *'frequency of service' waiting time* and refers to the time the patient has to wait until the next session is organised. Sometimes clinic sessions are of a specific type to allow for seeing a specific category of patients, for instance a fracture clinic. If this clinic is only organised once a week, the waiting time due to the frequency of service is on average half a week.

The overall waiting time of a patient is often due to a combination of the above causes. Similarly, the above illustrates the range of issues that might need to be addressed if a reduction in patient waiting times is to be achieved.

COORDINATION OF CHAIN OPERATIONS

Now that we have described the chain and are able to evaluate its performance, the last step to be taken in the OM approach is to consider the planning of the chain. Of relevance here are the design principles contained in the framework for production control that was introduced in chapter 2. The following issues need to be addressed:

- how to coordinate demand and supply;
- what variables should be controlled centrally (at the overall planning level of the chain) and what variables should be controlled locally (at the unit level);

■ what variables should be controlled in aggregates and what variables should be controlled in a detailed way.

The concepts of operational and structural coordination were introduced as means of balancing demand for resources and supply of resources (see Chapter 2). Operational coordination refers to the acceptance of the client orders and the ordering of resources, such that these are in balance with the orders accepted. Examples of operational coordination in the chain for treating patients with hip replacement are:

■ the coordination between the first visit, the X-ray examination and the second visit to ensure that these take place on the same day;
■ the coordination between pre-operative screening and admission to ensure that the timing of this screening does not delay the operation;
■ the coordination between the surgery and the ordering of the prosthesis that needs to be implanted during the procedure;
■ the coordination between the discharge of the patient and any follow-up activities required outside the hospital such as nursing home care or community physiotherapy.

When these forms of coordination do not take place, they result in a loss of capacity and a delay in the process. Important for the planning of the chain is to find out the earliest moment that information can become available to order resources for steps further down the chain, for instance, the point at which information can be provided to the home care agency about the expected discharge date of the patient (to ensure that home care is available when required and a delay in discharge is avoided).

Structural coordination refers to the setting of arrangements and conditions that allows for the operational coordination, including the target service level and resource utilisation level. Examples of questions that need to be answered about structural coordination in the chain for treating patients with hip replacement are:

■ Are there dedicated clinic sessions for patients with hip problems and dedicated operating theatre sessions for hip replacement surgery (in order to organise a separate product line for hip replacement patients) or are these patients seen in general clinics and treated in operating theatre sessions with a mixed composition?
■ How much capacity needs to be allocated to each processing point to allow for an undisturbed flow of patients through the chain?
■ Is capacity reserved at the radiology department for direct service to patients coming from the orthopaedic clinics?
■ What level of service (acceptable access time and waiting time on the waiting list) will be provided and what is the trade-off with the use of resources?

■ What are the decoupling points in the process? Why are they positioned as they are, and what do they try to accomplish?

From this elaboration of the operational and structural coordination it becomes clear that the variables controlled centrally, at the level of the chain, are:

■ the amount of capacity allocated to each station;
■ the balance between the allocations of different resources required for the chain;
■ the service levels to be realised for the chain.

The variables controlled locally, at the level of the units, are:

■ the occupancy level of resource use of the unit;
■ the performance of the unit in terms of delivery time.

Aggregate control, at the level of the total patient flow, takes place for:

■ the total amount of resources available for each processing point in the chain;
■ the reservation of capacity for the flow of patients expected from the orthopaedics clinics.

Detailed control, at the level of the individual patient, is required for:

■ the appointment with the orthopaedic surgeon for the second visit on the same day;
■ the booking of follow-up care at home after discharge.

An example of an analysis of the care chains within a specialty is illustrated in chapter 7.

QUESTIONS AND EXERCISES

1   Compare different approaches for classifying hospital products, i.e. International Classification of Diseases (ICD), diagnosis related groups (DRGs) and the patient grouping system as used in this book. What are their differences and similarities? What are their strengths and weaknesses?

2   What are the possibilities for improving the chain for patients with hip replacements (see Figure 5.1)? What will be the impact on the throughput time? What will be the impact on the use of resources?

3   Suppose hip replacements are going to be organised in a stand-alone treatment centre. The procedures are going to be performed by a group of orthopaedic

surgeons, who are also working at the hospital where they perform the other orthopaedic procedures. What will be the consequences for the chains of patient groups that can be distinguished in the patient flow of orthopaedics? What will be the impact on the throughput time? What will be the impact on the use of resources? What will be the impact on the need for coordination of the different chains?

REFERENCES AND FURTHER READING

Baas L.J.C. Producttypering medisch-specialistische ziekenhuiszorg (Dutch). *Medisch Contact,* 51, 1996, 356–358.

Bij J.D. van der, and J.M.H. Vissers. Monitoring health-care processes: a framework for performance indicators. *International Journal of Health Care Quality Assurance,* 12(5), 1999, 214–221.

De Vries G.G., J.M.H. Vissers and G. De Vries. The use of patient classification systems for production control of hospitals. *Casemix,* 2(2), 2000, 65–70.

Fetter R.B. *The new ICD-9-CM Diagnosis-related Groups Classification Scheme.* HCFA Pub. No. 03167. Health Care Financing Administration, U.S. Government Printing Office, Washington DC, 1983.

Fetter R.B. and A. Averill and others. Ambulatory visit groups: a framework for measuring productivity in ambulatory care. *Health Services Research,* 19, 1984, 415–437.

Fetter R.B. and J.L. Freeman. Diagnosis related groups: product line management within hospitals. *Academy of Management Review,* 11, 1986, 41–54.

Lillrank P. and M. Liukko. Standard, routine and non-routine processes in health care. *International Journal of Quality Assurance,* 17(1), 2004, 39–46.

NHS Modernisation Agency. *Improvement Leaders' Guides* (series 1, guide 1). Process mapping, analysis and redesign, 2002. Ipswich: Ancient House Printing Group.

Ploman M.P. Choosing a patient classification system to describe the hospital product. *Hospital and Health Services Administration,* 30, 1985, 106–117.

Plsek P.E. Systematic design of health care processes. *Quality in Health Care,* 6, 1997, 40–48.

Vries G.G. de, J.M.H. Vissers and G. de Vries. Logistic control system for medical multi-disciplinary patient flows. In V. de Angelis, N. Ricciardi and G. Storchi *Monitoring, Evaluating, Planning Health Services.* World Scientific, Singapore-New Jersey-London-Hong Kong, 1999a, 141–151.

Vries G.G. de, J.W.M. Bertrand and J.M.H. Vissers, Design requirements for health care production control systems. *Production Planning and Control,* 10(6), 1999b, 559–569.

Chapter 6

Frameworks for health operations management

Jan Vissers, Will Bertrand and Guus de Vries

THE PURPOSE OF DEVELOPING FRAMEWORKS

A framework for a hospital does not describe the optimal way to control hospital activities but instead describes a logical way of coordinating hospital activities within the perspective of the current hospital organisation. It is about what to do, and not about how to do it. Therefore, frameworks are not meant to be implemented as such. They rather serve as a reference background for the development of hospital production control systems, to show the weak spots where improvement is necessary, and to position contributions from logistic theories to issues of planning in the wider context of hospital planning.

THE FRAMEWORK USED IN THIS BOOK

The framework used as a reference in this book is a hierarchical framework for production control of hospitals that deals with the balance between service and efficiency at all levels of planning and control. It shows analogies to frameworks used in industrial settings for manufacturing organisations. The framework is based on an analysis of the design requirements for hospital production control systems (De Vries *et al.*, 1999) and builds on the production control design concepts developed in Bertrand *et al.* (1990). The design requirements are translated into the control functions at different levels of planning required for hospital production control. This translation is built on notions of the hospital as a virtual organisation with patient groups as business units and a focused factory approach for the production control per business unit. In short, we can distinguish a number of production control functions, which can be positioned at different levels of planning in a framework (see Table 6.1).

Table 6.1 *Production control functions distinguished in the planning framework for hospitals*

	Decision focus
1	Range of the services, markets and product groups, long-term resource requirements, centrally coordinated scarce resources; level of annual patient volumes, service philosophy, target service and efficiency levels
2	Contracted annual patient volume, amount of resources available at annual level to specialties and patient groups, regulations regarding resource use
3	Time-phased allocation of shared resources, involving specialist-time; detailed number of patients per period
4	Urgency and service requirements, planning guidelines per patient group
5	Scheduling of individual patients, according to guidelines at patient group level and resource-use regulations at resource level.

At the highest level decisions have to be made on the range of services provided, the markets one wants to operate in and the product groups for each market. Decisions also have to be made on the long-term resource requirements of the hospital, which scarce resources are centrally coordinated, what level of annual patient volumes one wants to achieve, what service philosophy will be used and what level of service one wants to aim for. These are all longer-term strategic decisions, which essentially do not belong to the domain of OM, but which have impact on the management of operations at shorter terms.

The next level focuses on the amount of resources that is available annually to specialties and patient groups, to ensure that the contracted annual patient volume can be realised. At this level the rules for using the resources also need to be established to ensure that the target service and efficiency levels are achieved. At the third level the focus is on the allocation of shared resources in time, taking into account the availability of specialists and seasonal developments. This requires more insight into the detailed numbers per patient group per period within the year. At level four the urgency and service requirements per patient group need to be established, and the planning guidelines per patient group. The fifth level regards the scheduling of individual patients, according to the planning guidelines for the patient group and the resource-use regulations for the resources involved.

Though the planning framework seems to be working only 'top-down', the needs for each level and the requirements for coordination are established 'bottom-up'. At the lowest level individual patients are coupled to resources in the day-to-day scheduling. This level in the framework is called *patient planning and control*. The way patients are operationally scheduled needs to be governed by rules established at patient group level. Oncology patients, for instance, have different urgency and service requirements from patients with varicose veins. Therefore, operational scheduling of patients needs to be governed by what we called *patient group planning and control*. To allow for the planning of a patient group, resources need to be allocated, taking into account the availability of specialists and personnel. This level is called *resources planning and control*, and also includes the time-phased allocation of resources. The level of resources required results from the annual patient volumes contracted, and the service and efficiency levels targeted for. This level is called *patient volume planning and control*. Finally, the volume level is governed by the strategic planning level, where, for instance, decisions are taken about which resources need to be shared or not. This level is called *strategic planning*. At this level there is no control involved.

These levels of planning can be further elaborated (Vissers *et al.*, 2001), resulting in the planning framework as shown in Figure 6.1 and Table 6.2.

The framework shows that every level needs a horizontal control mechanism to match patient flows with resources and that vertical control mechanisms are required to set the targets for lower levels (feed forward) or to check whether activities develop within the boundaries set by higher levels (feedback).

The lowest level of planning in our framework, *patient planning and control*, is equivalent to the operational control level mentioned by Anthony (1965; Anthony and Herzlinger, 1980). This level is concerned with the processes used in facilitating the day-to-day activities that need to be performed to deliver care for the patient group. These activities consist of rules, procedures, forms and other devices that govern the performance of specific tasks. Operational control is the process of assuring that specific tasks are carried out effectively and efficiently. The day-to-day activities of a hospital include scheduling of individual patients for admission, for outpatient consultation or for examinations. How these day-to-day activities are guided by higher level planning and how resources are made available to patient groups are determined by the next level.

The second level in our framework, *patient group planning and control*, focuses on decisions regarding the mix of patients that can be handled by the patient group but also their service requirements and the availability of resources for the patient group. At this level of planning, detailing of patient flows to production periods is required, taking into account seasonal influences, which allows for adjustments in the allocation of resources for high seasons and for low seasons.

This brings us to the next level where resources are made available to patient groups and specialties. The third level, *resources planning and control*, focuses on decisions concerned with the allocation of resources to specialties and patient groups. These decisions are taken approximately once each year or each quarter of a year. Allocation decisions are based on a detailed forecast of the patient flow per patient group or specialty. Therefore, the patient flow is broken down into patient groups that require the same constellation of resources (iso-process grouping). For each patient group the projected number of patients for the next period is determined and the amount of capacity required. When a shorter period of allocation is used,

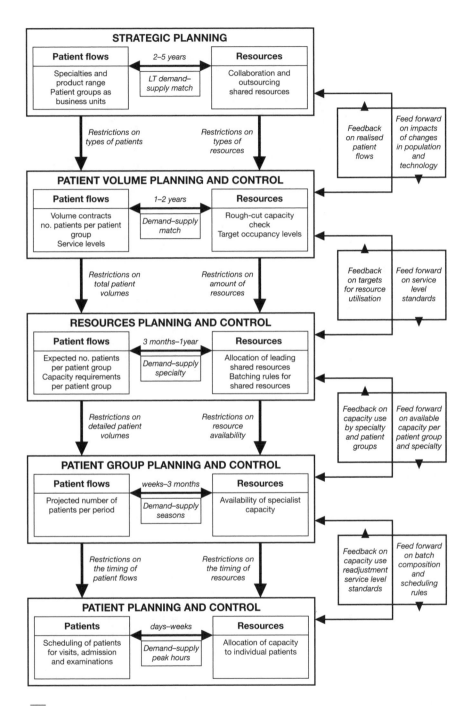

Figure 6.1 *Framework for production control of hospitals.*

Table 6.2 Framework for hospital production control

Framework level	Type of decision	Decision makers	Horizon	Decisions regarding patient flows	Decisions regarding resources	Control functions
Strategic planning	What is the range of services offered? (markets and product range)	Hospital management	2–5 years	catchment area; markets and target groups; specialties and product range; patient groups as business units	investment of resources; shared resources; collaboration; outsourcing	horizontal: coordination of demand and supply; vertical: feedback on realised versus target patient flows; feed forward: consequences of changes in population and technology; boundaries for patient flow volumes and aggregate resource requirements; target hospital resource utilisation rates and target service levels
Patient volume planning and control	What will be the development of hospital activities in the next year? (volumes and capacity requirements)	Hospital management	1–2 years	annual number of patients per patient group; service level per patient group; production volume agreements with health care insurers	indication of required capacities per patient group; target occupancy levels for leading and non-leading resources	horizontal: coordination of demand–supply; vertical: feedback on targets for resource utilisation; feed forward on service-level standards (maximum length of the waiting list and waiting times per patient group and specialty)

Table 6.2 (cont.)

Framework level	Type of decision	Decision makers	Horizon	Decisions regarding patient flows	Decisions regarding resources	Control functions
Resources planning and control	How are resources allocated to specialties and patient groups? (time-phased allocation)	Production unit managers and specialty	1 year – 3 months	expected number of patients per patient group and specialty; detailed capacity requirements per patient group	allocation of leading shared resources to specialties and patient groups; batching rules for leading shared resources	horizontal: coordination of demand–supply per specialty; vertical: feedback on aggregate capacity use by patient groups and specialty; feed forward on available capacity per patient group and specialty
Patient group planning and control	How is specialist-time scheduled at patient group level? (time-phased allocation)	Patient group management and specialty	3 months – weeks	projected number of patients per period (seasonal influence)	availability of specialist capacity	horizontal: coordination of demand–supply (seasonal variation); vertical: feedback regarding capacity allocated versus capacity used per patient group; re-adjustment of service-level standards; feed forward on batch composition and scheduling rules
Patient planning and control	Which patient is treated when? (operational planning)	Specialist, officers and patient	Weeks – days	scheduling of patients for admission, outpatient visits, diagnostic examinations	allocation of capacity to individual patients	horizontal: coordination of demand–supply (peak hours); vertical: feedback regarding performance on service-level standards; capacity utilisation per patient group

for instance three months, it is also possible to take into account seasonal holidays. Depending on the resource type, the allocation of resources can take place in different ways:

■ a lump-sum allocation of capacity (e.g. full time equivalents of nursing capacity);
■ a specific allocation of capacity in time (e.g. blocks of operating capacity during session hours within the week).

These time-phased allocations need also to be related to the allocation of specialist-time as a resource shared between patient groups. This makes production control of health care organisations different from production control structures for manufacturing systems. It is necessary to distinguish this more detailed level of allocation of resources in the production control structure of hospitals because of the characteristics of specialist-time as a special type of shared resource between patient groups. At the level of the specialty decisions are taken to allocate specialist-time to patient groups and to define restrictions for the use of specialist-time as a resource. As this also involves considering the availability of specialist-time, the planning horizon for this level is typically one to three months. Furthermore, some types of resources in hospitals involving specialist capacity (for instance operating theatres and outpatient clinics) are allocated to specialties, in the first stage in terms of a lump sum and in a later stage in a time-phased manner by allocating session hours within a week via a timetable. As the way in which these session timetables are set up can affect the performance in other parts of the hospital, this type of decision requires coordination at hospital level.

Patient volume planning and control is the fourth level of production control in the framework. Decisions regarding the patient mix consist of determining the number of patients per group. A patient group at this level could also be represented by the diagnoses within a specialty or based upon, for example, diagnosis related groups (DRGs), as long as the relationship with the iso-process grouping that we need further down the framework is clear. In order to determine the number of patients within such a group, the demographic characteristics of the population surrounding the facility, historical data regarding the number of patients in that group and patient volumes agreed upon with the health insurance companies, or commissioning organisations, are used as input data. A rough estimate of the resources needed per specialty and per resource department is required. In production control terminology this is called a rough-cut capacity plan. A decision must be made regarding how much capacity a patient group needs, based upon the number of patients within this group, and how much capacity is needed to guarantee that this number of patients can be treated in the next year, considering the targets set for the occupancy of resources and the levels of service. The patient volumes and resource requirements per group will be aggregated at the level of specialties and the hospital. Finally, it is necessary that the decisions concerning the patient mix and the resources are consistent with each other and with the decisions taken at the strategic planning level.

Strategic planning is the highest level of production control within this framework, although it is not a part of what is usually called production control. Nevertheless, this level is taken into account in our framework because of the planning and financial restrictions imposed on hospitals by national and regional governments and by health insurance companies. These restrictions significantly influence decisions taken by *strategic planning* and by *patient volume planning and control*. Strategic planning decisions concern the direction in which a hospital is heading for the next two to five years. Decisions are taken concerning the product range, i.e. the categories of patients the hospital wants to serve in the future, the target mix and the volumes of patients for the hospital. An important decision at this level is the acknowledgement of the patient groups that are run as business units, which will be proposed as such by specialties. Furthermore, decisions are taken regarding investments and divestment of resources. In addition, this is the level to decide whether to consider resources shared or non-shared.

OTHER FRAMEWORKS

Only a few references can be found in the literature on OM frameworks for health care. Smith-Daniels *et al.* (1988) in their extensive review study on capacity management in health care, made a distinction between decisions on acquisition of resources and decisions on the allocation of resources. The focus of their contribution, however, was a review of literature, and not the development of a framework. Butler *et al.* (1992) developed a multi-level modelling approach for hospital planning, which comes closer to our framework though it focuses more on the long-term planning. The framework developed, however, had only a capstone function for illustrating modelling contributions on the different levels distinguished.

Fetter and Freeman (1986) were the first to describe the possibility of developing product-line management in hospitals, using DRGs as a basis for organising product lines. By reference to the application of the matrix organisation concept to hospitals (Neuhauser, 1972), they distinguished between the clinical management of services (DRG product lines) by specialties and administrative management for clinical support services. Although their first application of product-line management was focusing on accountability and cost control, they also saw opportunities for managing operations in the product line. The potential of product-line management was further elaborated by Zelman and Parham (1990), who explored its consequences for marketing strategies, and by Rhyne and Jupp (1988), who considered its application for operations management. The second paper is most interesting as it describes a health care requirements planning system (HCRPS) as an application of the MRP concept (Material Requirements Planning) to health care, making use of the DRG classification system of products. This issue was also discussed earlier in this book in chapter 2. Chapter 2 also considered a framework on hospital resource planning (Roth and van Dierdonck, 1995) that builds on the work by Rhyne and Jupp (1988).

A SUPPLY CHAIN FRAMEWORK

Supply chain management (SCM) refers to the organisation of the production of goods produced by different organisations in the chain from raw materials to final products. The concept was first introduced in manufacturing when individual organisations further down the chain tried to reduce the risks of running out of supplies of materials or parts delivered by organisations further up the chain. By managing the supplies along the chain, the final products delivered to customers can be produced with shorter and more reliable delivery dates and with lower costs of inventories.

Health care is a special type of service industry, with a very close interaction between the client and the provider in the delivery of the service. The primary process in health care is represented by the flow of patients through the system. Providers add value to the patient by diagnostic and therapeutic services in order to find an answer for the patient's request for help. The flow of goods (supplies for wards, drugs, operating theatre supplies, food, office supplies) is secondary. Sometimes the goods flow is coupled on a one-to-one basis with the patient flow, for instance, a prosthesis that is implanted in a hip of a patient during a surgical procedure by an orthopaedic surgeon in an operating theatre. Most of the time the goods flow is decoupled from the patient flow by departmental stores.

There is as yet no framework developed for SCM in health care, so we can only sketch the development of such a framework (Huijsman and Vissers, 2004). The development of the control framework needs to be 'bottom-up', i.e. from the process level to the tactical level (where resources are allocated) and the strategic level (where objectives and targets are set). At each level of planning the require-ments for the patients flow and the resources required needs to be established and coordinated. Higher levels of planning should then be based on these lower-level requirements and have built-in guarantees that these requirements are met.

The resulting hierarchical planning framework for the chain can be used to check whether the plans for the contribution of the individual organisations are in line with the overall plan of the chain. This requires striking a balance between the logistics perspective for the care chain and the unit logistics perspective for the organisations that participate in the chain. This is not a simple task as it concerns potentially competing performance targets of each logistic perspective. A frame-work for patients with cerebrovascular accidents (CVA) is illustrated in Figure 6.2.

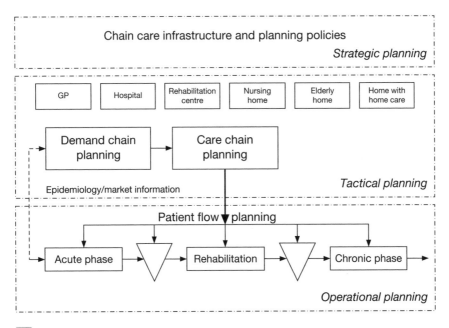

Figure 6.2 *Hierarchical control framework for care chain management.*

The framework shows that we distinguish three levels of planning: operational, tactical, and strategic. At operational level the day-to-day flow of the chain patients is managed through a function 'patient flow planning'. This planning function takes into account the number of patients in each phase and the lengths of the waiting lists for each phase. At the tactical level a function 'care chain planning' facilitates the operational planning by ensuring that the resources available to the chain are enough to fulfil the targets for production and service. At the same level, but with a longer planning cycle, one finds the function 'demand chain planning', which sets the parameters for the care chain planning, based on market information, i.e. epidemiological and demographic data. At the strategic level decisions are taken on the infrastructure of the care chain (i.e. the lay-out of the chain, the constellation of resources required for the chain, the participation of partners) and on the planning policies (i.e. the objectives and targets set for the chain).

QUESTIONS AND EXERCISES

1   Suppose we are going to develop a production control framework for a unit, i.e. the operating theatre department. What different levels of planning can be

distinguished? What are the decisions to be made at each level? Organise this information in a table.

2 Suppose we are going to develop a production control framework for a chain, i.e. stroke services. What different levels of planning can be distinguished? What are the decisions to be made at each level? Organise this information in a table.

REFERENCES AND FURTHER READING

Anthony R.N. *Planning and Control Systems: A Framework for Analysis.* Harvard University, Boston, 1965.

Anthony R.N. and R.E. Herzlinger. *Management Control in Nonprofit Organizations.* Revised edition. Richard D. Irwin Inc, Homewood Illinois, 1980.

Bertrand J.W.M., J.C. Wortmann and J. Wijngaard. *Production Control: A Structural and Design Oriented Approach.* Elsevier, Amsterdam, 1990.

Butler T.W., K.R. Karwan and J.R. Sweigart. Multi-level strategic evaluation of hospital plans and decisions. *Journal of the Operational Research Society,* 43(7), 1992, 665–675.

Fetter R.B. and J.L. Freeman. Diagnosis related groups: product line management within hospitals. *Academy of Management Review,* 11, 1986, 41–54.

Huijsman R. and J.M.H. Vissers. Supply chain management in health care: state of the art and potential. In T. Camps, P. Diederen, G.J. Hofstede and B. Vos (eds) *The Emerging World of Chains and Networks. Bridging Theory and Practice.* Reed Business Information, 's-Gravenhage, 2004.

Neuhauser D. The hospital as a matrix organization. *Hospital Administration* 17(4), 1972, 8–25.

Rhyne D.M. and D. Jupp. Health care requirements planning: a conceptual framework. *Health Care Management Review,* 13(1), 1988, 17–27.

Roth A. and R. Van Dierdonck. Hospital resource planning: concepts, feasibility, and framework. *Production and Operations Management,* 4(1), 1995, 2–29.

Smith-Daniels V.L., S.B. Schweikhart and D.E. Smith-Daniels. Capacity management in health services. *Decision Sciences,* 19, 1988, 898–919.

Vissers J.M.H., J.W.M. Bertrand and G. de Vries. A framework for production control in healthcare organisations. *Production Planning and Control,* 12(6), 2001, 591–604.

Vries G. de, J.W.M. Bertrand and J.M.H. Vissers. Design requirements for health care production control systems. *Production Planning and Control,* 10(6), 1999, 559–569.

Zelman W.N. and D.L. Parham. Strategic, operational, and marketing concerns of product-line management in health care. *Health Care Management Review,* 15(1), 1990, 29–35.

Part II

Case studies

Jan Vissers and Roger Beech

The case studies that follow in this second part of the book illustrate health OM at work in different health care settings. The first part of the book has offered a conceptual framework that acts as a reference for positioning these case studies in terms of their approach (unit, chain or network logistics) and in terms of the primary level addressed in the planning framework. To make it easier for the reader to position each contribution on these two dimensions, we use a visualisation as shown below.

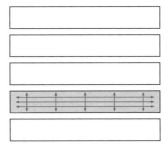

The planning framework discussed in chapter 6 indicates that there are five levels of planning: patient planning and control, patient group planning and control, resources planning and control, patient volume planning and control, and strategic planning. The above illustration indicates that the case study being presented is focusing on the second level: patient group planning and control.

A focus on unit, chain or network logistics is represented by arrows. Arrows in a vertical direction refer to the prevalence of unit logistics. The allocation and utilisation of resources play an important role in such case studies. Arrows in a horizontal direction refer to the prevalence of chain logistics. This means that the case study is focusing on processes for specific patient groups, and on ways to improve the performance of the chain in terms of service (waiting time) and throughput times. Arrows in both directions refer to a network logistics approach: a combination of unit and chain logistics. In the above illustration the case study is characterised by a network logistics approach, implying that the objective of the case study is to improve service performance in chains as well as the utilisation of resources by all chains combined.

Each of the case studies follows a similar format of elaboration. In principle, the following items will be covered:

- an introduction to the context of the case study;
- an introduction to the planning problem addressed, including the position of the problem in the reference framework for hospital production control, labelled in terms of unit/chain/network logistics, and a short review of the literature on the planning problem;
- the elaboration of the planning problem, including data on operational characteristics of processes and resources;
- a description of the model developed;
- a discussion of the results obtained;
- a reflection on the strength and weaknesses of the study and recommendations for the further development of the approaches used.

At the end of each case study you will find a list of questions, which aim to stimulate further reflection and discussion on the issues raised. Also presented are assignment exercises based upon the material in the case study. The order of presentation of the case studies is from operational to strategic.

Chapter 7

Description and analysis of hospital care processes

Jan Vissers

SUMMARY

We often talk about improving or redesigning hospital processes or process chains without having a description of their characteristics in terms of, for example, the volume of patients that they cover and the types and amounts of resources that they consume. This chapter describes an approach and a tool for describing and analysing hospital processes that enables hospital managers and professionals to visualise the process chains followed by patients within a specialty and the interactions of patients with resources such as outpatient facilities, diagnostic facilities, beds, IC beds, operating theatres, nursing staff and specialists. A case study undertaken within a project setting is used to illustrate the approach.

KEY TERMS

■ Description of care processes
■ Process mapping
■ Resource requirements of care processes
■ Analysis of care processes and specialty practice

INTRODUCTION

Many discussions in hospital organisational development revolve around the process chains followed by patients and the management of these processes, for example, discussions surrounding the re-design of services for elective patients by providing diagnostic and treatment centres or the possible expansion of community-based services for older people as a means of transferring care away from the acute hospital. It is, however, amazing to see that these discussions often take place without participants having a basic understanding of the process chains currently followed by the patient groups affected.

Alternatively, detailed process descriptions are increasingly being made for specific purposes, for example, the development of protocol-based care pathways for patients with a defined clinical profile that define the expected trajectory of patients and include indicators for measuring and monitoring the quality of care provided. However, such descriptions are often clinically focused and ignore the link with the use of resources or the interaction with other processes or shared resources. For example, a protocol for stroke care might include a statement that all admissions should undergo a CT scan within a set time limit. However, such a statement has resource implications for the CT scan facility and might restrict access to this service by other patient groups. Finally, the level of detail in clinically driven process descriptions often prevents the development of a system's perspective that allows an understanding of the totality of patient flows and resources.

What is required, therefore, is a way of describing processes at a level of detail and aggregation that allows for:

- a system's perspective of patient flows and resources that reflects the interaction of processes and resources;
- a broader context of the process that needs to be improved or redesigned;
- a fruitful discussion between medical specialists and management on problems or ideas for change;
- a trade-off between the level of service provided and the implications for the use of resources.

It is not intended that the method and tool 'processor' developed for this purpose should be the definitive answer to this issue. It has proven to be effective in the current state of hospital organisational development, in which the process is still to be regarded as a concept that is not yet fully crystallised.

BOX 7.1 THE CASE STUDY HOSPITAL

The case study hospital – one of the hospitals that has used the method and tool for describing hospital processes – is a 450-bed hospital in the centre of the Netherlands. The case study concerned the specialty of general surgery. We will use data of this specialty to illustrate the method and the tool.

The general surgeons had expressed concern to the hospital management that they were not able to keep the level of service at the level agreed upon. This was due to an increase in the numbers of patients seen as well as a change in patient mix. The outpatient department was a special cause for concern, with long access times for patients and long waiting times. But above all, their concern was the time available to handle the outpatient flow, with the average time available per patient being slightly more than five minutes. This also included oncology patients, and this specialty had shown a relative increase in numbers.

In the discussions with the hospital management the problem was initially formulated as a capacity problem in the outpatient department. When the hospital management suggested a benchmark to compare the amount of resources available to general surgery with a peer group of hospitals – a stereotype answer to capacity problems – the surgeons were not happy. Although they were not afraid of the outcome of such a benchmark, they did not have much confidence that it would contribute to a solution to their problem. They expressed this feeling to the hospital management, and together they decided that it would be more fruitful to develop a better insight into the processes of patients within general surgery. As a result of this, the issues of level of service in each of the processes and the efficiency in use of resources could then become clearer.

The next section provides further information on the planning problem by positioning it in a framework for production control of hospitals and by a short review of literature on methods for describing processes in hospitals. This is followed by a section in which the planning problem is further elaborated by providing data for the specialty general surgery, and by a section that describes the model that has been developed for this problem. The results of the application of the model to general surgery are then discussed and the final section reflects on our approach by formulating conclusions and recommendations for further research.

PLANNING PROBLEM

What level of knowledge do most hospital managers have about the core processes of a specialty? In the case of general surgery it will probably be limited to the number of general surgeons, their specialisations (trauma, vascular surgery, oncology, etc.), their total annual workload (admissions, visits, procedures, etc.), and perhaps some notion of the level of access time (waiting time for an appointment) and waiting time (for an elective admission). Their level of knowledge will probably not be in terms of a description of:

- the main patient groups served by general surgery;
- the trajectories (or process chains) of patients within patient groups;
- the numbers of patients served within patient groups, and the distribution over trajectories;
- the workload placed on outpatient and diagnostic facilities;
- the completion time for the trajectories.

Compared to the state of knowledge on processes in other types of manufacturing or service industries, one could consider this as a logical minimum description of the business process of a hospital.

Position in the planning framework

The planning problem addressed can be positioned at the second level of the framework for hospital production control, i.e. patient group planning and control, as presented in chapter 6 (see Figure 7.1). 'Patient group planning and control' or, alternatively 'patient group management', focuses on the challenge to develop a hospital planning approach that is based on patient groups. A patient group from a logistic point of view is defined as a target group of patients that can be easily defined in hospital practice by its correspondence in routing and in its use of specific types of resources, for instance, the diabetic patients group.

Patient group management is an application of the chain logistics perspective. It identifies the patient groups that have to be organised as product lines. However, in our approach we do not want to consider a process in isolation from its context. The context chosen is that of a specialty. By considering all processes within general surgery we are able to take into account the implications on the use of resources available to general surgery as a whole. By this approach we have created a network logistic approach, with an emphasis on chain logistics.

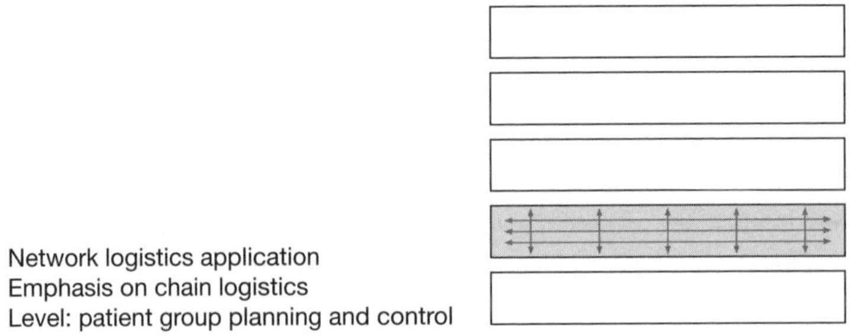

Network logistics application
Emphasis on chain logistics
Level: patient group planning and control

Figure 7.1 *Patient group management and planning framework.*

Literature review

There are many ways to describe a hospital care process, depending on the approach followed and perspective used, for example, quality management, clinical care pathways or logistics. Processes play an important role in the development of quality management systems in health care. The process is often the starting point for the improvement of performance by applying the plan-do-act cycle or by the 'isst-soll' comparison in the business process redesign (BPR) approach. In this case the focus of the description lies on identifying the steps that cause long waiting times and that can be speeded up by elimination or parallelisation of activities.

The recent development of (clinical) care pathways has also contributed to an increased insight into the care processes in a hospital. The UK Pathways Association describes care pathways in the following way:

> An integrated care pathway determines locally agreed, multidisciplinary practice based on guidelines and evidence where available, for a specific patient/client group. It forms all or part of the clinical record, documents the care given and facilitates the evaluation of outcomes for continuous quality improvement.
>
> (Luc, 2000)

Care pathways are multifaceted tools, comprising a number of different elements that have the primary purpose of supporting clinical processes. However, they can also be used for secondary purposes including monitoring the activity undertaken and commissioning services. Care pathways can also be used to deliver integrated care across traditional health care and agency boundaries.

The Supply Chain Operations Reference (SCOR) Model is a tool, developed by the Supply Chain Council (Supply Chain Council, 2000), for representing, analysing and configuring supply chains. SCOR is a reference model that describes terminology for defining standard processes at different detail levels of description of the supply chain. The SCOR model also supports performance management at each level by defining metrics, divided into four categories: reliability, flexibility and responsiveness, costs and assets. This also makes the SCOR model a useful tool to evaluate the performance of a supply chain.

Comparing the different approaches to describing health care processes, one could say that quality management/BPR often focuses on the improvement of a process in terms of its performance on the time dimension, care pathways try to visualise the medical decision-making process and often use a more detailed description, and logistics approaches use a process description with a clear linkage with the resources used for the process.

ELABORATION

The case study setting is the specialty of general surgery in a 450-bed hospital in the Netherlands. The specialty involves five general surgeons, who combine a general surgery practice with a specialisation. The specialisations are: trauma, vascular problems, gastroenterology and oncology. The specialty has facilities for outpatient clinics in the outpatient department. Specialists also see 'outpatients' in the emergency department.

The numbers of patients treated in 1999 were: 13,000 outpatient visits (including patients seen in the emergency department), 19,000 follow-up visits, 2,100 inpatient admissions and 1,100 day cases.

Information on the clinics held each week is given in Table 7.1. Each specialist has two sessions a week in which they see all types of patients and one session in which they primarily see patients fitting their specialisation. All specialists also have one session a week for minor procedures. One session a week is held by the senior registrar. For each session the number of time slots reserved for first and follow-up visits is given as well as the average time available for first and follow-up visits. The time available for first and follow-up visits in the specialised clinics is slightly longer.

Table 7.1 Information on weekly clinic sessions, general surgery specialty

Clinic type	Surgeon	Hours per week	First visits		Follow-up visits	
			Number of 'time slots'	Minutes allocated	Number of 'time slots'	Minutes allocated
General	Spec.1	6.5	11	8	66	4
	Spec.2	6.5	11	8	66	4
	Spec.3	6.5	11	8	66	4
	Spec.4	6.5	11	8	66	4
	Spec.5	6.5	11	8	66	4
	Sen. Reg.	2.0	4	10	9	5
	Total	34.5	59		339	
Specialised:						
trauma	Spec.1	2	3	10	12	5
vascular	Spec.2	2	3	10	16	5
oncology	Spec.3	2	3	10	9	10
gastroenterology	Spec.4	2	3	10	9	10
	Spec.5	1	1	10	5	5
	Total	9	13		51	
Minor procedures		13	4	10	71	10
Total		56.5	76		461	

Note: Sen. Reg = Senior Registrar; Spec. = Specialist

As one can see, the time allocated per patient in the oncology clinic is slightly longer than for patients visiting general clinics. This has implications if an increase in the expected volume of oncology caseload is anticipated.

One of the first things to find out in this case study was the amount of inflow of new outpatients for oncology in the current situation and the amount of time slots currently available for oncology patients. This was not an obvious problem as oncology patients entered the clinic not only via the oncology sessions but also via the general clinics: in other words, the process chains followed by oncology patients needed to be clarified. Investigation of the type of patients seen in each clinic provided information on the mix of patients per type of clinic (see Table 7.2).

As can be seen from Table 7.2, the mix of patients in the general type of clinics reflects the specialisation of the surgeons. This information shows that oncology patients concentrate mainly in the oncology clinic held by specialist 3 and in the general clinic of specialist 3. However, oncology patients also constitute 10–20 per cent of the session time of other surgeons. So, the amount of time available for oncology patients was indeed not an obvious issue.

Other questions were put forward in the meetings with the surgeons, such as, what would be the effects on the workload for the surgeons if we involved a nurse practitioner in the follow-up visits for oncology patients? This would require a separate clinic held by the nurse practitioner – what about the timing of such a session and the availability of rooms?

There were five examination rooms available for holding clinics. Based on office hours a room could be used on average for 30 hours a week, resulting in 150 hours of room capacity. There were two treatment rooms for performing small pro-

Table 7.2 Information on the mix of patients per clinic type, general surgery specialty

Clinic type	Specialist	Trauma %	Vascular %	Oncology %	Gastro-enterology %	Other %
General	Spec. 1	58	3	10	5	24
	Spec. 2	33	37	11	4	15
	Spec. 3	22	1	56	8	13
	Spec. 4	37	3	20	12	28
	Spec. 5	36	6	17	22	19
	Sen. Reg.	22	6	11	11	50
Specialised:						
trauma	Spec. 1	86	0	7	0	7
vascular	Spec. 2	7	85	8	0	0
oncology	Spec. 3	0	0	78	0	22
gastroenterology	Spec. 4	11	0	33	56	0
	Spec. 5	0	0	0	91	9
Small procedures		1	20	1	38	40

cedures, each available for 28 hours a week, resulting in 56 hours of treatment room capacity.

The series of questions put forward required a more in-depth analysis and a model that could support these questions but also allowed for making calculations of the resource consequences of changes in processes of patient groups.

MODEL

We have developed a computer model 'processor' that allows us to describe and model the processes of the different patient groups within the patient flow of a specialty. Use of the model first involves a discussion with the medical specialists belonging to the specialty as – given the state of development of hospital information systems – they are often the only ones who can provide the data required for this description.

The structure of the model – used for mapping the information on processes and resources – is illustrated in Figure 7.2.

Figure 7.2 shows the demand side of the model (upper part) and the supply side (lower part). The demand side starts with the inflow of new outpatients and the distribution over groups of patients that can be distinguished in the inflow and used for streamlining services and flows. Within these patient groups different treatment profiles are distinguished, representing the modes of treatment available for a patient group and the trajectories followed by patients. At the level of an individual trajectory the process of the patients from this patient group following this trajectory (iso-process grouping, see chapter 5) is described, using input from the medical specialist and information on examinations and treatments. The inflow and distribution of patients over patient groups, combined with the treatment profiles, allows for a calculation of resource requirements in the outpatient department and the diagnostic departments.

The supply side consists of a description of the available capacity in the outpatient and diagnostic departments, in terms of rooms, personnel and equipment. The information presented in Tables 7.1 and 7.2, for instance, make part of this description.

In the results part of the model demand and supply are matched, which allows for visualising throughput times of processes and calculation of resource utilisation.

RESULTS

We will illustrate the approach with data from general surgery in the case study hospital. Table 7.3 gives the distribution of the inflow of new patients over the patient categories distinguished.

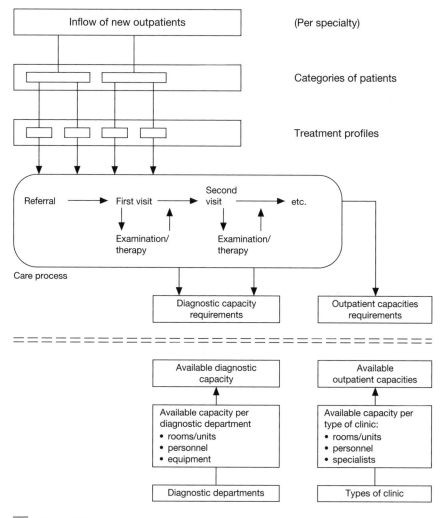

Figure 7.2 *Structure of the demand–supply model for hospital processes.*

The total inflow for general surgery is 260 patients per week. The majority of this inflow – more than 200 patients per week – enters via the emergency department; the rest enters via the outpatient department. Most patients at the emergency department are seen only once and return home or to their general practitioner; the rest are directly admitted as inpatients or return for outpatient follow-up. The outpatient inflow consists on average of 63 trauma patients with follow-up, 12 oncology patients, 15 gastroenterology patients, 11 patients with vascular problems, and a group of 18 patients with various medical problems. We must remark here on the flows of patients considered. Although we concentrate on

Table 7.3 *Overview inflow for general surgery patient groups over a week period (based on mean weekly averages)*

Inflow general surgery (per week)	Main patient groups			Subgroups		
	Name	Average number per week	Percentage total (%)	Name	Number per week	Percentage main group (%)
260	1. Trauma with follow-up	62.75	24	injuries/abscess	6	10
				ankle ligaments	6	10
				fractures-conservative	16	25
				fractures-inpatient/hip	3	5
				fractures-inpatient/rest	3	5
				rest	28.75	45
	2. Trauma with no follow-up	141	54	injuries	44	26
				contusions	45	26
				abdominal complaints	20	12
				inflammations	20	12
				various	40.75	24
	3. Oncology	12	5	mamma malign without diagnosis	2	17
				mamma malign with diagnosis	1	8
				mamma benign without diagnosis	3	25
				mamma benign with diagnosis	3	25
				colo-rectal	2	17
				melanoma	0.5	4
				rest	0.5	4
	4. Gastro-enterology	15	6	gall stones	3	20
				appendix	3	20
				haemorrhoids, etc.	6	40
				peri-anal fistula	2	13
				abdominal complaints	1	7
	5. Vascular complaints	11.5	4	varicose veins – referred	5	44
				varicose veins – own	3	26
				aneurism	1.5	13
				diabetic foot	0.5	4
				claudicatio-conservative	1	9
				claudicatio-procedure	0.5	4
	6. Various	17.75	7	hernia inguinal	3	17
				atheroom cyste, etc.	12	68
				sinus pilonidalis	1	6
				trigger finger	0.5	3
				scar rupture	0.5	3
				circumcision	0.5	3
				thrombose leg	0.25	1

the use of resources in the outpatient department, we have to take all the work of the specialists into account. Many people seen in emergency departments, or as inpatients, will continue as outpatients and want to use the time slots shown in Table 7.1. It demonstrates that even if the focus is the outpatient department, the complete workload of the surgeons must be understood because of the links between the different strands of work and activity generated in OP departments.

The six main patient groups are broken down into a number of subgroups that sometimes refer to a specific complaint or sometimes to a different treatment path. At this level a link can be made to the process of the patient. The descriptions of the processes of all these patient subgroups are based on expert opinion from clinical specialists. This information is structured with the help of the computer model that also returns the information to the specialists in the format of a process chart. As an example of one of these processes, Figure 7.3 shows the process for a trauma patient (ankle ligaments) with outpatient follow-up.

Figure 7.3 shows that the process for 'ankle ligaments' trauma patients with outpatient follow-up consists of up to five steps. The first step takes place at the emergency department. The patient is referred for an X-ray examination (upward arrow) and returns with the result to the emergency department (downward arrow). Everybody will return for a follow-up visit at the outpatient department in five days' time (not shown in this figure, but stored elsewhere in the model). The second step takes place at the outpatient department. Of all patients seen,

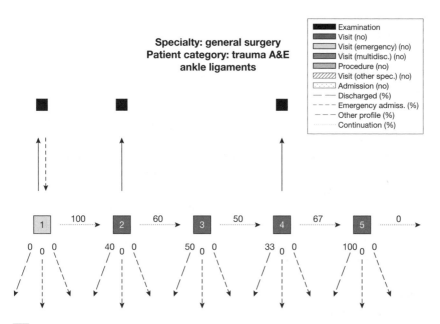

Figure 7.3 Graphical illustration of the care process for a trauma patient with outpatient follow-up.

40 per cent are discharged. The rest are given a plaster, and return on average in 21 days' time for a third visit. Then 50 per cent continue for a fourth visit; the other 50 per cent are discharged. At the fourth step all patients first go to the X-ray department, and then 33 per cent are discharged. The other 67 per cent return for a fifth visit and are then discharged.

The information that is used to describe the different steps in the process is summarised in Table 7.4.

For each step in the process information is given on the content of the step (in this case, first and follow-up visits, but it could also cover an admission or a procedure), the percentage of patients with diagnostics that are performed instantly (as a direct follow-up of the encounter with the specialist) or with an appointment on another occasion, the next step in the flow (percentage of patients that will return for a next step, will require immediate admission, will continue in another profile, or will be discharged), and the reappointment interval for patients that return.

As the model also contains information on the clinics organised on a weekly basis, it is possible to do checks on the balance between demand and supply. We show some of these results:

- average inflow of patients per patient group and the available slots in the clinics (Table 7.5);
- utilisation of outpatient department resources (Table 7.6);
- other clinical output (admissions, procedures, etc.) from patient groups (Table 7.7);
- workload for diagnostic departments (Table 7.8);
- throughput times of processes within patient groups (Table 7.9 and Figure 7.4).

Table 7.5 shows that the match between supply and demand is adequate when looking at the level of the total clinics offered, but that the match at the level of individual patient groups could be improved. It also provides evidence that more booking space is required for the flow of oncology patients. Secondary visits refer to return contact with the specialist in the same clinic session, after the diagnostic test. To illustrate for oncology patients, the demand is 12 slots per week (corresponding with the average inflow of new outpatients for oncology in Table 7.3). There are 11.6 slots per week available for oncology patients (three in the oncology clinics of specialist 3 and the rest in the general clinics of all surgeons). (To make this calculation you also have to take into account a 20 per cent reduction in the number of sessions held on average per week due to holidays, etc.)

By comparing the capacity of resources available for clinics in the outpatient department (consultation rooms, treatment rooms, clinic staff and clerical staff) with the amount of capacity required, it is possible to calculate the occupancy of

Table 7.4 Summary of steps in care process for 'ankle ligaments' trauma patients with follow-up

Patient group: trauma				Profile: ankle ligaments					
		Diagnostics		Flow data					Reappointment interval (in days)
				Percentages					
Step	Content	Direct: Examination without appointment	Examination by appointment	Continue in the same profile	Urgent admission	Continue in other profile	Discharge		
1	First visit (A&E) + second visit	Skeleton (25%)		100%					5
2	Follow-up visit	Plaster (100%)		60%			40%		21
3	Follow-up visit			50%			50%		10
4	Follow-up visit	Skeleton (100%)		67%			33%		21
5	Follow-up visit						100%		

Table 7.5 *Match between demand for and supply of time slots in clinics*

Patient group	First visits			Follow-up visits			Secondary visits		
	Demand	Supply	Occupancy (%)	Demand	Supply	Occupancy (%)	Demand	Supply	Occupancy (%)
Trauma				185.8	180.8	103	1.5	2.1	71
Oncology	12.0	11.6	103	57.6	55.7	103	0.5	1.2	35
Gastroenterology	12.0	12.3	98	37.8	37.2	102	0.2	0.6	33
Vascular surgery	11.5	11.5	100	41.0	44.6	92	0.2	0.6	33
Other	17.5	17.4	101	48.5	52.5	92	1.0	1.5	67
Total	53.0	52.8	100	370.7	370.8	100	3.4	6.0	57

resources in the outpatient department. This is illustrated in Table 7.6, which shows how resources are used in the outpatient department and how much space is left for a possible extension of clinic sessions.

As we have descriptions of all steps in the processes it is also possible to calculate the amount of other clinical output, generated per patient group: elective admissions, emergency admissions, multidisciplinary consultations and procedures. See Table 7.7.

The total clinical output for general surgery can easily be checked with the administrative data, available in the hospital information system. However, the information at the level of the patient group is new and illustrates the process-oriented way of improving insight into the functioning of care processes.

As the care profiles contain information on patient requirements for diagnostic tests it is also possible to visualise the workload of diagnostic departments resulting from processes for patient groups. See Table 7.8.

Another type of output is the throughput time of processes. Table 7.9 provides information on the number of activities per type and on the throughput times to complete all the steps in the process. For patient groups with a chronic condition, the process has been artificially cut off.

Table 7.6 Utilisation of resources in the outpatient department

Resource	Demand (hours per week)	Supply (hours per week)	Occupancy (%)
Consultation rooms	142.0	150.0	95
Treatment rooms	35.0	56.0	63
Clinic staff	79.5	97.5	82
Clerical staff	53.0	75.0	71

Table 7.7 Other average clinical output on a weekly basis per patient group (number of patients)

Patient group	Elective admissions	Emergency admissions	Multidisciplinary consultations	Procedures
Trauma		7.2		
Oncology	8.7			
Gastroenterology	8.6			
Vascular surgery	10.5		2.0	2.0
Other	5.0			12.5
Total	32.8	7.2	2.0	14.5

Table 7.8 Workload of diagnostic departments

X-ray department		Other diagnostic departments	
Diagnostic group	Hours per week		Hours per week
CT/MRI	1.8	Pathology	34.6
Thorax/skeleton	9.6	Bacteriology	6.5
Echo	9.2	Anatomy	7.3
Mammography	2.7	Nuclear medicine	0.4
Vascular test/duplex	4.5	Endoscopy	4.3
Total	27.8	Vascular tests department	1.0
		Heart tests	0.7
		Plaster room	12.7
		Physiotherapy	1.6

The throughput times between brackets are based on a cut-off point for chronic processes. The throughput times can also be visualised as shown for the trauma patient group in Figure 7.4. The difference between the current throughput time and the 'minimum' throughput time shows the gain to be made by better planning of patients in relation to the diagnostic tests.

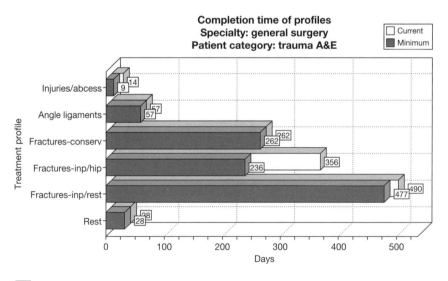

Figure 7.4 Throughput times for trauma patient group processes.

Table 7.9 Throughput times per process and patient group

Patient group	Treatment profile	Number of visits			Number of admissions	Number of visits to other specialty	Number of procedures	Through-put time (days)
		First	First (A&E)	Follow-up				
Trauma	injuries/abscess	1		4				14
	ankle ligaments	1		4				57
	fractures-conservative	1		8				262
	fractures-inpatient-hip	1		2	1			356
	fractures-inpatient/rest	1		7	2			490
	rest	1		4				28
Oncology	mamma malign without prior diagnosis	1		>13	1			(651)
	mamma malign with prior diagnosis	1		>13	1			(803)
	mamma benign without prior diagnosis	1		2	1			71
	mamma benign with prior diagnosis	1		2	1			140
	colo-rectal	1		>8	1			(1033)
	melanoma	1		>8	1			(1206)
Gastro-enterology	gall stones	1		2	1			125
	appendix		1	6	1			70
	haemorrhoids, etc.	1		5	1			141
	peri-anal fistula	1		5	1			106
	abdominal complaints	1		4	1			320
Vascular surgery	varicose veins-else	1		5	1			335
	varicose veins-own	1		4	1		1	147
	aneurism	1		>8	1	1		(1851)
	diabetic foot	1		>11	1	1		(943)
	claudicatio-cons.	1		3	1		1	250
	claudiatio-procedure	1		>7	1			(1802)
Other	hernia inguinal	1		4	1			86
	atheroom cyste	1		4			1	31
	sinus pilonidalis	1		9	1			179
	trigger finger	1		2			1	35
	scar rupture	1		3	1			94
	circumcision	1		2	1			64
	thrombose leg		1	1				10

REFLECTION AND FURTHER DEVELOPMENT

The results shown in the previous section illustrate what we would like to know from a logistics perspective about processes in health care. Of course, the descriptions given are just average representations of 'prototypes' of care processes as they actually occur in everyday reality. Prototypes of processes refer to a description that matches with the average picture of the processes followed by patients within this group and that is accurate enough to be used to diagnose problems in the handling of patient flows and to develop ideas for improvement. In the case study hospital the model was used to generate ideas for redesigning the clinic using more appropriate time slots for oncology patients.

It is important to have a realistic level of ambition when describing and analysing patient flows and processes in a clinical practice. One important aspect is the level of detail and the number of patient categories and profiles required. In the pilots that we have run with this approach in different hospitals we have been able to describe a specialty (e.g. neurology, orthopaedics, general surgery, cardiology, dermatology) in terms of 5–10 main patient groups, each further distinguished into 2–5 different routings, resulting in a total of 25–40 processes.

The computer model used to support the data collection provides process maps as well as insight into the match between the demand for resources and the availability of resources. The insights developed with this approach can be used to improve the performance of patient flow management around patient groups, for instance by redesigning clinics for dedicated patient groups (e.g. mamma oncology care), taking also into account the demand such a group makes on diagnostic departments.

If we take as starting point the current knowledge we have on processes in health care, then a good description of the processes as shown here opens a world of information around a process-oriented hospital practice. A good process description is, moreover, a powerful tool for communication between professionals and managers about a better-organised practice.

QUESTIONS AND EXERCISES

1 What are the differences in describing a process between the perspectives of clinical pathways, diagnosis related groups or patient flow logistics?

2 Re-calculate the number of average time slots available per week for oncology patients (i.e. 11.6) using the data in Tables 7.1 and 7.2, and a 20 per cent reduction in the number of sessions held on average per week (due to holidays, etc.).

REFERENCES AND FURTHER READING

Luc K. de. Are different models of pathways being developed? *International Journal of Health Care Quality Assurance*, 13(2), 2000, 80–86.

NHS Modernisation Agency. *Improvement Leaders' Guides* (series 1, guide 1). Process mapping, analysis and redesign, 2002. Ipswich: Ancient House Printing Group.

NHS Modernisation Agency. *Improvement Leaders' Guides* (series 1, guide 2). Measurement for improvement, 2002. Ipswich: Ancient House Printing Group.

NHS Modernisation Agency. *Improvement Leaders' Guides* (series 1, guide 3). Matching capacity and demand, 2002. Ipswich: Ancient House Printing Group.

Plsek P.E. Systematic design of health care processes. *Quality in Health Care*, 6, 1997, 40–48.

Supply Chain Council. *Supply chain operations reference model – version 3.1.* Technical paper, Pittsburgh PA. www. supply-chain.org/members/html/SCOR-model.cfm. 9 June, 2000.

Chapter 8

Aggregate hospital production and capacity planning

Jan Vissers

 SUMMARY

Most hospitals do not have a formalised and accepted method of allocating resources to the different specialties and revise these allocations when the annual contracts with purchasers or commissioners have changed. This case study describes a hospital-wide method used to translate annual target production outputs into capacity allocations to specialties, in such a way that: target production outputs per specialty are met, waiting lists are kept at a level that is acceptable, high but realistic targets are used for projecting occupancy levels and resource use, the use of beds is balanced with the use of operating theatres and with the workload for nurses on wards, systematic peaks and troughs in the weekly production cycle are reduced, and the characteristics of the patient flow per specialty (urgency, variability of resource use) are taken into account. The application of the method and experiences of its use in a number of Dutch hospitals will be discussed.

KEY TERMS

- Hospital-wide resource allocation
- Time-phased allocation of inpatient resources
- Balancing resource allocations
- Model support for resource allocation

INTRODUCTION

Allocation of inpatient resources such as beds, operating theatre facilities and nursing staff to specialties is an important issue for effective and efficient hospital operations management. The traditional approach to this allocation problem is a fragmented one. For example, one year the allocation of beds to specialties might be discussed because of the need to achieve a general reduction in the number of beds available at the hospital level. The next year the utilisation of operating theatre capacity might be scrutinised, resulting in a revised operating theatre timetable, and in the third year nursing workload might be the focus of discussion due to shortages of qualified nursing staff. However, these allocations of different resources, as required for inpatient admissions, are interconnected and should therefore be addressed in a combined effort.

Most hospitals do not have a formalised and accepted method to tackle this problem effectively. This contribution reports on a method, 'integral production and capacity planning on a logistic basis', that was developed for Dutch hospitals and implemented in more than 15 hospitals in the Netherlands. It is a hospital-wide method used to translate annual target production outputs into capacity allocations to specialties in such a way that:

- target production outputs per specialty are met;
- waiting lists are kept at a level that is acceptable;
- high but realistic targets are used for the occupancy level of resources;
- the use of beds is balanced with the use of operating theatres and with the workload for nurses on wards;
- systematic peaks and troughs in the weekly production cycle are reduced;
- the characteristics of the patient flow per specialty (urgency, variability of resource use) are taken into account.

BOX 8.1 THE CASE STUDY HOSPITAL

We present a case study that illustrates this method for a hospital that was faced by regular shortages of beds and by frequent admission stops. Previous investi-gations at this hospital had highlighted imbalances in the use of inpatient resources. One specialty had a shortage of operating theatre time with below-average use of beds; another had a shortage of beds. Allocation of resources was based on historical 'rights' rather than on real data on the demand for and use of resources. Up to then it had been almost impossible to discuss a reallo-cation of resources. However, a number of specialties asked the hospital manage-ment to reconsider the allocation of resources, as they faced increasing problems with long waiting lists. The bottleneck capacity at the hospital level was identified as beds, leading to many days when there was a stop on new admissions. The board of directors of the hospital decided to start a project with the aim of creating more flexibility in the allocation of resources through an annual revision of the allocation of inpatient resources. The project's objective was to develop a method for more dynamic capacity planning, taking into account developments in the catchment area, changes in technology and length of stay, and a balanced use of resources per specialty. The current, rather rigid allocation method – when considered at all – tended to result in a piecemeal approach to the separate resources: a new operating theatre allocation in the first year, a new bed-allocation plan the next year, only to find that the nursing staff allocation needed to be reconsidered the year after. The new approach was to look at the longer-term projection of patient flows and resource demands in order that there might be an annual allocation and balanced use of inpatient resources.

In the next section we will position the planning problem addressed in the planning framework as used for the case studies in this book and present a short literature review. The following section elaborates on the planning problem addressed in the case study and provides more detailed insight into the data that describe the problem. The decision support models used in the case study are then discussed, and the results of the case study and the developments of the method since then, based on its use in more than 15 hospitals, are presented. Finally, we reflect on the method and its further development.

PLANNING PROBLEM

The current practice of allocating resources to specialties within a hospital often results in capacity losses in beds, operating theatre time and other resources. There are three main reasons for this. First, the amount of a resource available to a specialty may not be in balance with the demand for that resource resulting from the average level of production. Second, the timing of the allocations in terms of the periods that a resource is made available to a specialty may lead to peaks and troughs in the workloads of departments. For example, if allocations of operating theatre sessions are not well distributed over the days of the week, large variations in the demand for beds and nursing staff might result. The third form of capacity loss may arise when the capacities of different resources that are required simultaneously for specialty production are not balanced, resulting in bottlenecks or under-utilisation.

The underlying reason for this capacity loss is that allocations of beds and operating theatre hours to specialties often tend to be based on historical rights rather than the requirements for resources resulting from the flow of patients. This is because there is a lack of procedures and methods available that hospitals can use to update resource allocations on a regular basis. When allocations are not patient flow based they can lead to over-capacity for one specialty and under-capacity for another. This can easily result in less optimal use of resources, i.e. fewer patients treated. This happens when requirements for capacity coordination are not well taken into account in the decision-making process of allocating resources to specialties.

Many resources in a hospital are shared by several specialties, such as beds, nursing staff, operating theatre facilities and diagnostic services. Scarcity results from the limited hospital budget or limited availability on the market for resources. When analysing the hospital's capacity structure, one can distinguish 'leading' and 'following' resources (see chapter 4 for definitions and terminology for unit logistics). 'Leading' resources act as triggers for production of 'following' resources. For example, a 'leading' resource for inpatient production of a surgical specialty is the operating theatre capacity allocated to this specialty, while beds and nursing staff are 'following' resources. This is an important distinction. The utilisation rate of a resource, defined as the ratio between its utilised capacity and available capacity, is often used as a measure of resource-use performance. One should, however, not only look at the average level of utilisation but also at the variations in the utilisation of resources at different times within a week, as these can cause knock-on variations in resource use in other parts of the hospital.

Apart from being the generator of hospital production, the clinical specialist is also one of the most important hospital resources. Almost all hospital production involves specialist-time as a resource, acting as a 'leading' resource for the workstations in the hospital. To improve hospital resource allocation it is therefore important to include specialist-time as a resource in the allocation procedure.

For some of the most important 'leading' resources hospitals use the concept of sessions as a batch-processing mechanism of patients. A session is a period of time allotted to a specialist in a workstation to treat a number of patients who require the same type of resources. Sessions are usually organised for a fixed period in the week and provide a short-term match between demand and supply of resources. Timetables regulate the allotment of sessions in a workstation to specialists. The most important ones are for operating theatre sessions and for clinic sessions. These timetables perform a similar function to master production schedules in an industrial setting, in that they define a production schedule per period (which in this case is a fixed schedule per week). The use of the session mechanism and timetables for scarce shared hospital resources leads to a number of requirements for coordination of capacity allocations (Vissers, 1994), which have already been discussed in chapter 4. Ignoring these coordination requirements may result in avoidable capacity loss or violations of the policy for planning specialty practice.

To illustrate the occurrence of capacity losses in health care we will provide some data on the use of resources by Dutch hospitals. Figure 8.1 shows weekly patterns in admissions, discharges and average bed occupancy rates averaged over all hospitals in the Netherlands (52 weeks, 1991).

From Figure 8.1 one can see that most admissions are concentrated in the beginning of the week and most discharges at the end of the week, resulting in a pattern of average bed occupancy rates with an accumulation in the middle of the week. The capacity loss resulting from this pattern could have been avoided by a better distribution of the inflow of patients over the days of the week. These activity profiles also exist at the individual hospital level and for other types of hospital resources (see also chapter 4).

Because of these characteristics, hospitals can benefit from an approach that enables capacity load levelling and also the development of workload target profiles for resources. To support hospitals in this planning effort we have developed a set of computer models that provide information for evaluating the links between resource allocation decisions and the need to coordinate capacity requirements. This was necessary as the current hospital information systems did not produce this information (De Vries, 1991). The approach involves the use of relatively simple 'what-if' models that visualise patient flows and resource requirements in different areas of hospital resource management decision making. The models that are used in the case study will be discussed in the section on capacity management models later in the chapter.

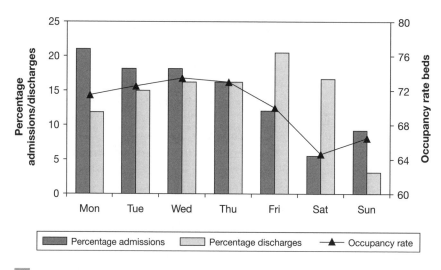

Figure 8.1 *Admissions, discharges and bed occupancy rates in Dutch hospitals (1991).*

The method we have developed for resource allocation, which takes into account capacity coordination requirements, is called 'Time-phased Resource Allocation'. This refers to the fact that not only the amount of resources allocated needs to match the level of demand, but that the timing of the allocation is also taken into account. This method allows for the development of capacity configuration plans that can be evaluated via detailed checks in the variation of capacity requirements throughout the week.

Position in planning framework

In this section we position the planning problem in the framework for operations management introduced in chapter 6. This framework describes the different planning levels required for hospital operations management and allows us to define the relationship between our planning problem and other planning issues in a hospital.

As shown in Figure 8.2, the method especially addresses the three upper levels of the planning framework and focuses on the long-term resource needs and annual allocation of resources. It combines the perspective of units (wards, operating theatres, etc.) with the perspective of chains (at the aggregate level of a specialty), although the emphasis is on efficient use of unit resources.

Literature review

Most literature in hospital patient scheduling and resource allocation focuses on a single resource. Much work has been done on bed planning for inpatient admissions (Wright, 1987; Bagust *et al.*, 1999; Ridge *et al.*, 1998), nursing workload in wards (Offensend, 1972; De Vries, 1987, Siferd and Benton, 1992), and scheduling surgical procedures in operation theatres (Blake, 2002; Dexter *et al.*, 2000; Gordon *et al.*, 1988; Guinet and Chaabane, 2003, Marcon *et al.*, 2003; Sier *et al.*, 1997). Much less has been published on the scheduling of patients who require

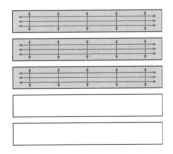

Network logistics application
Emphasis on unit logistics
Levels: strategic planning, patient volume planning
and control, and resources planning and control

Figure 8.2 *Production and capacity planning, and position in planning framework.*

121

multiple types of resources (Groot, 1993; Roth and Van Dierdonck, 1995; Kusters and Groot, 1996). Much of the work in this chapter is based on previous work by the author (Vissers 1994, 1998). In this chapter we focus on the allocation of resources. The case study in chapter 10 concentrates on the mix of patients to be admitted, i.e. the scheduling of patients (Adan and Vissers, 2002).

ELABORATION

The method 'integral production and capacity planning on a logistic basis' comprises a number of steps:

- demarcation of the scope of the method
- long-term resource requirements
- analysis of previous year's patient flows and resource utilisation
- reallocation of resources.

The emphasis of the method lies in the tactical level of planning. Nevertheless, when using the approach it is important to include also a longer-term perspective on resource requirements, so this is defined as a separate step in any project where the approach is followed.

We will now elaborate each of these steps as followed in the case study hospital. In a later section we will also report on our experiences with this approach in other hospitals and on the ways in which the method has been improved and developed over the years.

Demarcation of the scope of the method

The first step of the project in the case study hospital was to define what would be included in the production and capacity plan. Although this is a simple step, it is a very important one. It concerns the different types of resource that will be included in the production and capacity plan and the different sites of operation of the hospital. Apart from beds, operating theatres and nursing staff, it can include IC beds, outpatient clinic facilities and diagnostic departments. However, we would suggest that it is best to concentrate on a few resources initially and not to include all types of resource in the plan. The implementation of this new method will already be quite an effort. After the method has been introduced successfully, its scope can easily be increased every year. In the application of the approach in the case study hospital we concentrated on inpatient resources such as beds, operating theatre facilities and nursing staff.

A hospital can have different sites of operation. It might involve a larger and a smaller hospital with inpatient facilities on both sites, or a larger hospital on the main site and an outpatient facility on a second site. In such circumstances, we would suggest that both sites of the hospital are included in the scope of the project as the allocation of resources to the different sites is a major resource decision that is supported by the method. More importantly, key leading or following resources might be omitted. Our case study hospital operated only on one site.

Long-term resource requirements

Figure 8.3 illustrates the factors that affect the inflow of patients into a hospital. Potential demand for inpatient care delivered by a hospital is determined by the structure of its 'catchment' population and its needs for care. The actual demand for care from the hospital will depend upon its market share, i.e. the part of the population that uses its services rather than those provided by other hospitals in the area. Another important variable in the diagram is medical technology development (such as the use of non-invasive surgery), which can influence the throughput of patients by shortening the length of stay. Figure 8.3 is, of course, a simplification, as there are interactions between the factors mentioned that are omitted, for instance the influence of shorter length of stay on market share.

In the case study hospital, we investigated the ways in which changes in each of the above variables (population, demand for care, market share and length of stay)

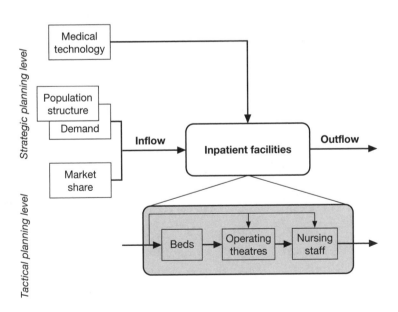

Figure 8.3 *Illustration of the variables included in the longer-term projections of patient flows and resource requirements.*

might affect its long-term resource requirements. The influence of each of these variables on the inflow of patients into the hospital and on the throughput of patients was investigated, first by varying one variable and keeping the other variables constant and next by looking at the combined effect of variables. To perform these analyses the model 'Patient Flows and Resources' was used, based on data giving population projections for the years 1990, 1995, 2000 and 2005 and the consumption of inpatient care by the inhabitants of the catchment area for the years 1989, 1990 and 1991 (see the section on capacity management models later in the chapter for a description of the model).

Population

Table 8.1 shows the changes in the projected total populations for the subregions in which the case study hospital was located. The case study hospital was based in the Central subregion.

From Table 8.1 it can be seen that the projected growth of the population in the central subregion was expected to lag behind that of the region as a whole. The projected regional increase by 1995 was 4.5 per cent while the expected increase in the population of the Central subregion was below 4 per cent. The number of inhabitants across the whole region showed a steady increase.

Using then current demand and market-share figures with the model 'patient flows and resources' we estimated the implications of the 1995 change in population on the inflow of patients for selected specialties. Figure 8.4 shows that the inflow of patients to the hospital in 1995 due to population developments was estimated to increase by more than 6 per cent, with variations between individual specialties.

Table 8.1 Changes in population projections within the region

Subregion	Number of inhabitants	Percentage change (base year 1990) (%)			Expected number of inhabitants
	1990	1995	2000	2005	2005
North-west	47.879	3.0	7.2	10.4	52.857
North-east	165.330	5.6	10.8	14.9	190.017
Central	191.467	3.8	6.8	9.3	209.220
South-west	140.063	4.7	9.7	13.4	158.901
South-east	102.035	4.3	8.5	11.5	113.797
Region total	646.774	4.5	8.8	12.1	724.792

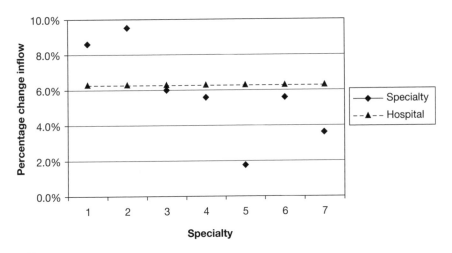

Figure 8.4 *Impacts of changes in population on inflow of patients (1995).*

Demand for care

As we had three years of data on hospital consumption available (1989, 1990, 1991), we were able to investigate only the direction of possible trends in the demand for care. Where consumption for a specialty was increasing three years in a row, we labelled this as an increasing trend. In this way we could track down trends in the demand for care in eight specialties, including general medicine (increase for males aged over 45, decrease for females aged 45–74) and cardiology (increase for males over 74, decrease for females over 74). However, an overall impact on specialty level was only noticeable for the specialties shown in Table 8.2, which shows the percentage deviation in the number of admissions to the hospital where 1990 is taken as base year. This implies that for general medicine the demand for care decreased over three years by about 3 per cent while for gynaecology the decrease was more than 7 per cent.

Table 8.2 *Influence of change in demand for care at study hospital*

Specialty	Percentage change in projected number of admissions (base year 1990)		
	1989	1990	1991
General medicine	+2.6	0	−0.3
Gynaecology	+4.4	0	−2.9
ENT	+1.6	0	−4.5
Neurology	−5.5	0	+10.3

Market share

We have also looked at the influence of market share of the hospital on the inflow of patients. Market share is defined as the number of patients admitted into the hospital divided by the number of patients from the region defined who have been admitted to any hospital in the Netherlands. It appeared that the hospital had a steady 14 per cent of the total market of about 67,000 patients per year. The market share per specialty varied from very low (dental surgery: 1 per cent) to average (general surgery: 15 per cent) and high (neurology: 21 per cent). Market shares per specialty showed minor changes over the three-year period. The influence of market-share development on the inflow of patients to the hospital showed major changes only for the specialties given in Table 8.3 (assuming population and demand for care as being constant).

We then considered the combined impact of long-term developments of population, demand and market share. Of the three variables discussed so far, only the population showed a clear trend for all specialties while the other variables (demand for care, market share) were more specialty specific. These could be regarded only as indications of actual trends because of the limited number of years that were available for analyses. Although the relative influence of some of these variables on the inflow of patients for some specialties was quite strong, we decided to include only the population development in the projection of future resource requirements.

Using the average length of stay, a target bed occupancy of 90 per cent and existing ratios between admissions and day cases and operations, we were able to make the projections for resource requirements as shown in Table 8.4. The calculations were made for the three base years available separately to get an impression of the sensitivity of the outcomes. We show here the results at hospital level, but these calculations have also been made at specialty level.

Table 8.3 Influence of change in market share on inflow to hospital

Specialty	Percentage change in the number of projected admissions (base year 1990)		
	1989	1990	1991
General surgery	−4.2	0	+0.7
Urology	+4.2	0	−5.8
Gynaecology	+4.4	0	−3.3
Plastic surgery	−27.6	0	+37.0
Neurology	+7.8	0	−1.5
Ophthalmology	−17.5	0	+14.0

Table 8.4 Resource impact projections for 1995 due to population development (hospital overall figures)

Base year of calculation	Occupancy rate in base year (%)			Projections of occupancy rate in 1995 (%)			Required resources in base year (numbers)			Resource requirements projections for 1995 (numbers)		
	1989	1990	1991	1989	1990	1991	1989	1990	1991	1989	1990	1991
Inpatient beds	86.7	85.4	85.0	93.1	90.8	89.3	267	263	262	287	280	275
Day-cases beds	101.7	104.7	112.4	108.4	111.6	119.1	12.2	12.6	13.5	13.0	13.4	14.3
Operating theatres	76.1	74.8	79.9	80.8	78.7	83.3	4.6	4.5	4.8	4.9	4.7	5.0

Looking at the results of Table 8.4 the following conclusions could be drawn:

- The current total number of beds of 276 would not be enough to cover future demand based on population development.
- The current number of day-case beds of 12 should be increased to at least 14.
- The current number of 6 operating theatres seemed to be enough to cover future demand in 1995.

Length of stay

The above calculations were based on the assumption that the average length of stay would stay the same. To get an impression of how future changes in lengths of stay might affect resource requirements we asked clinicians from some of the hospital specialties for their expert opinion on this issue. We preferred this approach to analysing, for example, national statistics because it allowed us to involve the clinicians in the project in order to make use of their local knowledge on conditions for length-of-stay development, such as the equipment likely to be available or the resistance of some specialists to using new operating techniques. The results of the interview rounds by specialty on length-of-stay development are summarised in Table 8.5.

According to Table 8.5 most specialties expected a decrease in the length of stay. These projections of the development in length of stay were then used to look at the consequences for resource use. Table 8.6 shows the results of these

Table 8.5 Development of length of stay for some specialties according to opinions of specialists

Specialty	Development of length of stay	Reasons for development
General medicine	Decrease: 0.5 day	shorter length of stay for younger patients
Cardiology	Decrease: 0.3 day	medical technology (non-invasive techniques for diagnosis)
General surgery	Decrease: 1.0 day	medical technology and short-stay development
Urology	Decrease: 0.5 day	not specified
Gynaecology	Decrease: 1.4 days	non-invasive surgery techniques
Orthopaedics	Increase: 0.3 day	increased percentage of elderly
Paediatrics	Decrease: 1.0 day	changed admission policy for early-born
Neurology	Decrease: 1.0 day	less 'wrong-bed' patients due to improved capacity of nursing homes

Table 8.6 *Resource impact projections for 1995 due to population and length-of-stay development (hospital overall figures)*

	Occupancy rate			Number of beds required		
	Base year	1995 (population)	1995 (population and length of stay)	Base year	1995 (population)	1995 (population and length of stay)
Inpatient beds	85.4	90.8	85.2	263	280	262

calculations at the overall hospital level for one base year of calculation (1990) and for inpatient beds.

It appeared that at hospital level the calculated increase of resource requirements of 6 per cent due to population development (see Figure 8.4) would be compensated for by a decrease in resource requirements due to a shorter length of stay. Similar results were obtained at specialty level.

This perspective on the long-term developments provided support for the next phase of the project: to develop a new bed allocation scheme that would meet the expected developments in the patient flow.

Analysis of previous year's patient flows and resource utilisation

In continuing this illustration of the approach, we will first look at the ways in which we analysed the case study hospital's flow of patients and its use of individual resources throughout the year. As beds were the bottleneck resource for hospital production, we initially concentrated on this resource. Then we considered the combined use of resources by a specialty. The analysis is based on data for the most recent year that we had available (1991).

Patient flows

To understand the development of bed occupancy throughout the year we analysed the number of admissions from week to week, as is shown in Figure 8.5.

According to Figure 8.5 on average 270 patients were admitted per week. Day-care patients, short-stay patients and 'regular' longer-stay patients each made up one-third of the number of admissions. For regular admissions, it appeared that there were no large peaks and troughs in the pattern of weekly admissions or seasonal trends. However, these were much more evident when considering short-stay patients and day cases. The dips here were assumed to be caused by the preference of patients not to be admitted during holiday periods. The peak and dip at

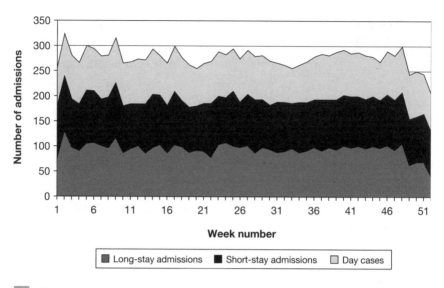

Figure 8.5 *Number of admissions per week (1991).*

the start and the end of the year are caused by a non-steady state due to sampling and should be ignored for interpretation as this refers to the way of counting patients whose stay includes New Year.

For surgical specialties the admission pattern within a week showed a definite shape. Figure 8.6 shows the admission pattern per day of the week for general surgery.

Figure 8.6 shows that there was clearly a pattern of admissions during the week for general surgery, which was linked with the number of operating theatre hours available per day. Patients with a length of stay of more than five days were, in general, admitted one day before the operation. On Sunday on average three patients were admitted to be operated on during Monday. Short-stay patients were admitted on the day of operation. General surgery would try to use fully its seven beds on the short-stay ward at the beginning of the week as this increased the likelihood of patients completing their rehabilitation without having to be transferred to a regular ward on Friday. As the week proceeded fewer patients were admitted. In general, surgical specialties in particular show such patterns, which seem to be related to the days that operating theatre facilities are available.

Bed allocation and bed occupancy

The hospital used a fixed allocation of beds to specialties. This allocation had not been changed for years. In practice, however, a specialty's bed allocation does not necessarily reflect the number of beds that are available for its admissions. In the

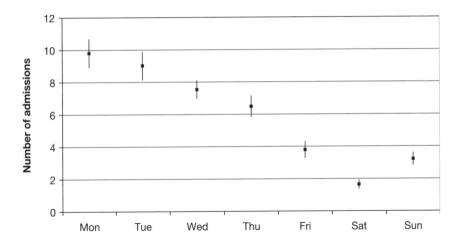

Figure 8.6 *Average number of admissions for general surgery (with 95% confidence limits) per day of the week.*

case study hospital, rules governing the availability of beds could be distinguished according to the length of stay of patients:

■ *Day-case beds* The hospital had a centralised facility for day cases of 12 beds that were used for one-day-surgery or one-day-observation patients. These beds were not allocated to specialties but could be used by all specialties.

■ *Short-stay beds* There was also a centralised facility of 39 beds for short-stay patients with a length of stay of not more than five days. In principle, the beds were allocated to specialties, but in practice they could be used for general purposes.

■ *Regular beds* The rest of the beds were scattered over the different wards and were used primarily for patients who had a length of stay of more than five days. These beds were more firmly allocated to specialties but again could be used by another specialty if it needed an extra bed.

The ways in which these beds were used by specialties can be seen in Table 8.7. As short-stay beds were not in use during the weekend, the average number of total allocated beds (short-stay and regular) per week was not always a whole number.

In Table 8.7 a distinction has been made between the use of beds by a specialty in the allocated wards and the use of beds outside these wards. This is an indication of the number of beds borrowed from other specialties. General medicine, for example, used on average 63.8 beds of which 3.2 beds were in wards where

Table 8.7 Utilisation of bed resources by specialty (based on monthly figures over 1991)

Specialty	Allocated number of beds	Average number of beds in use (n=12)	Standard deviation beds in use (n=12)	Percentage 'own' beds in use	Occupancy rate of allocated beds	Beds used from other wards	Number of day-case beds used	Number of admission stops
General medicine	64	63.8	2.8	94.7	99.6	3.2	1.1	30
Cardiology	17.7	18.3	1.5	99.0	103.5	0.8	0.1	67
Pulmonology	14	11.9	1.5	80.7	84.9	0.6	0.1	4
Rheumatology	14	10.4	2.2	72.3	74.5	0.3	–	12
Anaesthesiology	–	0.1	0.0	–	–	0.1	0.9	–
General surgery	52	44.2	4.3	79.8	85.0	2.7	1.3	2
Urology	14.1	9.8	1.8	64.4	69.2	0.7	1.0	1
Orthopaedics	25.2	22.1	2.6	76.2	87.6	2.9	2.2	6
Plastic surgery	4.7	3.6	0.8	73.2	75.4	0.1	0.6	1
Gynaecology	24	18.0	2.3	73.0	74.9	0.5	2.0	2
Paediatrics	24	15.0	2.9	53.6	62.4	2.1	0.2	5
Neurology	23.4	27.1	2.3	101.2	115.7	3.4	0.5	42
Dermatology	3	2.5	0.7	71.7	81.7	0.3	–	3
ENT	7.1	5.2	0.7	42.6	72.8	2.2	2.5	–
Ophthalmology	3.6	4.3	1.1	111.3	121.4	0.4	0.2	–
Radiology	0.7	0.8	0.0	112.7	112.7	0.0	0.3	–
Hospital total	304.1	257.0	9.0	86.5	86.5	–	13.0	175

no beds were allocated to this specialty. This resulted in an overall occupancy rate of 99.6 per cent, but of 94.7 per cent when looking at the occupancy of the beds on the wards allocated to general medicine. Also, neurology had a high occupancy rate of own beds combined with a large number of borrowed beds elsewhere. The occupancy rates of urology and paediatrics were below 70 per cent. The average occupancy rate at hospital level of more than 85 per cent was quite high, which indicated that beds could be considered as a bottleneck.

As the number of beds in use varied – as can be seen from the fluctuations (standard deviations) at monthly level – there were occasions when no bed was available to admit a patient. In this case the hospital was forced to use an 'admission-stop' for one or more days. During 1991 in total there were 175 'admission-stops', most of them within general medicine, cardiology and neurology. This large number of 'admission-stops' was a further indication of beds being the most important bottleneck in the case study hospital.

The simultaneous use of resources by specialties

To study the simultaneous use of different resources by a specialty we investigated two four-week samples: one 'busy' period and one 'average' period. The analysis was performed using the model 'Inpatient Capacity Management' (see the 'capacity management models' section for details of the model). This model visualises whether or not a specialty – given its admission pattern – uses its resources in a coherent way.

What in this hospital could be regarded as busy, average and below average periods can be seen in Figure 8.5. The first analysis was done for the busy period weeks 3–6 (January/February). The average number of admissions per week in this period was 290. As four weeks are a short period for analysis, a second 'average' period of analysis was chosen (weeks 35–38, August/September) to make it possible to compare a period with many 'admission-stops' with a period with few 'admission-stops'. The average number of admissions per week in the second period was 270. We will only show the results of the analysis for the busy period (see Table 8.8).

Table 8.8 shows that in a busy period on average 293 patients were admitted, of whom 89 were day-cases and 99 short-stay patients, resulting in an average level of bed occupancy of 99 per cent, an average nursing workload pressure of 95 per cent and an average operating theatre occupancy of 73 per cent. These results implied that it was not only beds that acted as a potential bottleneck but also the availability of nursing staff, while the utilisation of operating theatre resources remained relatively low. Or expressed in another way, the high bed occupancy and nursing workload prevented a higher utilisation of operating theatre resources.

The specialty bed occupancy figures only related to 'regular' beds. The overall hospital bed occupancy figure takes also day-case beds and short-stay beds into

Table 8.8 Simultaneous use of inpatient resources by specialty (January 1991)

Specialty	Number of admissions per specialty per week				Average occupancy rate per week (%)		
	Day cases	Short-stay cases	Regular admis-sions	Total admis-sions	Beds	Nursing staff	OT hours
General medicine	11	5	25	41	104	89	–
Cardiology	2	10	8	20	119	95	–
Pulmonology	2	0	4	5	51ᶜ	98	–
Rheumatology	0	0	4	4	101	97	–
Anaesthesiology	11	1	0	11	0	0	–
General surgery	11	15	19	45	98	101	74
Urology	3	5	4	12	70	96	23
Orthopaedics	11	10	7	29	111	110	68
Plastic surgery	5	3	2	10	91	157cᶜ	64
Gynaecology	9	11	10	31	83	98	75
Paediatrics	1	4	11	15	85	91	–
Neurology	4	13	10	27	139	101	35
Dermatology	0	0	1	1	103	97	–
ENT	18	12	1	31	143ᶜ	75	81
Ophthalmology	1	6	0	7	0	0	72
Radiology	2	2	0	4	0	0	–
Hospital total	89	99	105	293	99	95	73

Note: Figures marked ᶜ show deviations from expected values that can be explained by the short period of data collection (in the case of pulmonology), the inability to take into account short-stay beds (in the case of ENT) and the lack of good nursing workload measurement data (in the case of plastic surgery). Hospital totals and total admissions will not always add up correctly due to rounding off differences.

account. General surgery, orthopaedics, plastic surgery and neurology/neurosurgery showed the same picture as for the overall hospital: an imbalance between the use of bed resources and the use of operating theatre resources due to a shortage of beds or an over-capacity of operating theatre hours. Internal medicine and cardiology showed an imbalance between the use of bed resources and the use of nursing staff resources. Specialties with a well-balanced use of all inpatient resources were rheumatology, gynaecology, paediatrics and dermatology.

Important to note, but not shown here, is that the analysis for the second period produced an overall similar picture of the coherence in the use of resources, but on a lower performance level.

Reallocation of resources

The results of these analyses were used to develop a method for the flexible and coherent allocation of inpatient resources. The approach developed is, in principle, also applicable in other hospital settings. As the three resource types of beds, nursing staff and operating theatres are interdependent, a step-wise approach was chosen to allocate resources, starting with the bottleneck resource. The approach used was as follows:

1   Define the bottleneck resource as the resource that is most critical for hospital inpatient production. This is based on occupancy rate figures (average and standard deviation) as realised in the past.
2   Allocate the bottleneck resource to specialties or departments. This is based on the current use of the bottleneck resource.
3   Allocate the other resources to specialties or departments.

The allocation of the bottleneck resource is, in principle, based on the current utilisation of resources. Hospital management, however, can decide to increase or decrease capacity for the bottleneck resource based on strategic considerations for the future profile of the hospital. Information on current use and the analyses on population, demand and market-share development are used to support decisions concerning the actual allocation of the bottleneck resource. This is the first phase of resource allocation.

In the second phase, again the basis for allocation is the current utilisation of the resource at hand. When the current use of the resource does not produce any difficulties (e.g. sharp peaks and troughs), the current allocation can be maintained. Otherwise, some adaptations need to be made to alleviate resource impacts. To achieve coherence in resource use, every change in allocation of one of the resources needs to be checked on resource impacts for the other resources. The checks on coherent resource use can be supported by the model 'Inpatient Capacity Management'.

It is also important to include some reference points in terms of the target capacity loads to be achieved when there is a balanced use of inpatient resources. What analyses for the very busy and average busy periods in the case study hospital demonstrated was that the three resources showed different capacity load performances but that the differences between resources were, when considered relatively, the same in both periods. Based on the results of this case study, and also other studies, we would suggest the following hospital level capacity load targets for beds, operating theatres and nursing staff respectively: 90 per cent – 85 per cent – 100 per cent. Note that other studies in the UK (Bagust et al., 1999) advise 85 per cent for beds as reasonable. For specialties with more or less than average urgent admissions, these targets might be adjusted for beds and operating theatres by around $+/-$ 5 per cent. For nursing staff the target occupancy level is 100 per cent. This refers to the net availability of nursing staff for patient-related activities. As nursing staff is a very flexible type of resource a target of 100 per cent is acceptable; in reality the workload will vary between 85 per cent and 115 per cent.

As beds were the bottleneck resource for the case study hospital, the allocation procedure started with this resource. From the previous analyses it was clear that the available beds were, from time to time, not enough to cover all demand for specialties, resulting in 'admission-stops'. This indicated that there might be a need to develop managerial decisions to ensure that specialties that were important for the hospital strategic profile could meet their demand for beds: in other words, to make sure that other specialties did not borrow too many beds from these specialties in these busy periods. The then current use of beds by specialties differed from the historical-based allocations as has been shown in Table 8.7. In the setting of the case study hospital this did not result in capacity losses because the actual use of beds at operational level was very flexible. For example, on average, neurology used four beds more than its allocation and general surgery used eight beds fewer than its allocation. This illustrated that the actual use of beds by specialties had moved away from the allocated numbers, and that hospital management did not use bed allocation as a tool of management to implement scenarios that are in harmony with the hospital's strategic plan. To increase the allocated bed capacity of specialties where growth needed to be stimulated, different options could be considered: either extra beds could be allocated or measures to stimulate shorter length of stays could be introduced. We illustrate below an example of the first option, i.e. a review of the current bed allocation based on the actual use of beds. The results are shown in Table 8.9. The allocation of the other resources can be calculated in a similar way.

The bed allocation scheme suggested results in average bed occupancies of about 90 per cent for most specialties. Apart from the average use of beds, the fluctuations in bed usage also need to be taken into account. In this example the suggested number of beds allocated is equal to the upper confidence limit (95 per cent) for the average number of beds in use. It should be noted that this procedure benefits those specialties with high occupancy levels. Hospital management has again the task of checking that the allocations suggested do not harm specialties where growth needs to be stimulated. The allocation scheme shown leaves the allocation of about nine beds to the discretion of hospital management. The bed occupancy figures for most specialties are at about 90 per cent, which can be considered as a high bed utilisation performance.

CAPACITY MANAGEMENT MODELS

The two models that were used in the case study on the allocation of inpatient resources concern 'Patient Flows and Resources' and 'Inpatient Capacity

Table 8.9 Example bed allocation scheme based on actual resource use

Specialty	Allocated number of beds	Average number of beds in use	Standard-deviation average number of beds	New bed allocation	Old bed occupancy (%)	New bed occupancy (%)
General medicine	64	63.8	0.8	65.6	99.6	97.4
Cardiology	17.7	18.3	0.4	19.2	103.5	95.3
Pulmonology	14	11.9	0.4	12.9	84.9	92.2
Rheumatology	14	10.4	0.6	11.8	74.5	88.1
Anaesthesiology	–	0.1	–	–	–	–
General surgery	52	44.2	1.2	46.9	85.0	94.2
Urology	14.1	9.8	0.5	10.9	69.2	89.9
Orthopaedics	25.2	22.1	0.7	23.7	87.6	93.2
Neurosurgery	–	–	–	–	–	–
Plastic surgery	4.7	3.6	0.2	4.1	75.4	87.8
Dental surgery	–	–	–	–	–	–
Gynaecology	20	16.5	0.5	17.7	74.9	93.2
Paediatrics	24	15.0	0.8	16.8	62.4	89.3
Neurology	23.4	27.1	0.7	28.6	115.7	94.8
Dermatology	3	2.5	0.2	2.9	81.7	86.2
ENT	7.1	5.2	0.2	5.6	72.8	92.8
Ophthalmology	3.6	4.3	0.3	5.0	121.4	86.0
Radiology	0.7	0.8	–	0.7	112.7	–
Obstetric beds	4.0	1.5	–	4.0	37.5	37.5
Total allocated	291.5	–	–	276.4	–	–
Not allocated beds	–	–	–	9.2	–	–

Management'. The first model supports long-term decisions about the resources required to match future demand. The second model supports decision making at the medium-term level for balancing the resource requirements of inpatient services. The equations used to support analysis using these models are detailed below.

Patient Flows and Resources Model

Let $p_{i,j,k}(t)$ be the number of inhabitants in year t from age-category i, and sex-category j, living in community k. Let $x_{i,j,k,l,m}(t)$ be the number of patients in year t from age-category i, and sex-category j, living in community k, admitted in hospital l, for specialty m. Note that hospital l can also be a group of hospitals.

Then the number of patients expected for year $(t+a)$ in hospital l for specialty m, while demand is supposed to be at the same level as year t, can be derived using the equation:

$$PF_{l,m}(t + a) = \sum_{i,j,k} P_{i,j,k}(t + a) \times \frac{x_{i,j,k,l,m}(t)}{P_{i,j,k}(t)}, \text{ with } PF_{l,m}(t) \text{ is the patient flow expected for year } t \text{ in hospital } l \text{ for specialty } m.$$

In turn, the number of beds required in year $(t+a)$ in hospital l for specialty m is estimated using the equation:

$$BR_{l,m}(t + a) = \frac{PF_{l,m}(t + a) \times LOS_{l,m}(t + a)}{365 \times \text{target bed occupancy rate}}, \text{ with } BR_{l,m}(t) \text{ is the beds required for year } t \text{ in hospital } l \text{ for specialty } m, \text{ and } LOS_{l,m}(t) \text{ is the length of stay for year } t \text{ in hospital } l \text{ for specialty } m.$$

Inpatient Capacity Model

Let $x_{i,j}(l,t)$ be the number of patients admitted at day t for specialty l with a length of stay class i and an operation duration class j. Then the amount of beds required at day t for specialty l with a_i is the average length of stay of class i is derived as follows:

$$B(l,t) = \sum_{i} \sum_{u=a_i}^{0} \sum_{j} x_{i,j}(l, t - u)$$

Similarly, the amount of operating theatre hours required at day t for specialty l where v_i is day of operation length of stay class i, and:

$$v_i = 0 \text{ for } a_i \leq 5$$
$$v_i = 1 \text{ for } a_i > 5$$

and o_j is average duration of operation class j is estimated as follows:

$$O(l, t) = \sum_j \sum_i x_{i,j}(l, t - v_i) \times o_j$$

Finally, the amount of nursing staff required at day t for specialty l with $n(l,u)$ equals the amount of nursing staff required for admissions for specialty l at day u within the admission period (the nursing workload function), and is calculated as follows:

$$N(l, t) = \sum_i \sum_{u=a_i}^{0} \sum_j x_{i,j}(l, t - u) \times n(l,u)$$

RESULTS

The method as developed in the case study has been disseminated via one-day workshops in which participants from different hospitals can familiarise themselves with the method and its application. Up to now the method has been introduced in 15 hospitals in the Netherlands, and more than half of these hospitals now use the method on an annual basis to update their resource allocations. An important key to a successful implementation is the acceptance of the method by the relevant actors as an objective approach to this complicated planning problem.

The method is introduced and implemented in a hospital via a project. A task force is established, and its members familiarise themselves with the method and perform analyses into the logistics of patient flows at specialty level. It is important that key actors from the following aspects of operational planning and services are involved in the planning exercise: admission planning, operating theatre planning, nursing wards (day surgery, short stay and 'regular'), surgical and non-surgical specialties.

Figure 8.7 illustrates for the tactical planning level the steps to be performed by the project team, based on beds being the primary bottleneck resource. The most important change, compared with the approach followed in the case study hospital, is that the production volumes as agreed in the contracts for next year are the starting point for applying the method.

The allocations of beds per specialty are based on insight into the patient flows and bed requirements of recent years. Patient flows are analysed, taking into account seasonal effects and admission patterns during the week. It is important

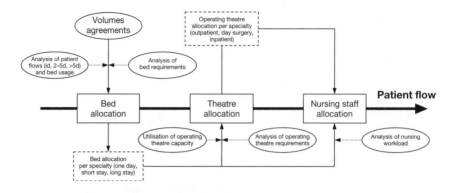

Figure 8.7 *Procedure for resource allocation.*

to distinguish in these analyses between day-surgery admissions (one day), short-stay admissions (two to five days), and long stay admissions (more than five days). This allows for a link with day-surgery bed requirements, short-stay bed requirements and long-stay bed requirements.

The bed allocation scheme resulting from this first step is the point of departure for the second step, i.e. the allocation of operating theatre capacity. The allocation of operating theatre capacity is based on an analysis of last year's utilisation figures and on the requirements of operating theatre resources for production of the volumes of patients agreed upon as target for next year.

The bed allocation scheme – as a result of step one – and the operating theatre allocation scheme – as a result of step two – are used to investigate the impact of these schemes on the nursing workload at the wards. The patient flows expected at the ward are translated into nursing workload using some workload classification scheme (for instance San Joaquin; De Vries, 1987) that allows not only analysis of the level of workload per ward but also the identification of structural peaks and troughs in the workload during the week.

Having completed the complete cycle of analysis, it is also possible to return to a previous step if the results – for instance on the workload of wards – indicate an unacceptable performance. Essentially, the procedure describes an iterative process. The outcome of the procedure should be that all resources involved in the production of inpatient care are checked on their availability and on a performance level that is according to standards. The procedure for allocation of the different resources should result in a balanced use of resources along the (aggregate) product line of each specialty.

There are a few points to mention in which the method as used nowadays has been developed further, compared with the case study approach:

■ *Prospective use* The case study illustrated the use of the method to reallocate resources based on current utilisation of resources, a retrospective use of

140

the method. Nowadays, the method is also used for prospective purposes. As illustrated in Figure 8.7, the reallocation also takes into account the production volumes agreed for next year's contracts. This is an extension as step 4 of the case study approach as discussed in the 'Elaboration' section under 'Reallocation of resources'.

■ *Target utilisation* The case study approach used as targets for utilisation of beds, operating theatres and nursing staff 90 per cent – 85 per cent – 100 per cent respectively. Nowadays we use a differentiation of these overall hospital figures for individual specialties. This is based on the notion that the characteristics of patient flows differ between specialties. We use as discriminating factors variation in the occupancy of resources and the level of urgency. A specialty with much variation in the use of resources from day to day, and with a high level of urgency, will have more difficulty in maintaining a high level of utilisation of resources. Based on this notion we have developed the rules of thumb shown in Table 8.10 for translating the overall hospital targets for the

Table 8.10 *Corrections on overall hospital targets for resource utilisation*

Variation in use of beds and percentage urgency admissions		Correction on target utilisation
Low variation in use of beds (CV < 25%)	Low level of urgency (< 20%)	plus 5%
	Average level of urgency (20–60%)	plus 5%
	High level of urgency (> 60%)	no correction
Average variation in use of beds (CV: 25–50%)	Low level of urgency (< 20%)	plus 5%
	Average level of urgency (20–60%)	no correction
	High level of urgency (> 60%)	minus 5%
High variation in use of beds (CV > 50%)	Low level of urgency (< 20%)	no correction
	Average level of urgency (20–60%)	minus 5%
	High level of urgency (> 60%)	minus 5%
Variation in use of OT and percentage urgency operations		Correction on target utilisation
Low variation in OT use (CV < 30%)	Low level of urgency (<15%)	plus 5%
	Average level of urgency (15–50%)	plus 5%
	High level of urgency (> 50%)	no correction
Average variation in OT use (CV: 30–50%)	Low level of urgency (<15%)	plus 5%
	Average level of urgency (15–50%)	no correction
	High level of urgency (> 50%)	minus 5%
High variation in OT use (CV > 50%)	Low level of urgency (<15%)	no correction
	Average level of urgency (15–50%)	minus 5%
	High level of urgency (> 50%)	minus 5%

Note: The coefficient of variation (CV) is used as measure for the variation of the use of resources, which is defined as the ratio between the standard deviation and the average. The cut-off points for low-average-high variation are case specific.

utilisation of beds and operating theatres to specific targets for individual specialties.

■ *Fixed and variable allocation* In the case study approach the number of beds allocated to a specialty was based on the average number of beds in use plus two standard deviations. Nowadays we make a distinction between a 'fixed' allocation (based on the target utilisation) and a variable allocation to deal with the variations within the week (based on one standard deviation). The variable beds are shared as pool beds between specialties.

■ *High season and low season allocation* In holiday periods production tends to be lower than in the normal season, and reductions in the resources available tend to occur. This can be a reason to develop two different schemes for the allocation of resources.

Our experiences with these amendments in the approach used for developing an approach for an annual production and capacity plan are positive. They contribute to a better fit between plans and reality.

REFLECTION AND FURTHER DEVELOPMENT

Based on the findings in this study on hospital resource allocation we now discuss some implications of this research in a wider context, and formulate recommendations for future research.

The method we have described provides a procedure for hospitals to update resource allocations on a regular basis. The long-term projections on patient flows and resource demands allow for investigation of the influence of developments in population, demand for care, market share and length of stay. This provides a firm basis for the annual allocation of resources. The 'Time-phased Resource Allocation' method takes into account the right level of allocations including the right balance between allocations of different resources, avoiding capacity loss, as well as the right timing of it, avoiding unnecessary peaks and troughs. The models that were used as analytical tools in this case study performed very well. They acted as a vehicle for the philosophy underlying the method and guided the analyses to be performed.

The approach to hospital resource allocation issues as described in this chapter can be applied to a wide range of problems. Potential areas of application are:

■ reorganisation of timetables for specialty activities, operating theatres and outpatient clinics;

■ improving workload and service levels of medical support services departments (X-ray, laboratories, organ examination departments) caused by interface problems with other parts of the hospital;

■ reallocation of inpatient resources (beds, operating theatres, nursing staff) due to shortages of (for instance) beds or structural overloading of (for instance) nursing staff;

- evaluating the impacts of the introduction of centralised facilities for day surgery or short-stay admissions;
- business planning for a new hospital;
- multi-location planning problems due to mergers.

Capacity load targets are needed to determine what can be considered as reasonable resource-use performance. This study shows that when resources used for the same production are allocated in a coherent way, high utilisation rates can be achieved. In the example of resources for inpatient production, capacity load targets for beds, operating theatres and nursing staff at overall hospital level could be set for 90 per cent – 85 per cent – 100 per cent. These are average figures for a busy season. When one goes beyond these levels there is reason to believe that the system will be overloaded, resulting in many admission stops or the by-passing of elective planning systems by specialists who misuse the label 'urgent case'.

To conclude this study on hospital resource allocation we present the following recommendations for future research in this area of hospital planning:

- *Capacity load targets* We used in this study as a heuristic for capacity load targets for beds, operating theatres and nursing staff at overall hospital level of 90 per cent – 85 per cent – 100 per cent. Further research could be done to find evidence for this heuristic or for adjustment of this heuristic. What are the impacts if, for instance, we would use 95 per cent – 90 per cent – 100 per cent instead? This could be done by simulation but also by experimenting with these targets in reality, as more and more hospitals are forced to operate under tighter budgets.
- *Model support* The models can be further improved, based on the experiences gained in this case study and otherwise. One of the principles used in modelling the current set was to make the models as simple as possible, avoiding claims for optimisation. This was done on purpose, as this level of support was considered more in balance with the current state of resource management in hospitals, and simple, transparent models encourage participation. It was judged more important to help hospitals on the way to a systematic review of resource use and resource allocation than to aim for optimal solutions. Perhaps after a few years' experience with the current tools there will be a need for more sophistication, to give broader support in the decision-making process than the current models do. It would be possible to superimpose on the current models a solution generator that would help the user in finding feasible solutions. This would bring the support of the models to a higher level, though still not at the level of optimisation. This level of support will probably remain out of reach, as resource allocation requires many variables to be taken into account at the same time, and the sophisticated models required would discourage the participation of those whose input is required for an effective solution.

QUESTIONS AND EXERCISES

1   The current case concentrates on inpatient resources. Figure 8.3 illustrates the method used for longer-term projections of patient flows and resource requirements. Expand the proposed method with outpatient and diagnostic resources. What resources would you suggest should be included? Develop a graphical illustration of the expanded model you suppose, in analogy to Figure 8.3.

2   In the section 'Analysis of previous year's patient flows and resource utilisation' a distinction is made between day cases, short-stay admissions and long-stay admissions. Why is this distinction so important from an operations management point of view?

3   What is the added value of the analysis of the simultaneous use of resources by a specialty (see the section 'Analysis of previous year's patient flows and resource utilisation') above the separate analysis of utilisation data of each of the resources involved? Do you expect the results of the analysis of the simultaneous use to show a higher or lower level of occupancy, compared with the results of data of the individual resources?

4   To define target utilisation figures for specialties, variation in the occupancy of resources and the level of urgency are used to translate overall hospital targets to specialty targets (see 'Results' section). Discuss other factors that could have been included to explain the capability of a specialty to maintain a high level of utilisation of resources.

REFERENCES AND FURTHER READING

Adan I.J.B.F. and J.M.H. Vissers. Patient mix optimisation in hospital admission planning: a case study. Special issue on 'Operations Management in Health Care', *International Journal of Operations and Production Management,* 22(4), 2002, 445–461.

Bagust A., M. Place and J.W. Posnett. Dynamics of bed use in accommodating emergency admissions; stochastic simulation model. *British Medical Journal,* 319, 1999, 155–158.

Blake J.T. Using integer programming to allocate operating room time at Mount Sinai hospital. *Interfaces,* 32, 2002, 63–73.

Dexter F., A. Macario and L. O'Neill. Scheduling surgical cases into overtime block time. Computer simulation of the effects of scheduling strategies on operating room labor costs. *Anaesthesia & Analgesia,* 90, 2000, 980–988.

Gordon T., A.P.S. Lyles and J. Fountain. Surgical unit time utilization review: resource utilization and management implications. *Journal of Medical Systems,* 12, 1988, 169–179.

Groot P.M.A. *Decision Support for Admission Planning under Multiple Resource Constraints.* Published doctoral dissertation, Enschede: Febo, 1993.

Guinet A. and S. Chaabane. Operating theatre planning. *International Journal of Production Economics,* 85, 2003, 69–81.

Kusters R.J. and P.M.A. Groot. Modelling resource availability in general hospitals. Design and implementation of a decision support model. *European Journal of Operational Research,* 88, 1996, 428–445.

Marcon E., S. Kharraja and G. Simonnet. The operating theatre planning by the follow-up of the risk of no realization. *International Journal of Production Economics,* 85, 2003, 83–90.

Offensend F.L. A hospital admission system based on nursing workload. *Management Science,* 19, 1972, 132–138.

Ridge J.C., S.K. Jones, M.S. Nielsen and A.K. Shahani. Capacity planning for intensive care units. *European Journal of Operational Research,* 105(2), 1998, 346–355.

Roth A.V. and R. Van Dierdonck. Hospital resources planning: concepts, feasibility and framework. *International Journal of Production and Operations Management,* 4, 1995, 2–29.

Sier D., P. Tobin and C. McGurk. Scheduling surgical procedures. *Journal of the Operational Research Society,* 48, 1997, 884–891.

Siferd S.P. and W.C. Benton. Workforce staffing and scheduling: hospital nursing specific models. *European Journal of Operational Research,* 60, 1992, 233–246.

Vissers J.M.H. *Patient Flow based Allocation of Hospital Resources.* Doctoral thesis, Eindhoven University of Technology, 1994.

Vissers J.M.H. Patient flow based allocation of hospital resources. *IMA Journal of Mathematics Applied in Medicine & Biology,* Oxford University Press, 1995, 259–274.

Vissers J.M.H. Patient flow based allocation of inpatient resources: a case study. In L. Delesie, A. Kastelein, F. van Merode and J.M.H. Vissers (eds) Feature Issue 'Managing Health Care under Resource Constraints', EJOR, 105(2), 1 March 1998, 356–370.

Vries G. de. Nursing workload measurement as management information. *European Journal of Operational Research,* 29, 1987, 199–208.

Vries G. de. De mythe van managementinformatie. In J.W. Hoorn, J. Lettink, H. van Tuijl, J. Vissers and G. de Vries (eds) *Sturing van zorgprocessen. Bedrijfskundig instrumentarium voor de ziekenhuismanager.* De Tijdstroom, Lochem, 1991.

Wright M.B. The application of a surgical bed simulation model. *European Journal of Operational Research,* 32, 1987, 26–32.

Chapter 9

How to take variability into account when planning the capacity for a new hospital unit

Martin Utley, Steve Gallivan and Mark Jit

SUMMARY

Providing the appropriate level of capacity for post-operative care to cater for the activity planned in operating theatres is an important planning issue affecting staffing levels as well as the provision of physical bed capacity and ward space. Over-provision of post-operative capacity is wasteful of resources while under-provision can cause operations to be cancelled and expensive operating theatre time to be wasted. This chapter addresses the problem faced by the planner who wishes to take account of unpredictable variability in post-operative length of stay. This planning problem is discussed with specific reference to planning capacity requirements for post-operative recovery within one of the new generation of health care centres being introduced within the UK NHS.

KEY TERMS

- Length of stay and stochastics
- Planning of bed capacity
- Model support for post-operative care

INTRODUCTION

The UK government has introduced a new class of health care centres that are dedicated to the delivery of diagnostic or routine elective services. Originally known as Diagnosis and Treatment Centres, such facilities are now being given the term Treatment Centres (TCs) by the government. Some of these TCs consist of entire newly built hospitals and others are housed within existing hospitals. This chapter describes how a mathematical model was used to support the planning process surrounding the delivery of elective general surgical services at one of these new centres.

Activity and capacity planning is required to support the development of these new centres and those managing a TC project need to address many complex and inextricably linked issues. Questions arise such as what patient groups will be treated in the new centre, how many operating theatres are required and what level of staffing and bed capacity is required for post-operative care. The focus of this chapter is on a model to support decisions made regarding the level of bed capacity required for post-operative care.

Capacity planning is one area where operational research, discussed briefly in chapter 1, has a large role to play in effective operations management. Operational research is the mathematical field that covers such topics, and many people work full time on such problems in a variety of contexts including manufacturing processes, telecommunications and transport. One key problem operational research deals with is the effect that variability in demand has on the capacity requirements of a system. It is important to draw a clear distinction between unpredictable variability and variations that can be predicted. For instance, it is well known that more patients are admitted to hospitals in the UK during the winter months. Seasonal variations in overall levels of demand for health care can thus be predicted and sensible planning will take account of these. By unpredictable variability we refer to processes such as emergency admissions for which, although the average number that arrive per day may be known, it is impossible to predict how many will arrive on a particular day. Similarly, managers might know the average duration of the post-operative recovery period associated with a certain procedure but would not be able to predict which patients will stay longer than average due to post-operative infections, etc. A key notion in much operational research work is that the more unpredictable variability there is, the more likely it is that operational emergencies will occur, particularly if systems operate close to capacity. Depending on the context, such operational emergencies might include unacceptable computer network delays, road traffic gridlock or bed crises.

It is perhaps fair to say that the importance of unpredictable variability is less widely recognised by those planning the delivery of health care services, at least in the UK. Various operational research studies have investigated such issues (for example Harper and Shahani, 2002, and Utley *et al.*, 2003), but there is little evidence that appropriate methods are applied in practice within the UK. Much is known about the average duration of patients' stays in hospital, but it has been uncommon to use information collected on a patient-by-patient basis to explore variability and its impact of service delivery. Indeed when the authors have requested such data from individual hospital managers, their requests have been met with some curiosity as to why anyone should need this.

The variability of patient length of stay has become more important to the operation of the UK NHS since a government policy was introduced that stated that hospitals should give patients a firm commitment regarding the date of their procedure. Such booking may occur some months before the event, so the booking manager does not know with any certainty what the status of the TC will be in terms of factors such as bed availability. This policy reduces the scope for hospital-initiated cancellations of elective procedures to be used to cope with bed crises. Effective booking means striking a balance between having too few admissions, leading to a waste of expensive health resources, and too many, which can lead to overload. This is a delicate balance to strike and unpredictable variability of length of stay plays an important role.

The case study discussed in the following sections concerns an actual planning problem that the authors were asked to advise about, and while factors such as data estimates may appear somewhat crude, this reflects the reality of NHS operational planning.

BOX 9.1 THE CASE STUDY SETTING

The study concerns one stream of clinical activity in a TC housed within a larger acute hospital. The TC manager had reached agreement with the wider hospital management concerning the level of patient throughput that the TC unit should deliver. This level of activity was largely influenced by the number of general surgery procedures that would be required to meet government targets concerning the maximum waiting time that patients should face. At the time of the planning exercise described in this chapter, the TC manager had agreed on an operating schedule with the available general surgeons and was in the final stages of arranging anaesthetic cover for this schedule and planning post-operative care facilities.

The questions the manager had to answer were:

- What level of bed capacity is appropriate to cater for expected demand for post-operative care?
- To what extent are bed capacity requirements affected by a pre-determined cyclic pattern of admissions for surgery?
- To what extent are bed capacity requirements affected by unpredictable variability in patient post-operative length of stay?

In the simplistic statement of the problem given in the box, the focus is on the provision of beds. It should be noted that along with the physical resource of beds, this planning problem also relates to the attendant level of nursing cover that is required for post-operative recovery and many other resource issues such as equipment requirements and demand on hospital catering.

The next section provides a more detailed description of the particular planning problem addressed and places it in within the planning framework presented in chapter 6. We also provide a brief summary of some of the different approaches to capacity planning and variability in patient length of stay that are available in the literature. The following section elaborates on the specific problem addressed and presents the data estimates that were used in the planning exercise. The mathematical modelling approach we used in this exercise is outlined in the next section and a summary of the analysis is presented. Mathematical detail is scant in this section and the emphasis is on the concepts behind the model and the mathematical expressions concerning bed requirements that are derived as a result of the analysis. The results of the planning exercise are then presented and the strengths, limitations and possible developments to our approach are discussed. We also raise some points for further consideration.

PLANNING PROBLEM

As the box shows, the management of the TC faces a number of complex planning problems. This section places the questions that the management needs to answer within the planning framework discussed in chapter 6, as well as similar questions discussed in the capacity planning literature.

Position in planning framework

With reference to the planning framework discussed in chapter 6, the problem of determining capacity requirements for post-operative recovery is an example of 'resources planning and control', a topic discussed in detail in chapter 4. Planning decisions made at this level are greatly influenced by the higher levels within the framework. The 'strategic planning' imposed by the UK government concerning the standard of services to be offered to patients includes maximum waiting times for elective surgery and very low hospital-initiated cancellation rates. The requirement to meet maximum waiting times influences the level and nature of the surgical activity decided upon by management at the 'patient volume planning and control' level, a key driver in determining the level of resources required for post-operative recovery. In addition, the strategic requirement of a low cancellation rate influences the extent to which post-operative resources need to cater for variability in demand.

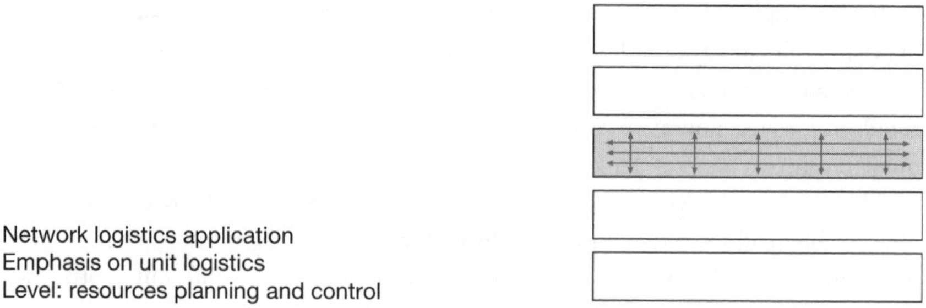

Network logistics application
Emphasis on unit logistics
Level: resources planning and control

Figure 9.1 *Variability and capacity planning, and position in planning framework.*

The focus of the problem is on resource allocation for a single activity within the hospital (post-operative recovery) and hence the planning process can be described as 'unit logistics'. However, there is an element of 'chain logistics' as decisions regarding the provision of resources for post-operative recovery are inextricably linked to the provision of resources at preceding stages of the patient journey, in this case operating theatre sessions.

Decisions made at the level of 'resource planning and control' will influence decisions made at the lower levels within the planning framework. A restriction on the number of patients that can be offered post-operative care at one time will influence the management of patient admissions and discharge at an organisational level ('patient group planning and control') and the management of individual patients during their post-operative stay in hospital ('patient planning and control').

Literature review

The academic literature contains several distinct approaches to hospital capacity planning. Much of this literature is concerned with the level of hospital capacity required to deal with changing patterns of demand for health care (Jones and Joy, 2002; Bagurst *et al.*,1999) or the relationship between hospital capacity, demand and waiting lists (see for example Worthington, 1987). This work is relevant to strategic planning decisions concerning the overall level and nature of provision for health care.

Of more relevance to this chapter are studies that examine variability in patient length of stay and the implications of this when planning the bed capacity required to cater for a known or desired average level of admissions. Rather than give an exhaustive literature review, we highlight a number of papers that take different approaches to this problem.

Shahani (1981) observed that capacity planning should not depend on average values of patient length of stay alone, as variability has a major effect on requirements. Harper and Shahani (2002) developed a computer tool to simulate patient flow in an adult medicine department where simulated patients are assigned a length of stay sampled from a user-specified random distribution.

An analytical alternative to such simulation techniques is the approach adopted by Harrison and Millard (1991). They found that the length of stay data for patients admitted to a geriatric ward could be successfully fitted by the sum of two exponentials, and developed a two-compartment Markov model of patient flows. Gorunescu et al. (2002) developed a model to determine the optimum number of beds given a desired rate of patient rejection. This used a queueing model with Poisson arrivals and a phase-type length of stay distribution.

Gallivan et al. (2002) discussed the heightened importance of length of stay variability in the context of a UK government initiative for hospitals to give a strong commitment to admitting a patient on a date arranged months in advance. They proposed analytical methods for estimating bed demand that incorporate empirical length of stay distributions and other sources of variability (Gallivan et al., 2002; Utley et al., 2003).

ELABORATION

The modelling approach described in this chapter has been used in a number of contexts. To illustrate the key features of the model, we focus on the application of the model to assist the planning of the capacity required for post-operative recovery for patients undergoing general surgery within a Treatment Centre. The key data that were used within the model related to the daily number of surgical cases that were planned and the post-operative length of stay distribution for the patient population concerned.

Planned theatre activity

The planned theatre activity was determined by the TC manager in response to two key constraints:

1   the number of patients that needed to receive an operation within the planning period required in order for the organisation to meet UK government targets relating to maximum waiting times;
2   the availability of general surgeons and anaesthetists.

After negotiation with surgeons and anaesthetists, the TC manager decided on the weekly schedule for theatre activity relating to general surgery given in Table 9.1 below.

Table 9.1 *The repeating weekly cycle of the planned number of general surgery cases*

Day of week	Number of patients planned
Monday	6
Tuesday	6
Wednesday	8
Thursday	8
Friday	9
Saturday	0
Sunday	0

Length-of-stay distribution

The exact distribution of length of stay for patients was not available since this was planning taking place before the new service came into operation, and thus direct observational data were not available. It was considered unwise to use length-of-stay distributions for patients from another hospital setting, since the new TC service was intended to treat only routine cases and this was expected to have the effect of curtailing the length-of-stay distribution. An estimated distribution was constructed by the research team in conjunction with the TC manager and the hospital's information manager to reflect the 'realistic target' average length of stay for surgical patients. Since the TC planned to select patients deemed less likely to have an extensive post-operative recovery, the shape of the distribution was chosen to have less of a 'tail' than is typical for post-operative care in traditional hospital environments. The distribution chosen for use in generating planning estimates is given in Table 9.2.

Table 9.2 *The post-operative length-of-stay distribution used to generate the planning estimates of post-operative capacity requirements*

Length of stay (days)	Proportion of patients (%)
1	36
2	47
3	10
4	5
5	2

It was assumed in this case that the length of stay for all patients using the TC could be approximated using this distribution. However, as discussed in 'Reflections and further development' section below, the techniques employed could be extended to consider the case where the length-of-stay distribution could differ for patient subgroups (representing different surgical specialties).

It was also assumed for the purposes of generating the planning estimates that patients could be discharged on any day of the week, including weekends, and that patients' length of stay was not affected by which day they received surgery. Although this might be an unrealistic assumption in some hospital contexts, weekend discharging is one change in practice that is being encouraged within TCs.

THE ABACUS CAPACITY PLANNING MODEL

Preamble

The mathematical model developed by the authors to address planning problems of this nature has been used as the basis of a computer tool called ABACUS (Analysis of Booked Admissions and Capacity Use). It was initially formulated to assess the impact of three factors that can cause unpredictable variability in bed requirements: patient length of stay, patient-initiated cancellations and emergency admissions. The model presented in this chapter is a simplified version of the full ABACUS model as it does not incorporate emergency admissions or patient-initiated cancellations.

The ABACUS model is based on techniques from a branch of mathematics called probability theory. To use the method, the planner supplies information about the length-of-stay distribution and the number of patients booked for admission on each day of the week. The computer model then calculates estimates related to the demand for beds and how this varies through the week. This is done without recourse to complicated and time-consuming simulation techniques. Unlike other analytical approaches to this type of problem, the structure of the analysis does not require that the length-of-stay characteristics of the patient population conform to a particular mathematically derived statistical distribution.

Assumptions

Consider a ward that operates a booked admissions system. For the initial stage of our analysis we make the assumption that the ward has unlimited capacity and can hence meet all demand, no matter how many patients are booked. This assumption might seem like a bizarre contrivance but it allows one to use the standard results of probability theory to derive formulae for the expectation and variance of the bed demand. These indicate the probability that the number of beds required exceeds a given level. Depending on the actual number of beds allocated to the ward, this reflects the proportion of booked operations for which additional capacity would have to be made available.

Another assumption in our analysis is that the lengths of stay of patients can be treated as identically and independently distributed. Here, the assumption of independence is crucial. Assuming that all patients have lengths of stay that are identically distributed is less critical and the analysis can be extended to consider different streams of patients with different length-of-stay distributions, although this is beyond the scope of the present discussion.

Notations and model

We use the following notation.

We assume that there is a fixed admissions planning cycle of duration C days. Typically this will be the seven-day week, although other planning cycles may be preferred.

For $1 \leqslant c \leqslant C$ suppose that N_c is the number of elective booked admissions planned for day c of the planning cycle. Note that we assume cyclic operation whereby the same pattern of elective admissions are planned from one cycle to the next.

Variation in length of stay is a central feature of our analysis and we reflect this using probability distributions associated with the patients' length of stay. For $j \geqslant 0$ let p_j denote the probability that a patient is still an inpatient j days after being booked for admission. Note the assumption that these length-of-stay distributions do not depend on the day of admission; however more refined analysis might allow for the possibility that factors such as the occurrence of weekends may influence discharge decisions.

It is notationally convenient to assume that p_j is defined and has the value 0 for values of j that are negative.

We are interested in estimating bed demand and how this varies during the planning cycle depending on the parameters discussed above. We stress that this is different from a typical queueing theory analysis, which would take into account the consequences of sufficient capacity being unavailable. We thus make the somewhat artificial assumption that there is sufficient capacity such that all bookings are honoured and that all emergencies can be admitted. In these circumstances, results from Utley et al. (2003) can be used to derive closed form analytical expressions for the mean and variance for the number of patients requiring beds on a given day of the planning cycle depending on the factors discussed above. These have a somewhat simpler form than in the original paper (Utley et al., 2003) due to the simplified nature of the current example.

A central and simplifying feature of our analysis is that the assumption of cyclically repeating admissions means that steady state probabilities are also cyclic. Also, one can reinterpret length-of-stay survival distributions in cyclic terms. A concrete example helps to motivate the particular form taken by our formulae for bed demand. Suppose a planning cycle of one week. Suppose that each week there is a single admission and that this always occurs on a Monday. The expected bed demand for each Monday is the sum of contributions corresponding to the current admission, the admission on the previous Monday, the admission the week before, etc. In order to derive an analytical expression for this expectation, one simply adds terms in the length-of-stay survival distribution corresponding to 0 days, 7 days, 14 days, etc. Equally, to determine expected bed demand on a Tuesday, one sums the survival distribution terms corresponding to 1 day, 8 days, 15 days, etc.

Extending this notion to the more general case, $X_{d,i}$ the contribution to the mean bed requirements on day d of the cycle from an admission on day i of the cycle is given by:

$$X_{d,i} = \sum_{w \geq 0} P_{wC + d - i}$$

Note that given the general definition of p_j, terms of this series for which the second subscript is negative are zero.

Then μ_d, the total mean bed requirements on day d of the cycle, is simply given by:

$$\mu_d = \sum_{i=1}^{C} N_i X_{d,i}$$

$$= \sum_{i=1}^{C} N_i \sum_{w \geq 0} P_{wC + d - i}, \qquad 1 \leq d \leq C.$$

Similarly, the contribution to the variance of the number of beds required on day d of the cycle from a single admission on day i of the cycle, $Y_{d,i}$, is given by:

$$Y_{d,i} = \sum_{w \geq 0} P_{wC + d - i}(1 - P_{wC + d - i})$$

and σ_d^2, the variance of the bed requirements on day d of the cycle, by:

$$\sigma_d^2 = \sum_{i=1}^{C} N_i Y_{d,i}$$

$$= \sum_{i=1}^{C} N_i \sum_{w \geq 0} P_{wC + d - i}(1 - P_{wC + d - i}), \qquad 1 \leq d \leq C.$$

RESULTS

The mathematical model outlined in the section above was used to calculate the distribution of requirements for post-operative care beds, based on the data relating to length-of-stay variability and patient admissions given in the 'Elaboration' section. These calculations were performed using a Visual Basic for Applications (VBA) routine written by the authors to implement the model within the Microsoft Excel spreadsheet environment.

Distributions of post-operative bed requirements

As the number of patients undergoing surgery varies throughout the week, the distribution of bed requirements is different for each day of the week. Figures 9.2 and 9.3 show the distribution of bed requirements for a Monday and a Friday respectively.

To summarise the results, we plotted for each day the mean bed requirements and the upper 95 percentile of bed requirements. The graph showing the weekly cycle of bed requirements is given in Figure 9.4.

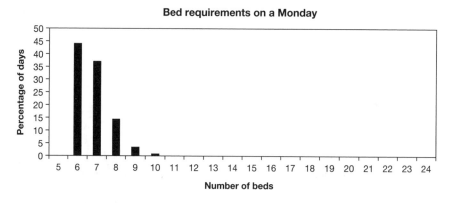

Figure 9.2 *Distribution of bed requirements on a Monday.*

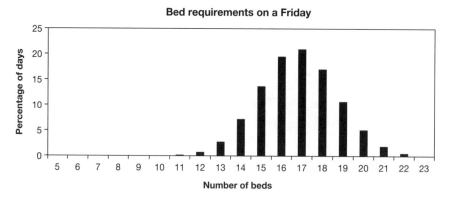

Figure 9.3 *Distribution of bed requirements on a Friday.*

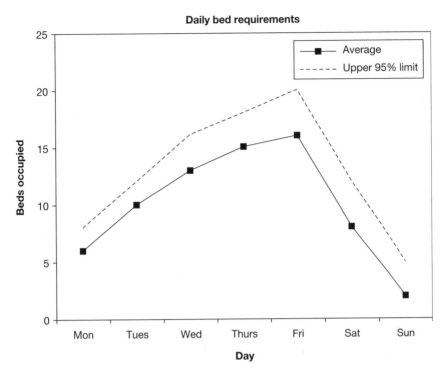

Figure 9.4 *Mean post-operative bed requirements and the upper 95% limit of bed requirements for each day of the week.*

Evaluating a particular level of post-operative bed provision

The distributions of bed requirements presented in the previous section were calculated using the assumption that no operations would be cancelled due to a shortage of post-operative beds. These results can be used to explore the likely impact on the TC of providing a given number of post-operative care beds. This is done by using the calculated distributions of bed requirements to calculate the proportion of days when requirements would exceed a given capacity. This provides an estimate for the proportion of days on which the TC would face operational difficulties whereby extra post-operative beds would have to be provided to avoid the cancellation of scheduled operations. For the current example, Figure 9.5 shows the proportion of Fridays on which bed requirements exceed capacity for different levels of capacity that could be provided. To highlight the folly of basing capacity plans on average lengths of stay, the capacity corresponding to average bed requirements is marked.

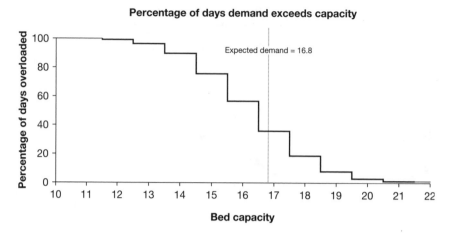

Figure 9.5 *The percentage of Fridays on which demand exceeds capacity for a range of possible operational capacities (the dashed line shows the capacity that corresponds to average requirements).*

REFLECTIONS AND FURTHER DEVELOPMENT

The methods presented here allow one to calculate the probability distribution of the demand for beds for a hospital department implementing a particular admissions schedule in the situation where no scheduled admissions are deferred or cancelled due to bed availability. These methods can be extended to incorporate other sources of variability such as emergency admissions and patient-initiated cancellations (Utley *et al.*, 2003). Such calculations can then be used to estimate the proportion of days where bed demand exceeds a given capacity. The effect of unpredictable variability in availability of capacity due to staff absences or unforeseen bed closures could potentially be examined at this stage of the analysis although this has not been examined in detail.

It should be noted that our modelling approach makes no allowance for what might happen if demand should exceed capacity. In practice, many things might happen if this arises. For example, patients' admissions for surgery might be deferred or other patients might be discharged earlier than otherwise intended. If such events are thought of as operational emergencies, then our model can be used to give an estimate of the proportion of days that such operational emergencies occur, assuming that a bed is available for the majority of booked admissions. Given that one of the main stated aims of the TC programme is to keep TC-initiated cancellations to an absolute minimum, this would seem a reasonable assumption.

Our modelling implicitly assumes that the lengths of stay being planned for are those that are judged to be clinically necessary. In practice, length of stay may reduce if there is high occupancy in response to fears of a potential bed crisis. If this is expected to be a major effect, then this would introduce a source of error.

It could be argued that our method is over-simplistic, as it does not model the actions of hospital managers when faced with such excess demand. The hypothetical situation for which the probability distribution of bed demand is estimated is indeed highly artificial. However, the estimates derived from this simple scenario can provide useful information for those introducing a booked admissions system in the 'real world', where capacity is most definitely limited. Conversely, the independence of the estimates from the particular decision processes employed in the instance of operational emergencies could be regarded as an advantage. Rather than reflecting the virtues or ills of a particular strategy for dealing with operational emergencies, our methods give an indication of the intrinsic level of operational emergencies that could be expected due to the characteristics of the operating schedule itself, the patient group being catered for and the operational capacity decided upon. For *planning* purposes, this would seem to be the crucial information.

The problem presented to health care delivery by unpredictable variability is not so much the variability but the fact that it is unpredictable. If one can somehow predict variations, system design can take account of this and compensate. For example, we know ahead of time that winter months bring an increase in admissions for respiratory conditions. This is predictable variability, and sensible planning takes account of it.

In the modelling approach described in this chapter, all patients are assumed to have the same distribution of possible lengths of stay. If subgroups of patients can be identified that have different length of stay characteristics, then this information could potentially be used to lessen the adverse impact of variability in terms of capacity requirements. For the extreme case where distinct groups of patients that have a known and certain length of stay can be identified prior to admission, the capacity requirements associated with a given admission schedule show no unpredictable variability. Chapter 10 on 'Admission planning and patient mix optimisation' gives an excellent account of the type of sophisticated planning that is possible in this circumstance. In reality, there is always likely to be some residual unpredictable variability within a particular subgroup of patients due simply to the unpredictable course of many health care processes and the response or possible reaction to treatment by individual patients. That said, knowledge about systematic differences between different patient groups could be used to minimise fluctuations in capacity requirements and this will be the focus of future work.

QUESTIONS AND EXERCISES

1   How do the requirements for a model intended to support capacity planning differ from those of a model intended to support capacity management at an operational level?

2   Under what circumstances would the assumptions that underpin the ABACUS model not hold?

3   Is a health care system that seems efficient from the point of view of the users efficient in terms of capacity usage?

4   A surgical unit plans to operate on 2 patients every day of the week, Saturdays and Sundays included. Consider the implications of the three different length-of-stay distributions given in Table 9.3 below.

Table 9.3 Length-of-stay distributions for three different capacity planning scenarios

Length of stay (days)	Scenario 1 (%)	Scenario 2 (%)	Scenario 3 (%)
1	0	25	31
2	100	50	47
3	0	25	15
4	0	0	5
5	0	0	2

Using the equations given in the section on the ABACUS Capacity Planning Model or otherwise, show that the mean and variance in the bed requirements for the three scenarios are as given in Table 9.4 below. Further, show that for scenario 2, six beds are required on 3.52 per cent of days.

Table 9.4 Mean and variance for bed requirements for the scenarios of Table 9.3

Scenario	Average bed requirements	Variance of bed requirements
1	4	0.0
2	4	0.75
3	4	0.98

REFERENCES AND FURTHER READING

Bagust A., M. Place and J. W. Posnett. Dynamics of bed use in accommodation emergency admissions: stochastic simulation model. *British Medical Journal*, 319(7203), 1999, 155–158.

Gallivan S., M. Utley, T. Treasure and O. Valencia. Booked inpatient admissions and hospital capacity: mathematical modelling study. *British Medical Journal*, 324(7332), 2002, 280–282.

Gorunescu F., S. I. McClean and P. H. Millard. A queuing model for bed-occupancy management and planning of hospitals. *Journal of the Operational Research Society*, 53(1), 2002, 19–24.

Harper P.R. and A. K. Shahani. Modelling for the planning and management of bed capacities in hospitals. *Journal of the Operational Research Society*, 53(1), 2002, 11–18.

Harrison G.W. and P. H. Millard. Balancing acute and long-stay care: the mathematics of throughput in departments of geriatric medicine. *Methods of Information in Medicine*, 30(3), 1991, 221–228.

Jones S.A. and M. P. Joy. Forecasting demand of emergency care. *Health Care Management Science*, 5(4), 2002, 297–305.

Shahani A.K. Reasonable averages that give wrong answers, *Teaching Statistics*, 3, 1981, 50–54.

Utley M., S. Gallivan, T. Treasure and O. Valencia. Analytical methods for calculating the capacity required to operate an effective booked admissions policy for elective inpatient services. *Health Care Management Science*, 6, 2003, 97–104.

Worthington D. Queuing models for hospital waiting lists. *Journal of the Operational Research Society*, 38(5), 1987, 413–422.

Chapter 10

Admission planning and patient mix optimisation

Jan Vissers, Ivo Adan and Miriam Eijdems

SUMMARY

Admission planning is an important area of planning hospital operations for elective patients that do not need emergency care. Its purpose is not only to admit patients according to medical priority but also to take into consideration the resource use of admitted patients in order to balance the workload of departments along product lines. Admission planning will be further elaborated and an integer linear programming model will be developed that can be used by hospitals to balance the workload of admissions by taking into account the resource requirements of different patient categories within a specialty. An application in a hospital will be used to illustrate principles of planning and the results obtained.

KEY TERMS

- Admission planning and multiple resources
- Patient groups and resource requirements
- Patient mix optimisation and an integer linear programming approach

INTRODUCTION

Patients can enter a hospital in three ways: as an outpatient after a referral from a general practitioner, as an emergency patient in the case of immediate need of specialist treatment and as an inpatient. Inpatient admissions can be of two types:

scheduled or unscheduled. Scheduled inpatient admissions, also called elective patients, are selected from a waiting list or are given an appointment for an admission date. Unscheduled inpatient admissions, emergency admissions, concern patients that are admitted immediately as a consequence of a medical decision by a specialist at the outpatient department or at the emergency department. In this chapter we will concentrate on elective inpatient admissions.

Admissions planning is the planning function that places patients on the waiting list, is in charge of waiting lists, schedules patients for admission and communicates with patients about their scheduled admission. Admissions planning can be centrally coordinated for all specialties, or it can be decentralised. Although this is a point of discussion in hospital organisation development, it is not of importance to this contribution. We will consider the admissions planning as a regulating mechanism for a specialty, whether performed centrally or decentralised.

Admission planning decides on the number of patients admitted for a specialty each day, but also on the mix of patients admitted. Within a specialty different categories of patients can be distinguished according to their requirement for resources. The type of resources required for an admission may involve beds, operating theatre capacity (in the case of a surgical specialty), nursing capacity and intensive care (IC) beds. The mix of patients is, therefore, an important decision variable for the hospital to manage the workload of the inflow of inpatients.

The current way of dealing with this issue is based on the experience of planners rather than on a formal procedure. Often the only focus is the operating theatre capacity, because it is important that this resource is used to its maximum capacity. Admission planning in such a case comes down to operating theatre planning, as the other resources involved are not considered. Most hospitals do not have a tool available to evaluate the patient admission profile (i.e. the number and the mix of patients to be admitted) or the consequences for the combined resources involved.

BOX 10.1   THE CASE STUDY HOSPITAL

The case study hospital – that acted as the pilot setting for the development of the model – is a 400-bed hospital in the south-east of the Netherlands. The pilot concerned the specialty of orthopaedics. We will use data from this specialty to illustrate the model.

The orthopaedic surgeons as a group were very concerned to improve the planning of inpatient admissions. The number of surgeons was at a stable level after a few years of ups and downs, and the number of admissions had been rising since the previous year. The questions raised in the group were, among others:

■   What resources do we need to fulfil the contracts agreed with hospital management?

> ■ What is a good balance between beds, operating theatre hours and nursing staff to accommodate effectively the planning of admissions as well as the efficient use of resources?
>
> ■ What is the mix of patients to be admitted each day of the week to optimise the use of available resources?
>
> The orthopaedic surgeons discussed this problem with the hospital management. Together they decided to start a pilot project to develop a tool for supporting this problem.

The next section provides further information on the planning problem by positioning it in a framework for operations management of health care organisations, and by a short review of literature. In the following section the planning problem is further elaborated by providing data for the specialty orthopaedics. The model that has been developed for this planning problem is then described and we discuss the application of the model to orthopaedics and the results, illustrating the functioning of the model and the contribution to the planning problem of orthopaedics. Finally, we reflect on our contribution to this planning problem, by formulating conclusions and recommendations for further research.

PLANNING PROBLEM

For the development of the model we concentrated on the third question posed by the group of orthopaedic surgeons – the optimal mix of patients to be admitted – as their first two questions are included in providing an answer to this. In this contribution we will therefore concentrate on the following planning problem: how can one generate a patient admission profile for a specialty, given targets for patient throughput and utilisation of the resources and while satisfying given restrictions?

Position in planning framework

In this section we position the planning problem in the framework for operations management introduced in chapter 6. This framework describes the different planning levels required for hospital operations management and allows us to define our planning problem in relationship with other planning issues in a hospital.

As shown in Figure 10.1, the planning problem addressed in this case study is positioned at the second level of the framework, i.e. patient group planning and control. The approach followed is defined as a network logistics approach, although

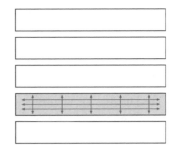

Network logistics application
Emphasis on unit logistics
Level: patient group planning and control

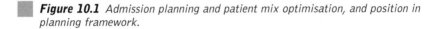

Figure 10.1 *Admission planning and patient mix optimisation, and position in planning framework.*

the emphasis is on unit logistics. We will provide some further information on the position of the case study in the framework.

The main focus of the planning problem and approach followed in the case study is on the level 'patient group planning and control'. A key issue is to define the mix of patients, selected from different patient groups, that need to be admitted for each day of the week to realise targets for resource utilisation and throughput. This is a relevant planning issue at weekly or monthly planning level. It uses aggregate information on patient groups and their resource profiles. Although the resource profiles of the patient groups provide information on the use of different resources (regular beds, operating theatres, IC beds, nursing staff), the resource profile cannot be used for scheduling individual patients. Its main function is to allow for visualisation of the impact of different admission profiles on the use of resources. Although a combination of chain logistics (patient groups and multiple resources) and unit logistics (resource use), the emphasis lies with the unit logistics perspective, as we are most interested in a balanced use of resources that is optimal with respect to targets set.

The emphasis lies on the second level of the framework, but there are also links with the other levels. At the level of 'strategic planning' the categories of patients distinguished for admission planning need to checked with the profile of the hospital. The throughput used for admission planning needs to be checked with the annual volumes agreed upon at the level of 'patient volume planning and control'. At this level, where annual patient volumes are translated into capacity allocations, the amount of resources available to a specialty also needs to be checked. It is also at this level that decisions are taken to set beds apart or reserve beds for emergency admissions. The link with the level 'resources planning and control' is clear, as the planning of patient groups needs to be performed within the restrictions of the available capacity for the sum of patient groups served by the specialty. The admission profile developed at the level of patient groups can be of guidance to the level 'patient planning and control'. When admission planning uses the admission profiles as a target mix to be filled in with daily admissions, one may expect results similar to the projections.

Literature review

The literature on admission planning and patient classification is rather extensive. See Gemmel and Van Dierdonck (1999) for a recent state of the art on admission planning. Although many studies are concerned with scheduling of admissions and resources (see, for instance, Fetter and Thompson, 1986; Roth and Van Dierdonck, 1995), developing policies for admission based on the mix of different categories of patients within a specialty has not been investigated much before (Vissers *et al.*, 2000; Adan and Vissers, 2002). Patient classification studies and patient mix studies are mostly used for marketing and finance purpose (see, for instance, Barnes and Krinsky, 1999) and not so much for patient flow planning.

ELABORATION

The model has been applied to the specialty of orthopaedics in a general hospital setting. We will discuss in this section the different data required to analyse the problem and to develop a model.

Patient inflow and throughput

In 1998 about 760 inpatients were admitted and there were 700 day cases. About 15 per cent of the inpatients were admitted as emergencies, while the remaining were admitted on an elective basis using a waiting list. Day cases are always elective admissions. The average length of stay of inpatients (excluding day cases) was 12.4 days. There were 11 categories of patients that could be distinguished in orthopaedics.

We recorded the actual admissions over a number of weeks, but we will use the inflow of week 12 in 1998, which was considered to have a representative inflow pattern, to illustrate the model. We will also use the average inflow, based on the annual output, as a reference inflow pattern. Table 10.1 provides information on the number of admissions per category of patients in the sample week and the average week.

Demand requirements

The patient groups can be characterised on a number of features, such as length of stay, nursing workload, day and duration of operation, use of IC beds and days of using an IC bed. These features are given in Table 10.2 and Box 10.2.

Table 10.1 Number of admissions per category of patients in the sample week and the average week

Patient category	Patient mix Week 12	Patient mix average
1	14	13
2	2	1
3	0	1
4	1	2
5	0	1
6	0	1
7	1	2
8	3	1
9	2	2
10	1	1
11	2	1
Total	26	26

Table 10.2 Characteristics per category of patients

Patient category	Length of stay (days)	Nursing workload	Day of operation	Operation duration (minutes)	Use of IC beds	Days IC bed start	duration
1	1	L1	0	20	N		
2	1	M1	0	30	N		
3	2	M1L1	0	38	N		
4	3	M2L1	0	40	N		
5	4	M2L2	0	50	N		
6	5	M3L2	0	46	N		
7	9	Z4M4L1	1	77	N		
8	14	Z6M6L2	1	70	N		
9	18	Z6M8L4	1	80	N		
10	24	Z24	1	120	Y	0	1
11	29	Z29	1	92	N		

Notes: Nursing workload profile is expressed in number of days with Z workload (5 points), number of days with M workload (2 points) and number of days with L workload (1 point)

If a patient is operated on the day of admission, it is labelled as day 0; IC days are counted with the day of operation as starting point

BOX 10.2 CATEGORIES OF PATIENTS

Eleven categories of patients are distinguished. Each of the groups is described below and examples of procedures are given.

Category 1: Day surgery procedures that generate little nursing workload. Patients can take care of themselves. Example procedures are arthroscopy of the knee and small procedures on hands or feet. The procedure does not take more then 20 minutes.

Category 2: Day surgery procedures that generate medium nursing workload because these patients cannot use an arm or leg after the operation. Example procedures are carpal-tunnel syndrome, arthroscopy of the knee and removing osteosyntheses.

Category 3: Surgical procedures in short stay with a length of stay of 2 days. The nursing workload is medium for the day of operation, usually because the patient cannot move a hand or foot for a couple of hours. Examples in this category are menisectomies by arthroscopy and small operations on hands and feet.

Category 4: Surgical procedures in short stay with a length of stay of 3 days. Operations are osteotomies of toes and osteotomies of hand or foot and a classical menisectomy.

Category 5: Operations in short stay with a length of stay of 4 days. Examples are small osteotomies on legs or elbow.

Category 6: Operations with a length of stay of 5 days. Examples are osteotomies on the ankle or shoulder.

Category 7: Operations with an average length of stay of 9 days. Operations are extensive osteotomies on the thigh or hips, and operations to repair the rupture of the knee ligament. The nursing workload for these patients is high for the first four days because they are not allowed to leave their bed.

Category 8: Operations with an average length of stay of 14 days. Examples are surgical procedures for a total hip replacement.

Category 9: Operations with an average length of stay of 18 days. Examples are surgical procedures for a total knee replacement.

Category 10: Operations with an average length of stay of 24 days. This group of patients contains the spine operations. These patients need to go to the IC unit the night after the operation because of the high risks.

Category 11: The last category is a mixture of different types of procedure. A characteristic of the patients in this group is that most of them are older than 60 and end up in a nursing home. It usually takes a while before they have a place in a nursing home.

Available resources

Orthopaedics has 28 beds allocated in a ward, including beds for short-stay patients. There are also beds for day-surgery patients, shared with other specialties, but we will concentrate on inpatients. The four orthopaedic surgeons each have day operating theatre sessions, in total 6 hours a day. There are about 12 full-time-equivalent nurses available for the ward, but nursing capacity is expressed in terms of nursing points. On Wednesday one IC bed is reserved for elective admissions from category 10. Table 10.3 summarises the available resources for orthopaedics.

Table 10.3 Available resources for orthopaedics

Day of the week	Operating theatre (minutes)	Beds (number)	Nursing (points)	IC beds (number)
Monday	360	28	80	0
Tuesday	360	28	80	0
Wednesday	360	28	80	1
Thursday	360	28	80	0
Friday	360	28	80	0
Saturday	0	20	70	0
Sunday	0	20	70	0

As one can see, the availability of resources can be less during the weekend. During the weekend there is no operating theatre capacity available and there are no IC beds; there are also no short-stay beds available and there are fewer nursing staff.

Capacity load factors and resource importance

The different resources each have a target occupancy level, which defines the level of occupancy that reflects a realistic target workload. This can be different during the weekend. Table 10.4 provides information on the target occupancy level for each type of resource.

The data in Table 10.4 are required to describe the production system of the specialty. We also need to specify the relative importance of the different resources. Table 10.5 gives the weights used to reflect the relative importance of the different resources involved, according to the participants in the hospital. As one can see, operating theatres and IC bed use are considered very important, bed use is considered important, and nursing workload is considered of medium importance.

Table 10.4 Target occupancy levels per type of resource

Day of the week	Operating theatres (%)	Nursing (%)	Beds (%)	IC beds (%)
1	85	95	90	0
2	85	95	90	0
3	85	95	90	100
4	85	95	90	0
5	85	95	90	0
6	0	95	80	0
7	0	95	80	0

Table 10.5 Relative weights per type of resource

Resource type	Weight
Operating theatres	5
Nursing	3
Beds	4
IC beds	5

Note: weight range: 0 =ignore, 1 = not important, 2 = barely important, 3 = medium importance, 4 = important, 5= very important

Restrictions

It is also important to be aware of any restrictions imposed on the planning problem. In reality many restrictions can play a role that will make it difficult to realise a feasible admission profile. We will illustrate this with two examples of restrictions in the case of orthopaedics. The first restriction that plays a role in the planning problem is that category 6 patients, having a length of stay of 5 days, need to be admitted on Monday in order to have them discharged before the weekend. Furthermore, the number of category 1 patients is limited to six patients a day from Monday to Friday, in order to avoid a concentration of day-surgery patients (leading to extra handling for the nurses) on one day.

MODEL

In this section we translate the planning problem into a mathematical model in the form of an integer linear program (ILP). In the next section we describe the various factors that are relevant to the planning problem. Then, in the following section, the mathematical model will be formulated.

Relevant factors

It will be clear from the discussion in the previous sections that the following factors play an important role in the planning problem:

Planning period This is the complete time period (typically several months or a year) over which the admittance of patients has to be planned.

Patient categories There is usually such a wide variety of patients that they need to be categorised to make the planning problem more manageable. Patients are categorised according to their utilisation of resources. Patients in the same category have a similar length of stay and require on average the same amount of nursing and operating theatre time.

Resources The relevant resources are beds, IC beds, operating theatres and nursing staff.

Available capacity of the resources The bed and IC bed capacity are the total number of beds available to the specialty at the wards and IC unit, respectively. The operating theatre capacity is the total operating time available per day. Nursing workload is measured in points; the nursing capacity is the number of points that is available per day. Typically, the availability of resources varies over the planning period, and the capacities will be allocated in a cyclic (e.g., weekly) pattern.

Planning cycle Since the capacities are allocated cyclically, it is natural to consider cyclic admission patterns, too. On one hand, the cycle length should not be too short, because then patients with a low admission occurrence cannot be included in the admission cycle. On the other hand, a long cycle length results in a planning problem that is computationally too big to handle. In practice, the cycle length typically varies from one week to four weeks.

Admission profile The admission profile describes the inflow of patients, i.e. the number and mix of patients admitted on each day within the planning cycle.

Target patient throughput This is the target number of patients that should be admitted within the planning cycle. Of course, this number can be easily deduced from the target number of patients set for the whole planning period.

Target utilisation of the resources This is the desired utilisation (or occupancy rate) of the resources on each day of the planning cycle. It should be realised as closely as possible.

Restrictions on admission profiles An admission profile realising the target throughput and resource utilisation may still be unacceptable for the specialty for a number of reasons. The specialty may want to fix the number of patients from a specific category admitted at a specific day in the admission cycle, for example, or the number of patients from a certain combination of categories who can be nursed (or operated) on a single day may be limited. These options will be treated as additional restrictions for admission profiles.

This completes the description of the relevant factors. Clearly, the important decision variable is the admission profile, and the planning problem can now be reformulated as follows: to find an admission profile for a given planning cycle such that the desired target utilisation of the resources is realised as closely as possible, while satisfying the target patient throughput and restrictions.

Mathematical model

In this section we translate the planning problem into a mathematical model. Let T denote the length (in days) of the planning cycle, and let M denote the number of patient categories. The patients are categorised according to their workloads for the resources. To describe the workloads of patients from category i, $i = 1, \ldots, M$, we introduce the following variables:

- b_i = number of days that a patient from category i stays in the hospital and needs a bed;
- p_i = number of pre-operative days for a patient from category i;
- c_i = number of days that a patient from category i needs an IC bed;
- o_i = the operation time (in minutes) for a patient from category i;
- n_{it} = the nursing workload (in points) for a patient from category i on day t of his stay in the hospital, where t runs from 1 to b_i.

On each day of their stay in the hospital a patient needs a nursing bed at the wards. Here we assume that a nursing bed is also reserved while the patient is in the IC unit. The number of IC days are counted with the day of operation as the starting point. Typically, the nursing workload is high on the day of operation, after which it gradually diminishes. Finally, the target throughput of patient category i over the planning cycle is denoted by THR_i.

It is convenient to number the resources 'operating theatre', 'nursing', 'beds' and 'IC beds' from 1 to 4. For resource r, $r = 1, \ldots, 4$, we then introduce the following quantities:

- C_{rt} = available capacity of resource r on day t of the planning cycle;
- U_{rt} = target utilisation of resource r on day t of the planning cycle.

The important decision variables in the planning problem are the number and mix of patients admitted on each day of the planning cycle. Let X_{it} denote the number of patients from category i admitted on day t of the planning cycle. Clearly, X_{it} is a nonnegative integer. Thus:

$$X_{it} \in \{0,1,2,\ldots\}, \quad i = 1,\ldots,M, \, t = 1,\ldots,T,$$

and they should satisfy the target patient throughput, i.e:

$$\sum_{t=1}^{T} X_{it} = THR_i, \quad i = 1,\ldots,M.$$

We now want to find X_{it}'s for which the absolute deviation of the realised and target utilisation of the resources is minimised. For this problem we introduce the auxiliary variables V_{rtk} satisfying:

$$V_{rtk} \geq 0, \, r = 1,\ldots,4, \, t = 1,\ldots,T, \, k = 1,2;$$

and formulate linear constraints forcing these variables to be equal to the absolute deviation of the realised and target utilisation. We first explain this for resource 1, i.e. the operating theatre. Since patients of category i are operated after being p_i days in the hospital, the realised utilisation of the operating theatre on day t is equal to:

$$\sum_{i=1}^{M} o_i X_{it-p_i}.$$

Here we adopt the convention that subscript t in X_{it} should be read modulo T (so, e.g., $X_{iT+1} = X_{i1}$). Hence, if we require that:

$$\sum_{i=1}^{M} o_i X_{it-p_i} \leq U_{1t} + V_{1t1}, \quad t = 1,\ldots,T,$$

$$\sum_{i=1}^{M} o_i X_{it-p_i} \leq U_{1t} - V_{1t2}, \quad t = 1,\ldots,T,$$

and minimise the sum:

$$\sum_{t=1}^{T} (V_{1t1} + V_{1t2}),$$

then it is readily verified that the minimum is realised for:

$$V_{1t1} = \max\left(\sum_{i=1}^{M} o_i X_{it-p_i} - U_{1t}, 0\right), \quad V_{1t2} = \max\left(U_{1t} - \sum_{i=1}^{M} o_i X_{it-p_i}, 0\right).$$

So, indeed, $V_{1t1} + V_{1t2}$ is equal to the absolute deviation of the realised and target utilisation of operating theatre on day t of the planning cycle. For the other resources we formulate constraints similar to the ones above. That is, for nursing staff, beds and IC beds we subsequently obtain:

$$\sum_{i=1}^{M} \sum_{d=1}^{b_i} n_{id} X_{it-d+1} \leq U_{2t} + V_{2t1}, \quad t = 1, \ldots, T,$$

$$\sum_{i=1}^{M} \sum_{d=1}^{b_i} n_{id} X_{it-d+1} \leq U_{2t} - V_{2t2}, \quad t = 1, \ldots, T,$$

$$\sum_{i=1}^{M} \sum_{d=1}^{b_i} X_{it-d+1} \leq U_{3t} + V_{3t1}, \quad t = 1, \ldots, T,$$

$$\sum_{i=1}^{M} \sum_{d=1}^{b_i} X_{it-d+1} \leq U_{3t} - V_{3t2}, \quad t = 1, \ldots, T,$$

$$\sum_{i=1}^{M} \sum_{d=1}^{c_i} X_{it-p_i-d+1} \leq U_{4t} + V_{4t1}, \quad t = 1, \ldots, T,$$

$$\sum_{i=1}^{M} \sum_{d=1}^{c_i} X_{it-p_i-d+1} \leq U_{4t} - V_{4t2}, \quad t = 1, \ldots, T.$$

The realised utilisation of the resources may, of course, not exceed the available capacity. Thus:

$$U_{rt} + V_{rt1} \leq C_{rt}, \quad r = 1, \ldots, 4, \quad t = 1, \ldots, T.$$

Then, minimising the absolute deviation of the realised and target utilisation of the resources amounts to minimising the sum:

$$\sum_{r=1}^{4} w_r \sum_{t=1}^{T} (V_{rt1} + V_{rt2}).$$

In this sum, the absolute deviation of the utilisation of resource r is weighted with coefficient w_r, defined as:

$$w_r = \frac{a_r}{\sum_{t=1}^{T} U_{rt}}.$$

where a_r is some nonnegative number. The coefficients are introduced to make the sum dimensionless (i.e. independent of the units used) and to control the relative importance of the resources (by means of a_r). Finally, we have to take into account the restrictions on admission profiles mentioned in the previous section. The first restriction just means that we fix certain variables X_{it} to prescribed values. For the second restriction we introduce B indicating the maximum number of patients from categories $i \in S$ that can be nursed on a single day, where S is a subset of $\{1, \ldots, M\}$. The second restriction then translates to:

$$\sum_{i \in S} \sum_{d=1}^{b_i} X_{it-d+1} \leq B, \ t = 1, \ldots, T.$$

Summarising, our planning problem can be formulated as the following ILP:

$$\min \sum_{r=1}^{4} w_r \sum_{t=1}^{T} (V_{rt1} + V_{rt2})$$

subject to the following constraints:

$$\sum_{t=1}^{T} X_{it} = THR_i, \ i = 1, \ldots, M,$$

$$U_{1t} - V_{1t2} \leq \sum_{i=1}^{M} o_i X_{it-p_i} \leq U_{1t} + V_{1t1}, \ t = 1, \ldots, T,$$

$$U_{2t} - V_{2t2} \leq \sum_{i=1}^{M} \sum_{d=1}^{b_i} n_{id} X_{it-d+1} \leq U_{2t} + V_{2t1}, \ t = 1, \ldots, T,$$

$$U_{3t} - V_{3t2} \leq \sum_{i=1}^{M} \sum_{d=1}^{b_i} X_{it-d+1} \leq U_{3t} + V_{3t1}, \ t = 1, \ldots, T,$$

$$U_{4t} - V_{4t2} \leq \sum_{i=1}^{M} \sum_{d=1}^{c_i} X_{it-p_i-d+1} \leq U_{4t} + V_{4t1}, \ t = 1, \ldots, T,$$

$$\sum_{i \in S} \sum_{d=1}^{b_i} X_{it-d+1} \leq B, \ t = 1, \ldots, T,$$

$$U_{rt} + V_{rt}1 \leq C_{rt}, \ r = 1, \ldots, 4, t = 1, \ldots, T,$$

$$V_{rt1} \geq 0, \ V_{rt2} \geq 0, \ r = 1, \ldots, 4, t = 1, \ldots, T,$$

$$X_{it} \in \{0,1,2, \ldots \}, \quad i = 1, \ldots, M, t = 1, \ldots, T.$$

This completes the description of the mathematical model.

Solution approach

To solve the above ILP problem we used the solver MOMIP. This is an optimisation solver for middle-sized mixed integer programming problems, based on the branch-and-bound algorithm. It has been developed by W. Ogryczak and K. Zorychta (1996) from the International Institute for Applied Systems Analysis (IIASA). A nice feature of this solver is that it allows the user to control the computation time (by limiting the number of nodes examined), of course without the guarantee of finding the optimal solution. In the application presented in the next section we bounded the computational effort for each scenario, and always found a good (but maybe not optimal) solution in a few minutes' computer time on an ordinary PC. The model has been implemented in a decision support system called OptiMix.

RESULTS

The results presented are twofold. The results in the next section will illustrate the behaviour of the model on different parameter settings of the weighting function using data on orthopaedics. The results in the following section illustrate the contribution of the model to the planning problem in the case of orthopaedics.

Sensitivity analysis

This section contains results produced by the model to illustrate the behaviour of the model on the use of the weighting function for the relative importance of the different resources. The outcomes of the model provide evidence that the model does what it should do.

We will start with the current settings for the weighting function provided in Table 10.5 and use the average weekly throughput of patients in Table 10.1. The other parameters are set according to the settings in the current situation described earlier. The output of the model for the current setting is shown in Table 10.6. The numbers between brackets (following the resource type) indicate the weights used in the objective function.

As can be seen from Table 10.6, operating theatre utilisation shows the least performance due to an over-capacity that is made available to orthopaedics. The use of beds follows the target utilisation reasonably well and the nursing workload and the IC use are according to their targets. The score of the solution, based on

Table 10.6 Occupancy levels for the current setting

Day no.	Operating theatres (5) (minutes)		Nursing (3) (points)		Beds (4) (number)		IC beds (5) (number)	
	Target	Realised	Target	Realised	Target	Realised	Target	Realised
1	306	293	76	76	25	25	0	0
2	306	272	76	77	25	25	0	0
3	306	200	76	76	25	22	1	1
4	306	90	76	76	25	23	0	0
5	306	245	76	75	25	25	0	0
6	0	0	66	64	16	16	0	0
7	0	0	66	65	16	16	0	0

the objective function, is 1.56. The score is the outcome of formula (1) and represents the weighted sum of the deviations between the realised and the target utilisation of the resources involved per day of the week. A lower score represents a better fit between realisations and target. The admission profile suggested by the model is shown in Table 10.7.

As can be seen from Table 10.7, the restrictions regarding patient categories 1 and 6 have been dealt with properly. Also, the category 10 patient is admitted on Tuesday to be in need of an IC bed on Wednesday.

Table 10.7 Admission profile for current setting (number of admissions)

Day category	1	2	3	4	5	6	7
1	4	3	0	1	5	0	0
2	0	0	0	0	1	0	0
3	0	0	0	0	1	0	0
4	1	1	0	0	0	0	0
5	1	0	0	0	0	0	0
6	1	0	0	0	0	0	0
7	1	0	0	0	1	0	0
8	0	0	0	1	0	0	0
9	0	1	1	0	0	0	0
10	0	0	1	0	0	0	0
11	0	1	0	0	0	0	0

Suppose we want to reduce the operating theatre resources to find a better fit between demand for and supply of resources. Table 10.8 shows the utilisation figures with a reduction in operating theatre resources available to orthopaedics to 260 minutes a day. As can be seen, the reduced operating theatre capacity is sufficient to handle the demand, and the occupancy levels follow the target levels reasonably well. The objective function score of this solution is 0.53. This shows that the deviations from the target utilisation levels in Table 10.8 are less than the deviations in Table 10.6.

Suppose we change the weight function, focusing on optimising one resource type, say operating theatres; we give operating theatres capacity a maximum weight of 5 and the other resources a minimum weight of 1. Table 10.9 shows the utilisa-

Table 10.8 *Occupancy levels for the current setting with reduced operating theatre capacity*

Day no.	Operating theatres (5) (minutes)		Nursing (3) (points)		Beds (4) (number)		IC beds (5) (number)	
	Target	Realised	Target	Realised	Target	Realised	Target	Realised
1	221	243	76	73	25	22	0	0
2	221	220	76	77	25	24	0	0
3	221	200	76	78	25	23	1	1
4	221	227	76	77	25	25	0	0
5	221	210	76	74	25	25	0	0
6	0	0	66	64	16	16	0	0
7	0	0	66	64	16	17	0	0

Table 10.9 *Occupancy levels with maximum weight for operating theatre use*

Day no.	Operating theatres (5) (minutes)		Nursing (1) (points)		Beds (1) (number)		IC beds (1) (number)	
	Target	Realised	Target	Realised	Target	Realised	Target	Realised
1	221	206	76	69	25	21	0	0
2	221	222	76	76	25	25	0	0
3	221	220	76	79	25	24	1	1
4	221	232	76	80	25	24	0	0
5	221	220	76	78	25	25	0	0
6	0	0	66	65	16	16	0	0
7	0	0	66	62	16	17	0	0

tion figures of this change in the parameter setting of the weight function. As can be seen, the use of operating theatre capacity has improved and the use of beds and nursing workload had slightly worsened; the use of the IC beds is unaltered.

Application to orthopaedics

We will illustrate the contribution of the mathematical model to the planning problem of orthopaedics with the output of the model for the following situations:

- What if we use the programme of week 12, the sample week, in combination with the original settings?
- What is an adequate availability of resources for the average week programme?

We first evaluate the feasibility of the programme of week 12 (see Table 10.1). The total number of patients is the same as for the average week programme, but there is a substitution towards patient groups requiring more resources (categories 8 and 11). Using the model for this inflow of patients results in no feasible solution within the restrictions defined for the planning problem. Looking at Table 10.6, one may suspect that the nursing capacity and the bed capacity have acted as the bottle-necks obstructing a solution, and not the operating theatre capacity. The conclusion is that although the number of patients is adequate, week 12 has a mix of patients that does not fit within the capacity constraints for orthopaedics. The orthopaedic surgeons probably only considered the operating theatre capacity when deciding the week programme, and not the bed and nursing capacity.

So, the first decision orthopaedics has to make is the week programme that reflects the maximum number and mix of patients that can be admitted as elective patients, given the capacity constraints. This can be calculated from the target volumes at annual level, given the number of weeks operating theatres are available to orthopaedics. Perhaps it is necessary to make different week programmes for each season, but in total it has to result in the annual target volumes.

Suppose we use the average week programme as given in Table 10.1. How many resources do we need to fit adequately the demand of resources? We follow a step-wise procedure. First, we observe in Table 10.8 that operating theatre capacity is on average at the target level, so further reduction will not be wise. The only resource worthwhile to consider is the bed capacity. By reducing the bed capacity during the week to 27 beds, we arrive to the results as shown in Table 10.10.

Clearly, there are different answers possible to the question put forward on the amount of resources that would adequately fit to the demand required for the average week programme, but the solution presented does show good results. The objective function produces a score of 0.21. This is a better fit, compared to the fit in Table 10.8 with a score of 0.53.

Up to now we have only considered constant target levels during the week, with a shift of level during the weekend. One step further would be to consider solutions with a different amount of resources allocated within the days of the week. Suppose we increase the operating theatre capacity in the beginning of the week and decrease the capacity at the end of the week. See Table 10.11 for the allocations used per day, and Table 10.12 for the utilisation results.

As can be seen from Table 10.12, by allocating more operating theatre resources and bed resources in the beginning of the week but increasing the number of beds available during the weekend, we seem to get a better fit between demand and supply. The objective function score is 0.24, showing that even this solution is slightly worse than that in Table 10.10. As both scores are almost equal, one could say that both solutions are resulting in a similar performance.

Table 10.10 Finding the proper allocation of resources

Day no.	Operating theatres (5) (minutes)		Nursing (3) (points)		Beds (4) (number)		IC beds (5) (number)	
	Target	Realised	Target	Realised	Target	Realised	Target	Realised
1	221	216	76	77	24	24	0	0
2	221	227	76	75	24	23	0	0
3	221	220	76	77	24	24	1	1
4	221	217	76	79	24	24	0	0
5	221	220	76	74	24	24	0	0
6	0	0	66	66	16	17	0	0
7	0	0	66	61	16	16	0	0

Table 10.11 Allocated resources per day of the week

Day of the week	Operating theatres (minutes)	Beds (number)	Nursing (points)	IC beds (number)
Monday	280	27	80	0
Tuesday	280	27	80	0
Wednesday	260	27	80	1
Thursday	240	25	80	0
Friday	240	25	80	0
Saturday	0	23	70	0
Sunday	0	23	70	0

Table 10.12 *Occupancy levels with varying amounts of allocated capacity per day*

Day no.	Operating theatres (5) (minutes)		Nursing (3) (points)		Beds (4) (number)		IC beds (5) (number)	
	Target	Realised	Target	Realised	Target	Realised	Target	Realised
1	238	243	76	75	24	24	0	0
2	238	230	76	76	24	25	0	0
3	222	220	76	76	24	23	1	1
4	204	197	76	74	22	22	0	0
5	204	210	76	73	22	22	0	0
6	0	0	66	68	18	18	0	0
7	0	0	66	67	18	18	0	0

The total amount of resources used in Table 10.12 is almost the same as in Table 10.10: the total amount of operating theatre capacity used is the same, the total amount of beds used is slightly better (1 bed less on three days) and the nursing capacity is unaltered. Perhaps a similar approach to the allocation of nursing capacity (following the availability of beds) would result in a small improvement in the use of nursing capacity. The day-dependent allocation makes it possible to reflect better the resource demands caused by the short-stay policy followed for many orthopaedic patients. On the other hand, the fixed allocation is perhaps more easy to implement, and does not result in a loss of performance, providing the right level of availability of resources.

REFLECTION AND FURTHER DEVELOPMENT

Based on the results described in the previous section, we can conclude that the model is able to generate an optimal admission profile per category. By an 'optimal admission profile' we mean a profile that results in the smallest possible deviation between the realised and the target resource utilisation, while the total available capacity of the different resources is not exceeded, the target patient throughput is met and the given restrictions are not violated.

The model has been implemented in a decision support system called OptiMix. It has been developed primarily to support the tuning of the demand on and the availability of capacities at a tactical level of decision making, but it can also be used at the strategic and operational level. Determining how many resources are required for the coming years is a strategic decision. If the volumes of patients per category for the next couple of years can be predicted, then OptiMix can calculate the minimum amount of capacity that is required to treat these patients. Although OptiMix does not use detailed information, it can still be used to balance the demand on and the availability of capacities in the short term. If in the short run patients are already scheduled for the dates in the planning period, Optimix can be used to define an optimal mix for the remaining admissions, while fixing the already scheduled admissions and treating these as restrictions for the planning problem. Further research and development is required to develop planning policies for defining reserve capacity for emergency patients and buffer capacity required to cope with variations of the resource requirements per patient category.

The approach also has possibilities for wider application. It is easy to adapt the model to another combination of resources that would fit better to the situation investigated. For instance, the model has also been used for thoracic surgery planning, where more use is made of intensive care facilities.

QUESTIONS AND EXERCISES

1   Verify the score of the current setting in the 'sensitivity analysis' part of the 'Results' section by using the information in Table 10.6 and formulas (1) and (2).
2   Formulate the basic assumptions underlying the mathematical model and investigate the degree to which the model fits reality.
3   Formulate one or more scenarios as a follow-up of the scenarios presented in the 'Application to orthopaedics' part of the 'Results' section that would be interesting to investigate to improve the performance of orthopaedics.
4   Reflect on the wider applicability to other specialties or other planning issues in a hospital. How should the model be adapted to these alternative circumstances?

REFERENCES AND FURTHER READING

Adan I.J.B.F. and J.M.H. Vissers. Patient mix optimisation in hospital admission planning: a case study. Special issue on 'Operations Management in Health Care,' *International Journal of Operations and Production Management*, 22(4), 2002, 445–461.

Barnes C. and T. Krinsky. Classification systems, case mix and data quality: implications for international management and research applications. *Case mix*, 1(2), 1999, 112–115.

Fetter R.B. and J.D. Thompson. A decision model for the design and operation of a progressive patient care hospital. *Medical Care*, 7(6), 1986, 450–462.

Gemmel P. van and R. Van Dierdonck. Admission scheduling in acute care hospitals: does the practice fit with the theory? *International Journal of Operations & Production Management*, 19 (9 and 10), 1999, 863–878.

Ogryczak W. and K. Zorychta. *Modular optimizer for mixed integer programming – MOMIP version 2.3. WP-96–106*, IIASA, Laxenburg, Austria, 1996.

Roth A. and R. Van Dierdonck. Hospital resource planning: concepts, feasibility, and framework. *Production and Operations Management*, 4(1), 1995, 2–29.

Vissers J.M.H., M. Eydems-Janssen, R. de Kok and F. Myburg. Optimisation of the patient mix for hospital admission planning. In E. Mikitis (ed.) *Information, Management and Planning of Health Services. Proceedings ORAHS99* (ISBN 9984–19146X), Riga, Latvia: Health Statistics and Medical Technology Agency, 2000, 161–178.

Chapter 11

Master scheduling of medical specialists

Erik Winands, Anne de Kreuk and Jan Vissers

SUMMARY

Medical specialists perform different activities in hospitals: seeing patients in clinics in the outpatient department, performing surgical procedures on patients in sessions in operating theatre departments, seeing patients at the ward during a ward round, being on call for seeing unscheduled patients at the emergency department. To coordinate these activities the group of specialists belonging to the same discipline uses a schedule that describes the timing of these activities on a weekly basis.

This case study deals with the process of developing master schedules for the activities of medical specialists organised in a specialty practice in a hospital. A model has been developed to describe and analyse the problem. The model has been implemented in a tool called MediPlan that not only increases the performance of the master schedules but also decreases the process time needed to generate such schedules. The optimisation procedure implemented in MediPlan is based on simulated annealing, a well-known local search technique. The performance of the tool is tested by means of a case study for the specialty of orthopaedics within a hospital in the Netherlands.

KEY TERMS

- Master scheduling of specialist activities
- Specialty practice organisation
- Optimisation via local search technique

INTRODUCTION

Medical specialists are the key operators in hospital processes. Patients will see a medical specialist in different phases of their journey through the hospital: during a visit to the outpatient department for discussion about the complaint, the diagnosis, the therapy or the follow-up after an admission; during a diagnostic procedure in a diagnostic department or a surgical procedure in the operating theatres department; during a ward round in cases where the patient is admitted. These activities of medical specialists are organised in sessions: a clinic session in the outpatient department, in which the specialist sees a number of outpatients; an operating theatre session in the operating theatre department; a ward round, visiting all patients admitted to a nursing ward.

From the perspective of the operations management of hospitals, medical specialists represent a very important hospital resource. However, the topic of planning of medical specialists is often not covered in hospital planning. Frequently, the availability of specialists is a bottleneck for the efficient use of other resources. Therefore, the planning of capacity of specialists, in terms of their availability for performing operations, is an important area for improvement. This is a challenge as specialists do not like to be scheduled or regarded as a resource. One area and opportunity for working together with specialists on improving the performance of specialist planning is to develop a schedule for the different activities of specialists in a hospital, for instance, outpatient clinic sessions, operating theatre sessions, ward rounds, etc.

BOX 11.1 THE CASE STUDY HOSPITAL

The case study hospital that acted as a pilot setting for the development of the model is a 400-bed hospital in the Netherlands, operating on two sites separated by a distance of 20 kilometres. The pilot concerned the specialty of orthopaedics. This specialty struggled with their schedule as they had to operate on the two sites of the hospital, with only five orthopaedic surgeons available. The questions they wanted to answer were:

- What is the performance of the current schedule of activities?
- What would be the gain in performance if activities were concentrated on one site per day instead of time being lost changing sites during the day?
- Could a schedule be developed that took better account of the preferences of individual specialists in terms of the order of activities within the day but which did not compromise the overall performance of the specialty ?

We will use data of this specialty to illustrate the planning problem and the model.

The rest of the chapter is organised as follows. The next section gives a more detailed description of the planning problem, together with the positioning of the case study in the reference framework of this book, and a short review of the relevant literature. In the following section we elaborate on the planning problem of master scheduling of medical specialists and discuss the components of a model that would allow the evaluation and optimisation of master schedules. The model developed for the problem, including the solution approach implemented in MediPlan, is then described, and we show how the developed model can be applied in practice. Finally we reflect on the strength and the weakness of the study and make some recommendations for further research.

PLANNING PROBLEM

Consider the following situation. A group of specialists wanted to develop a new schedule for their activities in a two-location hospital setting. Based upon interviews about their current schedule and their objectives and ideas for a revised schedule, a proposal was developed that was thought to meet their objectives. The proposal was discussed with the group of specialists and received much criticism. Some of the objectives were not properly understood and formulated, new objectives were added, and many arguments that were not very concrete were used to propose further changes. The project team – consisting of one of the specialists, a manager and the external management consultant – developed a new schedule, taking into account the comments of the group of specialists. The process described here went on for about four months, during which eight different proposals were put forward before a final proposal was accepted and implemented (Vissers, 1994).

In the evaluation of the process the project team concluded that the process could have been speeded up considerably if they had possessed a tool that would be able to handle the different performance criteria and capacity restrictions related to the planning problem and that would be able to generate a number of alternatives. In this contribution we will concentrate on the planning problem for a single specialty within a hospital. More specifically, the present case study deals with the evaluation and optimisation of the basic schedules for a specialty, the so-called 'master schedules'. Each specialty has its own master schedule. These schedules may vary a little from week to week, due to the absence of specialists, but in principle each week schedule is derived from this master schedule. A complicating factor in the development of a master schedule is the fact that not all activities have to be carried out every week. A small fraction of the activities follows a bi-weekly, or even a four-weekly, pattern.

In the case study hospital we wanted to avoid the pitfalls described above by developing a tool that enabled the generation of master schedules for specialist activities in hospitals. In this contribution we aim to answer the following research question:

> How, in a reasonable amount of time, could we construct for the activities of specialists master schedules that deliver good performance while satisfying given capacity restrictions?

There are a number of criteria that need to be taken into account to develop a good master schedule. First of all, a master schedule needs to meet the output targets for the hospital at annual level. From the point of efficient use of resources, it is also important to have activities of one type (for instance operating theatre sessions) well spread throughout the week. Then preferences of individual specialists also have to be taken into account, for instance, the order of activities within one day or the avoidance of a transfer within one day between different sites of a hospital.

Position in the planning framework

Figure 11.1 illustrates the position of this case study in the framework for operations management introduced in chapter 6. The planning problem addressed in this case study is positioned at the third level of the framework, i.e. resources planning and control. We concentrate on one key resource, i.e. specialist capacity, but also consider the use of other related resources such as outpatient clinics and operating theatre facilities. Therefore, the approach followed is according to the unit logistics perspective. The next level above in the planning framework – 'patient volume planning and control' – defines the amount of sessions of each type to be organised in order to meet the volumes agreed upon at an annual level.

The level we consider in this case study is concerned with the issue of how to organise these sessions in order to provide the service levels agreed upon, while maintaining an efficient organisation of activities. Efficiency is a key issue at this level, because the way sessions in outpatient departments and the operating theatre department are allocated determines whether or not peaks and troughs are introduced in the workload of diagnostic departments and wards. See also the

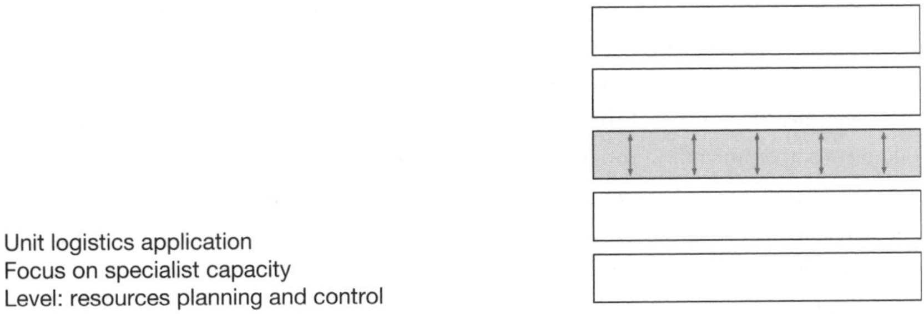

Unit logistics application
Focus on specialist capacity
Level: resources planning and control

Figure 11.1 *Master scheduling of medical specialist, and position in planning framework.*

distinction between 'leading' and 'following' resources in chapter 4 on unit logistics. The way resources are allocated at the level of 'resources planning and control' acts also as a restriction for scheduling patients and resources at the next level below in the planning framework, i.e. 'patient group planning and control'. The issue discussed in this chapter, therefore, is an important link between the more strategic and the more operational planning levels of the framework.

Literature review

The issue addressed in this chapter, i.e. specialist capacity planning, has received little attention previously. Most literature on the scheduling of hospital resources concerns beds (Wright, 1987; Bagust et al., 1999; Ridge et al., 1998), operating theatres (Blake, 2002; Guinet and Chaabane, 2003; Sier et al., 1997; Bowers and Mould, 2001), outpatient departments (Brahimi and Worthington, 1991; Lehaney and Paul, 1994; Rising et al., 1973; Cayirli and Veral, 2003; Bowers and Mould, 2005). These all refer to departments where interaction takes place between resources of a specific department and specialist capacity. However, the above illustrations only focus on a part of the capacity of the specialist. Literature references to papers that take into account the total capacity of a specialist, and concentrate on scheduling all the activities of specialists are scarce and hard to find.

The planning problem as such was first addressed by Vissers (1994); a very simple spreadsheet type of model was developed to describe master schedules for specialists and analyse their resource effects. As a follow-up of this study a decision support tool called SOM (Schedule Optimisation Model) was developed (Klaasen, 1996; Vissers 1996). Although the tool developed has been used in a number of hospitals in the Netherlands, it has one serious shortcoming. The tool cannot handle activities with a bi-weekly or four-weekly pattern.

ELABORATION

This section elaborates on the planning problem of master scheduling for medical specialists. In particular, we will discuss the data of a specialty of orthopaedics in a two-site hospital. We start by presenting the current master schedule used by the orthopaedic surgeons and then reflect on the different components that should be taken into account when modelling the planning problem. We emphasise here that the presented schedule is a stylised reflection of the original schedule used by the specialty of orthopaedics. Several minor and major adjustments have been made to the data of the pilot hospital in order to facilitate the problem description, the model formulation and the presentation of the results. Nevertheless, the case study still clearly demonstrates the problematic nature of master scheduling for medical specialists as well as the virtues of the developed model in a practical setting.

Table 11.1 Current master schedule orthopaedic surgeons

	Monday		Tuesday		Wednesday		Thursday		Friday	
	AM	PM	AM	PM	AM	PM	AM	PM	AM	PM
Surgeon 1	OT A	Other A	Other A	OPD A	OT A	Ward A	OPD A		OPD A	
Surgeon 2	OPD A	Ward A	DIAG A^2	Ward B	OPD B	OT B	OT A	OT A^2	OPD B	DIAG B
Surgeon 3	OPD B	Ward B	OT A	Ward A	OT B	OPD B	OPD A	OPD A	OT A	
Surgeon 4		OT B	Ward A	Ward B	OPD A	OT A	OPD B	OPD B	OPD A	OT A
Surgeon 5	OPD A	OT A	OPD A	OT A^2		Ward A	OPD B		OT B	OPD B

Note: OT: operating theatre; OPD: outpatient department; DIAG: diagnostic procedures; Ward: scheduled ward round; A: location A; B: location B; Other: other activities; OT A^2: bi-weekly operating theatre session at location B, etc.)

Suppose we deal with a group of five orthopaedic surgeons working on two locations, Location A and Location B. Table 11.1 provides information on the activities of each of the surgeons per day of the week.

Based on this schedule and also some interviews with surgeons and managers from operating theatres and outpatient departments, one can make the following observations that play a role in a proper description of the planning problem:

■ the surgeons perform a number of different types of activity;
■ most of these activities are organised on a weekly basis, a few on a bi-weekly basis;
■ each day of the week is divided into two parts: AM and PM;
■ the number of activities that need to be scheduled each week should be sufficient to meet the annual output targets;
■ the way sessions of one type (for instance, operating theatre sessions) are distributed over the days of the week, is bounded by a restriction on the availability of this type of resources (for instance, only one operating theatre available for orthopaedics per day of the week);
■ preferences in order of activities within a day exist at the level of individual specialists;
■ in evaluating the performance of a schedule different criteria play a role.

We will discuss these components of the planning problem below.

Frequency of activities

Each day of the week is divided into a fixed number of blocks, so-called *day-parts*. The specialty of orthopaedics uses two day-parts for planning during a day. Tables 11.2 and 11.3 provide information on the weekly and bi-weekly activities that have to be carried out by the individual specialists. The majority of the activities follow a normal weekly pattern. Notice that the orthopaedic surgeons do not have to carry out activities with a four-weekly pattern.

Table 11.2 Weekly activities for the specialists

	Operating (sessions)		Outpatient (sessions)		Wards (rounds)		Diagnostic (sessions)		Other (day halves)	
	A	B	A	B	A	B	A	B	A	B
Surgeon 1	2	0	3	0	1	0	0	0	2	0
Surgeon 2	1	1	1	2	1	1	0	1	0	0
Surgeon 3	2	1	2	2	1	1	0	0	0	0
Surgeon 4	2	1	2	2	1	1	0	0	0	0
Surgeon 5	1	1	2	2	1	0	0	0	0	0

Table 11.3 Bi-weekly activities for the specialists

	Operating (sessions)		Outpatient (sessions)		Wards (rounds)		Diagnostic (sessions)		Other (day halves)	
	A	B	A	B	A	B	A	B	A	B
Surgeon 1	0	0	0	0	0	0	0	0	0	0
Surgeon 2	1	0	0	0	0	0	1	0	0	0
Surgeon 3	0	0	0	0	0	0	0	0	0	0
Surgeon 4	0	0	0	0	0	0	0	0	0	0
Surgeon 5	1	0	0	0	0	0	0	0	0	0

Capacity restrictions

The coordination between the specialty under consideration and the rest of the hospital (for instance, other specialties and departments) takes place via so-called *capacity restrictions*. These restrictions may under no circumstances be violated by the master schedule. The following capacity restrictions are to be included in the model:

- All activities of an individual specialist have to be scheduled in the master schedule in order to meet the production targets of the specialty.
- The number of operating theatres and outpatient units available for the specialty at each day-part and at each location is limited.

The capacity restrictions for the number of operating theatres are listed in Table 11.4, in which the number of available operating theatres is given for each day-part on both locations. Furthermore, there are always two outpatient units at Location A and one outpatient unit at Location B available for orthopaedics. Notice that the capacity restrictions for the number of operating theatres at Location B are tight, i.e. the specialty needs at least four operating theatre sessions a week at this location to perform all the operations and this is exactly the number of sessions available each week.

Table 11.4 Capacity restrictions for operating theatres (number of sessions)

	Monday		Tuesday		Wednesday		Thursday		Friday	
	AM	PM	AM	PM	AM	PM	AM	PM	AM	PM
Location A	1	1	1	1	1	1	1	1	1	0
Location B	0	1	0	0	1	1	0	0	1	0

Evaluation criteria

To be able to evaluate the performance of a master schedule, different *criteria* should be included in the model. These criteria may be violated if necessary, but each violation decreases the performance of the master schedule. The criteria address the following issues:

1   the need to sequence activities in any day such that a transfer between locations for an individual specialist is avoided;
2   the need to accommodate the wishes of individual specialists in terms of their preferred day-part for a specific activity or preferred sequencing of activities;
3   the need to spread activities (operating theatre sessions and outpatient clinic sessions) over the day-parts of the week per group of specialists and per location;
4   the need to spread activities (operating theatre sessions and outpatient clinic sessions) over the day-parts of the week per individual specialist.

We held interviews to investigate the preferences of the orthopaedic surgeons with respect to day-parts for activities or sequences of activities:

- Surgeon 1 preferred to have the activities indicated by *other* at Location A on Monday afternoon and Tuesday morning;
- Surgeon 2 preferred to perform the *diagnostic sessions* at Location B on Thursday afternoon;
- Surgeon 3 wanted the *half day off* to be preceded by a *ward round* at Location B;
- Surgeon 4 wanted to do the *wards round* at Location A on Tuesday morning;
- Surgeon 5 had no specific preferences.

Moreover, we used these interviews to discuss the importance of the above evaluation criteria according to the orthopaedic surgeons. Table 11.5 shows the weighting factors that reflect the relative importance of the criteria. This means that the preferred sequences of activities are very important, whereas transfer between locations within one day and preferred day-parts for specific activities are considered only of medium importance. Finally, spreading of activities for both the individual specialists and within the specialty is of (almost) no importance to the orthopaedic surgeons.

Table 11.5 Weighting factors for relative importance of criteria

Criteria	Weight
Location transfer	5
Preferred day-part	7
Preferred sequence	10
Spreading of activities for specialists	0
Spreading of activities within the specialty	2

MODEL

In this section we translate the presented scheduling problem into a mathematical model in the form of an integer quadratic program (IQP). In the next section we first describe the solution approach. In the following section, the mathematical model is formulated. The final section describes the implementation of the solution approach in a software tool called MediPlan. For more detailed information, see De Kreuk and Winands (2001).

Solution approach

To find optimal master schedules for medical specialists in which the bi-weekly and four-weekly activities are integrated, three steps have to be followed:

1   Construction and optimisation of a schedule with the *weekly activities*;
2   Addition of the *bi-weekly activities* to the weekly schedule and optimisation of this bi-weekly schedule;
3   Addition of the *four-weekly activities* to the bi-weekly schedule and optimisation of this four-weekly schedule.

Integer quadratic programming (IQP) is used to formulate a mathematical model that finds the optimal schedules. In the optimal schedules the capacity restrictions mentioned in the previous section have to hold, while the number of criteria that are violated is minimised.

Mathematical model

In this section the optimisation model is described mathematically. For the ease of presentation, we show only the mathematical model for the weekly activities. Let t denote the day-parts in one week ($t \in \{1, \ldots, 10\}$), and let S denote the total number of specialists. All possible activities get a number, which is shown in Table 11.6.

To describe the capacity restrictions, the following parameters are introduced:

■ $f_{a,s}$ is the number of day-parts for which specialist s ($s \in \{1, \ldots, S\}$) has to perform activity a ($a \in \{1, \ldots, 11\}$). So $\sum_{a=1}^{11} f_{a,s} = 10$;

■ $g_{a,t}$ is the maximum number of specialists that can perform activity a on day-part t ($t \in \{1, \ldots, 10\}$).

To describe the criteria, for which the violations have to be minimised, the following parameters are introduced:

■ c_i is the weight of a violation of criterion i ($i \in \{1, \ldots, 5\}$);
■ $w_{s,t}$ is equal to the number corresponding to the activity that specialist s wants to perform on day-part t ($w_{s,t} \in \{1, \ldots, 11\}$). $w_{s,t}$ equals zero if specialist s has no preference on the corresponding day-part.

Table 11.6 *Activities in mathematical model*

No.	Activity	No.	Activity
1	Operating theatre, location 1	6	Operating theatre, location 2
2	Outpatient clinic, location 1	7	Outpatient clinic, location 2
3	Ward rounds, location 1	8	Ward rounds, location 2
4	Diagnostics sessions, location 1	9	Diagnostics sessions, location 2
5	Other, location 1	10	Other, location 2
		11	Day-part off, no location

For every day-part an activity has to be assigned to every specialist. This gives the following decision variable:

- $x_{s,t}$ is equal to the number corresponding to the activity that specialist s has to perform on day-part t ($x_{s,t} \in \{1, \ldots, 11\}$).

The capacity restrictions form the constraints of the optimisation model. The first capacity restriction is that all activities of an individual specialist have to be scheduled in the master schedule in order to meet the production targets of the specialty, i.e:

$$\sum_{t=1}^{10} 1[x_{s,t} = a] = f_{a,s} \text{ for all } a \in \{1, \ldots, 11\}, s \in \{1, \ldots, S\}.$$

($1[x]$ is the indicator function, which becomes one if x occurs). The second type of capacity restrictions is that the number of operating theatres and outpatient units available for the specialty at each day-part and at each location is limited. This is given by:

$$\sum_{s=1}^{S} 1[x_{s,t} = a] \leq g_{a,t} \text{ for all } a \in \{1,6\}, t \in \{1, \ldots, 10\},$$

$$\sum_{s=1}^{S} 1[x_{s,t} = a] \leq g_{a,t} \text{ for all } a \in \{2,7\}, t \in \{1, \ldots, 10\}.$$

The criteria that have to be minimised form the objective of the optimisation problem.

The first criterion is that it is preferable that no sequence of activities is scheduled in one day that requires a transfer between locations for an individual specialist. This criterion is described by:

$$\sum_{s=1}^{S} \sum_{t=1}^{5} 1[x_{s,2t-1} \leq 5 \wedge 6 \leq x_{s,2t} \leq 10] + \sum_{s=1}^{S} \sum_{t=1}^{5} 1[6 \leq x_{s,2t-1} \leq 10 \wedge x_{s,2t} \leq 5]$$

A second criterion is that a violation should be given if the preferred day-part for a specific activity for an individual specialist is not assigned, i.e:

$$\sum_{s=1}^{S} \sum_{t=1}^{10} 1[w_{s,t} \neq 0 \wedge x_{s,t} \neq w_{s,t}].$$

There are also (non)-preferred sequences of activities for individual specialists. Here, only the mathematical formulation is given to violate if preferred sequences of activities do not occur, but the formulation for the non-preferred sequences is almost identical. That is:

$$\sum_{s=1}^{S} \sum_{t=1}^{10} 1[x_{s,t} = a \wedge x_{s,t+1} \neq b],$$

where a and b represent the first and second activity in the preferred sequence, respectively. The other criteria have to do with the spreading of the activities over the day-parts per week per group of specialists and per location and also the spreading per individual specialist. These criteria are included in the model by calculating the spreading of the activities in the usual way. The mathematical formulations are not given here, since it would make the model look unnecessarily complex. For more information on these formulations, see De Kreuk and Winands (2001).

Summarising, the problem of master scheduling of medical specialists can be formulated by the following IQP:

Minimise

$$c_1 \left(\sum_{s=1}^{S} \sum_{t=1}^{5} 1[x_{s,2t-1} \leqslant 5 \wedge 6 \leqslant x_{s,2t} \leqslant 10] + \sum_{s=1}^{S} \sum_{t=1}^{5} 1[6 \leqslant x_{s,2t-1} \leqslant 10 \wedge x_{s,2t} \leqslant 5] \right) +$$

$$c_2 \left(\sum_{s=1}^{S} \sum_{t=1}^{10} 1[w_{s,t} \neq 0 \wedge x_{s,t} \neq w_{s,t}] \right) + c_3 \left(\sum_{s=1}^{S} \sum_{t=1}^{10} 1[x_{s,t} = a \wedge x_{s,t+1} \neq b] \right)$$

Subject to

$$\sum_{t=1}^{10} 1[x_{s,t} = a] = f_{a,s} \text{ for all } a \in \{1, \dots, 11\}, s \in \{1, \dots, S\}$$

$$\sum_{s=1}^{S} 1[x_{s,t} = a] \leqslant g_{a,t} \text{ for all } a \in \{1,6\}, t \in \{1, \dots, 10\}$$

$$\sum_{s=1}^{S} 1[x_{s,t} = a] \leqslant g_{a,t} \text{ for all } a \in \{2,7\}, t \in \{1, \dots, 10\}$$

$$x_{s,t} \in \{1, \dots, 11\}$$

Implementation

The model described in the previous section is implemented in a software tool called MediPlan. MediPlan uses the solution approach consisting of three steps, i.e. constructing and optimising a schedule with weekly activities, addition of the bi-weekly activities and addition of the four-weekly activities. Each of the steps in the solution procedure consists of two parts: the construction of an initial schedule and the development of alternative schedules with a higher performance. The development of alternative schedules in each step is continued until the decision maker is satisfied with the schedule and wants to proceed to the next step.

The following two steps are followed to construct the initial weekly schedule:

1   Schedule the weekly activities for which capacity restrictions are imposed (i.e. operating theatre sessions and outpatient clinic sessions) in such a way that these capacity restrictions are satisfied.

2   Schedule the rest of the weekly activities (i.e. diagnostics sessions, ward rounds and other activities) randomly over the idle day-parts of the schedule.

It is important that the number of activities that have to be scheduled does not exceed the number of day-parts that are available for the different activities. The initial bi-weekly schedule is made in the same way. This means that we first schedule the bi-weekly activities with capacity restrictions in the doubled weekly schedule without violating these capacity restrictions. Second, the remaining bi-weekly activities are randomly added to the schedule. The initial four-weekly schedule is constructed by applying exactly the same procedure to the bi-weekly schedule.

To generate an alternative schedule, two different activities of a specialist in the schedule are selected and exchanged. When generating alternative weekly schedules all activities may be chosen and exchanged. However, in the optimisation of the bi-weekly schedule the weekly activities are fixed, which means that they cannot be selected for exchange. When optimising the four-weekly schedule, the weekly and bi-weekly activities are fixed. In the exchanging process, capacity restrictions are constantly checked. In this way a variant of the current schedule is made that is feasible given the capacity restrictions.

After the exchange of the activities, the score of this schedule variant is computed. In order to decide whether the variant will be accepted or not, we make use of simulated annealing, a 'local search' technique (see, for example, Aarts and Korst, 1989). Local search methods have the goal of finding a solution in a large solution-set in a smart and fast way and concentrate on problems that can be formulated unambiguously in terms of mathematical terminology and notation. Furthermore, it is assumed that the quality of a solution is quantifiable and that it can be compared to that of any other solution. Finally, it is assumed that the set of solutions is finite.

Simulated annealing comes down to the following steps:

1   Generate a variant of the current schedule as explained above.

2   Calculate the score of the variant.

3   If the variant has a higher performance than the current schedule, accept the variant as a new schedule; if not, the variant is accepted as the new schedule with a pre-determined probability (the probability of acceptance of lower performing variants gradually decreases).

4   Continue with step 1.

The probability of acceptance of a variant with a lower performance helps to overcome local optima. Local optima are schedules that have a better score than all the schedules that can be obtained by exchanging activities, but are not the best possible schedule (global optimum). By gradually reducing the probability of accepting lower performance variants, the algorithm is able to find an optimal (global) solution by using only a limited number of runs.

RESULTS

In this section we will show the output of MediPlan for this case study, i.e. the optimal schedule together with its score, and present a discussion of the output.

The master schedule for the specialty of orthopaedics generated by MediPlan is shown in Table 11.7. For the ease of presentation, we only depict and discuss the weekly schedule. This master schedule was constructed in only a couple of minutes, which is a significant reduction in process time compared to the old situation as sketched in the 'Planning problem' section earlier in this chapter.

Table 11.8 summarises the performance of the master schedule in Table 11.7 on the different criteria included in MediPlan. This master schedule satisfies the imposed capacity restrictions with respect to the limited number of operating

Table 11.7 Final weekly master schedule for the specialty of orthopaedics

	Monday		Tuesday		Wednesday		Thursday		Friday	
	AM	PM	AM	PM	AM	PM	AM	PM	AM	PM
Surgeon 1	OPD A	Other A	Other A	OPD A	Free	OT A	Ward A	Free	OT A	OPD A
Surgeon 2	OT A	Free	Free	OPD B	OT B	OPD B	Ward B	DIAG B	OPD A	Ward A
Surgeon 3	Ward A	OT A	OPD A	OPD A	OPD B	OT B	OPD B	OT A	Ward B	Free
Surgeon 4	Ward B	OT B	Ward A	OT A	OT A	OPD A	OPD A	Free	OPD B	OPD B
Surgeon 5	OPD B	OPD B	Free	Ward A	OPD A	Free	OT A	OPD A	OT B	Free

Table 11.8 Score for the master schedule

Criteria	No. of violations	Score
Location transfer	1	5
Preferred day-part	0	0
Preferred sequence	0	0
Spreading of activities for specialists	–	0
Spreading of activities within the specialty	–	3.8
TOTAL		8.8

theatres and outpatient units. It immediately strikes the eye that the generated schedule violates no criteria concerning preferred sequences and day-parts of activities. Furthermore, in the entire week only one orthopaedic surgeon has to transfer between locations within one day. The bottom line of Table 11.8 shows the total score of the master schedule.

If we compare this with the performance of the original schedule (Table 11.1), we can make the following observations:

■ The original schedule also showed one transfer on Tuesday (Surgeon 4) between locations, contributing 5 points to the score.
■ In the original schedule one wish for a preferred day-part (Surgeon 2 on Thursday afternoon) was violated, contributing 7 points to the score.
■ The sequence order of activities for Surgeon 3 (half day off preceded by ward round at location B) was violated, contributing 10 more points to the score of the original schedule.
■ Spreading of activities was not considered in the original schedule, and will certainly produce a higher contribution to the score for the original schedule than the revised schedule.

Summarising, the score of the original schedule is much higher than that of the revised schedule. The new schedule shows fewer violations and a better spreading of activities.

REFLECTION AND FURTHER DEVELOPMENT

We want to start this section with a discussion of the quality of the model on both the performance of the generated master schedules and the speed of the process involved. After all, the aim of the present research was the development of a method or a tool that could both *improve* and *speed up* the process of constructing master schedules. Besides the case study presented, MediPlan has been tested on various theoretical examples and on the specialty of gynaecology within the same hospital (see De Kreuk and Winands, 2001), for more details). Based on these implementations of MediPlan we may conclude that the model worked successfully with respect to the performance of the generated master schedules. Furthermore, MediPlan also reduced the process time of developing master schedules significantly in the practical implementations. Once the decision maker had been able to define relevant performance criteria and capacity restrictions, the generating of a schedule with maximal performance took only a couple of minutes. Although further testing is needed, the first (positive) applications of the model encourage further use for other specialties and other hospitals.

We would like to end with a possible extension of MediPlan that can support hospitals in the coordination of schedules for specialties and departments such as operating theatres and outpatient departments. After all, most of the work of the specialist is regulated by these department schedules. Between these department schedules large degrees of dependency exist, i.e. a delay in one department may cause delays in successive departments. For example, if an operating session takes more time than scheduled, the specialist might not be able to start, at the correct time, a clinic session in the outpatient department. This dependence is often a bottleneck when one wants to redesign a schedule for a specific department. If, for instance, some shifts are to be made in the clinic schedule, what will be the consequences for the other activities of the specialist? A further complication is that the workload of the medical service departments is, to a large extent, dependent on the outpatient clinic schedule. At times of a fracture clinic, for example, many patients will visit the X-ray department. Therefore, a direct relationship exists between the clinic schedule of the outpatient department and the workload of some medical service departments. When looking at changes in the working day of a specialist these *second-order effects* also have to be taken into account. Therefore, an interesting topic for further research would be to analyse the match between the master schedules for individual specialties generated by MediPlan and the department schedules. Undoubtedly, there is great demand from hospitals for a decision support tool visualising and optimising the coordination between and within the individual specialty schedules and the department schedules.

QUESTIONS AND EXERCISES

1 Based on the data of Tables 11.2 and 11.3, what is the minimum number of operating theatres and outpatient units needed by the specialty of orthopaedics in a week at location A?

2   What is the relationship between the master schedule of a specialty on the one hand and the production targets and waiting lists of the specialty on the other hand?

3   Define one or more capacity restrictions for a master schedule in addition to the ones presented in the 'Capacity restrictions' subsection of the 'Elaboration' section. By who are these restrictions imposed (e.g. another specialty, another department or the hospital board)?

4   Define one or more performance criteria for a master schedule in addition to the ones presented in the 'Evaluation' subsection of the 'Elaboration' section.

REFERENCES AND FURTHER READING

Aarts E. and J. Korst. *Simulated Annealing and Boltzmann machines.* John Wiley & Sons, New York, 1989.

Bagust A., M. Place and J.W. Posnett. Dynamics of bed use in accommodating emergency admissions; stochastic simulation model. *British Medical Journal,* 319, 1999, 155–158.

Blake J.T. Using integer programming to allocate operating room time at Mount Sinai hospital. *Interfaces,* 32, 2002, 63–73.

Bowers J. and G. Mould. Organisational implications of concentration of emergency orthopaedic services. *Health Bulletin,* 59, 2001, 381–387.

Bowers J. and G. Mould. Ambulatory care and orthopaedic capacity planning. *Health Care Management Science,* 8, 2005, 41–48.

Brahimi M. and D.J. Worthington. Queuing models for out-patient appointment systems – a case study. *Journal of the Operational Research Society,* 42(9), 1991, 733–746.

Cayirli T. and E. Veral. Outpatient scheduling in health care: a review of literature. *Production and Operations Management,* 12(4), 2003, 519–549.

Guinet A. and S. Chaabane. Operating theatre planning. *International Journal of Production Economics,* 85, 2003, 69–81.

Klaasen S.A.M. *Beslissingsondersteuning bij roosteroptimalisering in ziekenhuizen.* In Dutch. MSc-thesis, University of Technology, Eindhoven, 1996.

Kreuk de A.C.C. and E.M.M. Winands. *MediPlan: het optimaliseren van meer-weke-lijkse roosters van specialisten in een ziekenhuis.* In Dutch. Project report, Faculty of Mathematics and Computer Science, University of Technology, Eindhoven, 2001.

Lehaney B. and R.J. Paul. Using SSM to develop a simulation of outpatient services. *Journal of the Royal Society of Health,* 114, 1994, 248–251.

Ridge J.C., S.K. Jones, M.S. Nielsen and A.K. Shahani. Capacity planning for intensive care units. *European Journal of Operational Research,* 105(2), 1998, 346–355.

Rising E., R. Baron and B. Averill. A system analysis of a university health service outpatient clinic. *Operations Research*, 21(5), 1973, 1030–1047.

Sier D., P. Tobin and C. McGurk. Scheduling surgical procedures. *Journal of the Operational Research Society,* 48, 1997, 884–891.

Vissers J.M.H. *Patient Flow based Allocation of Hospital Resources.* Doctoral thesis, University of Technology, Eindhoven, 1994.

Vissers J.M.H. Generating alternative solutions for hospital resource scheduling under multiple resource constraints. Paper presented at ORAHS, Lisbon, 1996.

Wright M.B. The application of a surgical bed simulation model. *European Journal of Operational Research,* 32, 1987, 26–32.

ACKNOWLEDGEMENT

The authors would like to thank Marko Boon for the implementation of the user interface for MediPlan. Furthermore, the authors are indebted to Jacques Resing for his helpful comments and valuable suggestions.

Chapter 12

A patient group based business planning model for a surgical specialty

Jan Vissers, Ivo Adan, Miguel van den Heuvel and Karin Wiersema

SUMMARY

In this contribution we present an approach for a business planning model for a surgical specialty, based on modelling of all patient processes as well as of the dynamics involved in planning and managing resources. An important basis of the model is the description of the processes of all patient groups served by the specialty. The data for this description are based on the expert knowledge of medical specialists and administrative data from the hospital information system. Furthermore, the planning of scheduled patients and the handling of emergency patients in the model takes into account the workload generated by leading resources, such as operating theatres, for following resources, such as beds. The model allows, therefore, decision support for resource management issues as well as process design issues.

KEY TERMS

- Business modelling of hospital practice
- Patient groups, trajectories and resources
- Process design and resource impacts
- Utilisation of unit resources

INTRODUCTION

There is much interest in developing business approaches for hospital practice. In applying such an approach, a major obstacle to overcome is the state of development of the product and process concept in health care. The introduction of DRG systems – or similar systems – in many countries as a way of financing health care has stimulated enormously the further development of these concepts. This allows for using process descriptions as a basis for developing a business model for hospital practice.

In this study we concentrate on the planning of activities of a group of surgeons in a hospital that operates on one or more sites. Planning the business of such a specialty involves decisions on the frequency of activities and on the allocation of resources to activities. The case study hospital was facing difficulties in dealing with these issues.

BOX 12.1 THE PILOT HOSPITAL

The pilot hospital experienced serious problems with the management of patient flows and resources for the specialty general surgery. The group of six general surgeons had sessions at the two sites of the hospital. At the main site all types of services were offered: emergency services, outpatient clinics, operating theatre sessions and ward rounds. At the second site only outpatient clinics were held. Problems faced by the group of surgeons were, among others:

■   loss of capacity in outpatient clinics and operating theatre sessions, which were not used in an optimal way;
■   the long access times for a first visit to the outpatient clinic and long waiting time on the waiting list for a patient requiring surgery;
■   concerns about the functioning of the A&E department linked to patients with differing urgency having to be seen.

The group of surgeons discussed these problems with the board of directors, and the decision was taken to start a broader project with the support of the internal management consultancy staff. Different project teams were installed to investigate the practice problems at the different units involved: the accidents and emergency department (A&E), the outpatient department (OPD), the operating theatre department (OTD), the ward and the admissions department. Furthermore, a decision was made to develop a patient flow model that would support decision making from two perspectives. The objective of the model was to generate information that indicated the ways in which changes in process design or in available resources within departments affected services for patients as well as the use of resources.

In the next section we will position the planning problem in the framework of health OM as used in this book. The following section gives a more detailed description of the planning problem. The different parts of the patient flow model are then explained, and the application of the model is discussed. Finally, we formulate conclusions and suggestions for further research.

PLANNING PROBLEM

The problems faced by the group of surgeons can roughly be categorised under two headings:

- practice management problems: the distribution of outpatient activities over both sites, and the allocation of resources to activities;
- process design problems: the management of a patient's journeys through the system and the management of related waiting times.

In this section we relate the planning problem to the framework for operations management introduced in chapter 6 and provide a short literature review.

Position in planning framework

The framework describes the different planning levels required for hospital operations management and allows us to define the relationship between our planning problem and other planning issues in a hospital.

As shown in Figure 12.1, the planning problem addressed in this case study is positioned at the second level of the framework, i.e. patient group planning and control. The approach followed is defined as a network logistics approach, with equal emphasis on unit logistics and chain logistics. We will provide some further information on the position of the case study in the framework.

The primary level addressed in this case study is 'patient group planning and control'. Much of the effort is linked to generating a good description of the care processes utilised by the different categories of general surgery patients. There is also a link to the next level of 'resources planning and control', as it is possible to aggregate data at the level of one year. Nevertheless, the focus is in on short-term planning and time horizons of one week.

The problem faced by the group of general surgeons clearly needs to be approached from a unit logistics as well as chain logistics perspective. Unit logistics considers the logistics of an individual unit (an inpatient ward, an outpatient department, an operating theatre department) and aims to optimise the use of the resources available for the unit. Efficiency is a strong point of unit logistics, but the contribution of the unit to the optimal flow of patient processes can be a weak

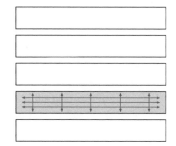

Network logistics application
Emphasis on unit logistics as well as chain logistics
Level: patient group planning and control

Figure 12.1 *Patient group based business planning model, and position in planning framework.*

point. Units are more concerned with the total flow of patients serviced by the unit than with the flow of individual patient groups. Chain logistics is concerned with the logistics of an individual chain or process (a process for a specific patient group, for instance patients requiring hip replacements) and aims to optimise the flow of this patient group through the hospital system. Service is a strong point of chain logistics, but the efficient use of resources can be a weak point. The focus is most of all on eliminating waiting times, combining or parallelising steps. The optimal use of resources is not very well looked at, as this can often be evaluated only at the aggregate level, for instance at the level of a specialty, where resources are allocated. Therefore, a combination of unit logistics and chain logistics is required, i.e. a network logistics approach. In a network logistics approach a hospital is represented as a network of units, coupled by chains that represent the process for individual groups of patients. Using a network logistics approach for developing the model will allow support for issues dealing with the units' perspectives as well as issues dealing with the chains' perspective. See also chapters 4 and 5.

Literature review

The development of hospital product definitions and process descriptions over time is reflected in the way business models for hospital practice have developed. From the beginning, business models revolved around the specialty as an entity. Most of them, however, stayed at this level of aggregation; see, for example, the Hospital Planning Model (Beech *et al.*, 1990). This model made projections for the output at the level of a specialty, using monthly figures on available resources and average productivity per unit of capacity (for instance the number of patients operated per operating theatre session. The specialty was considered as one patient flow. Within the patient flow of the specialty no distinction was made between patient groups that could have quite different resource profiles. In another attempt by Bowen and Forte (1997) a Business Planning Model was developed to support planning issues for a surgical specialty. They concentrated on the flows between the A&E department, the outpatient department and the operating theatre department. Again, no distinction was made between patient groups within a specialty. Furthermore, the process of patients was not completely covered, as patients also visit diagnostic departments and can be admitted to wards. However, it was probably the best model possible, given the state of development of process thinking in health care at that time. Process descriptions were not available and data on the realisation of processes by patients were lacking. Then there were other approaches that included more detailed patient groups based on diagnosis related groups (DRGs), such as the Hospital Resource Planning model by Roth and van Dierdonck (1995). For each DRG all material and capacity requirements are based on average results from the analysis of hospital data. The DRG approach uses a sort of process description, but it differs in many respects from the logistic approach followed in this book. The limitations of their approach are: routing of patients and uncertainty are not included; outpatient activities are not included; interaction between resources over time (for instance between operating theatres and wards) is not considered.

In our previous approaches to the problem we developed a model based on more aggregate data, first at the overall specialty level (van der Lei, 1998) and later for the level of patient groups (van Leeuwaarden and van der Linden, 2001), based on transitions between states in the model (A&E, outpatient, inpatient, etc.). Again, this is also a flow approach, but it is not yet based on a process description of patient groups. It uses a description at the level of a patient group in which the flow between the A&E department, the outpatient department and the ward is described in terms of the percentage of patients who continue after a previous state. This is in contrast to the approach in this chapter, which is based on a detailed description of all the steps in the process followed by patient groups.

ELABORATION

The annual flow of patients of general surgery in the pilot hospital can be characterised by 13,000 first visits, 19,000 follow-up visits, 1,250 day cases, 2,200 admissions and 16,600 bed days (2003). The process most of these patients follow after the referral by the general practitioner is a first visit to the general surgeon in the outpatient department, possibly followed by some diagnostic tests to support the diagnosis, and then a second visit where the diagnosis and treatment options are discussed. For emergency patients the start of the process is at the emergency department, and when an admission is required, the patient is admitted without further delay. When an admission is required for an elective patient, the patient is put on a waiting list. Before the patient can be admitted and operated on, the patient needs to be screened and informed on the procedure for anaesthetics. Then the patient is admitted to a ward, operated on and returned to the ward to recover.

After the discharge the patient will often be seen once or twice for follow-up at the outpatient department.

The units encountered in this process are:

- the outpatient department
- the emergency department
- the pre-operative screening unit
- the ward
- the operating theatre department.

These are all units that can be characterised by an amount of capacity available to process patients, and by a procedure for scheduling patients. In the outpatient department and the operating theatre department the available amount of resources is defined per specialist, i.e. the number of minutes per day of the week that a specialist can see patients in the outpatient department or operate on patients in the operating theatre department. The capacity of the outpatient department is also broken down into that available at the two sites of the hospital. The capacity of the ward can be broken down further into types of beds: day cases, short stay, long stay and intensive care.

This is only a first description of the planning problem at a very global level. It needs to be specified more precisely, as patients can move through the system in different ways. This is illustrated in Figure 12.2.

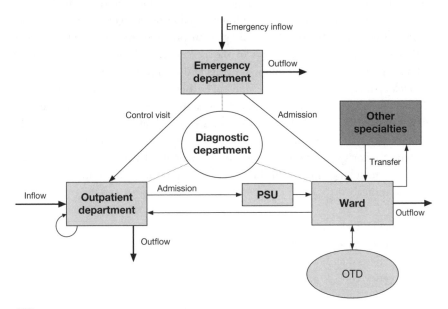

Figure 12.2 *Representation of the system at the level of the specialty (PSU = pre-operative screening unit, OTD = operating theatre department).*

Figure 12.2 illustrates that patients can enter the general surgery system in three ways:

- as outpatients referred by a general practitioner;
- as emergency patients;
- as patients initially of another specialty, but transferred to general surgery (for instance patients referred to general medicine for stomach complaints, but transferred to general surgery for surgical procedures).

Each of these flows behaves differently and has different characteristics. The emergency patient enters the system via the emergency department. Most of these patients (about 60 per cent) are attended to only once and then are referred back to the general practitioner. A part of the emergency flow (about 10 per cent) are immediately admitted as inpatients and operated upon at a short notice. The rest (about 30 per cent) are attended to and further follow-up will be provided at the outpatient department. The outpatient enters via the outpatient department, and revisits the clinic until the diagnosis has been made. Then part of the flow (about 60 per cent) continues treatment on an outpatient basis, while the rest (40 per cent) needs an admission. The patients that need admission are given an appointment for the admission date or are put on a waiting list. These patients first have to visit the pre-operative screening unit to test their condition for undergoing the surgical procedure and to be informed about the mode of anaesthetics used for the operation. After the admission follow-up care is given in the outpatient department. So, in the outpatient department the outpatient follow-up flow of emergency patients mingles with the new outpatients referred by general practitioners. These subflows have different characteristics, in terms of the percentage of patients continuing for admission or the number of follow-up visits in the outpatient department.

Delays in the process can be due to bottleneck capacities or waiting lists. To be able to show these dynamics in the system we have to include the time dimension in the model. That will enable us to look at the development of the state of the system. But this is not the only complicating factor. We also have to include a priority rule as the urgency of the patient's demand plays an important role in scheduling patients. In this case the hospital uses the following urgency classification:

- urgency code 1: immediate admission
- urgency code 2: admission within one week
- urgency code 3: admission within three weeks
- urgency code 4: admission when capacity is available.

When patients are selected from the waiting list, and scheduled for operation, these urgency codes are taken into account.

Up to now all complications discussed have been dealt with before in model-ling approaches. But we need to go further as we are still using the total patient flow as the basis for modelling, while all the characteristics discussed before can vary widely between different patient groups. So, the important step that we have to add in order to deal effectively with the problem faced by the pilot hospital is to be able to model at the level of individual patient groups. Then we will see that these different patient groups will use the general surgery system as illustrated in Figure 12.2 in a very different way.

MODEL

We will illustrate the different parts of the model and then discuss the assumptions made.

Demand side

For modelling the demand, we followed a procedure as illustrated in Figure 12.3. The total inflow of new outpatients is broken down into a number of patient groups. A patient group is a group of patients that is recognisable in the patient flow and that is used to organise specialty practice at a more detailed level. Often they will be distinguished by their use of resources, for instance fracture patients using the plaster room. In order to make it manageable, the number of patient groups needs to be limited to 5–10 groups (see also chapter 7).

For a patient group a number of trajectories can be distinguished that can further help to expose similarity between the routing of patients (for instance conservative treatment versus surgical intervention) or their use of resources. Again, to make it manageable the number of trajectories per patient group should be on average not more than five. This will make the total of processes (patient groups times trajectories) distinguished for modelling the flow of a specialty between 25 and 40. This makes a classification scheme used for logistics a more global one than one for hospital financing: for example general surgery can include more than 250 DRGs.

Then the care process for each of the combinations of patient groups and trajec-tories is modelled, as illustrated in the lower part of Figure 12.3. In Figure 12.4 this is illustrated in more detail for patients undergoing laparotomy or laparoscopy.

We see from Figure 12.4 that 72 per cent of patients enter the system as elec-tive patients via the outpatient department, while 28 per cent enter as emergency patients via the A&E department. For the elective patients the process starts with a first visit at the outpatient department. No diagnostic tests are asked for. Then 82 per cent of the patients follow the trajectory of laparoscopy. This requires an admission at a short-stay ward for, on average, three days and a surgical procedure

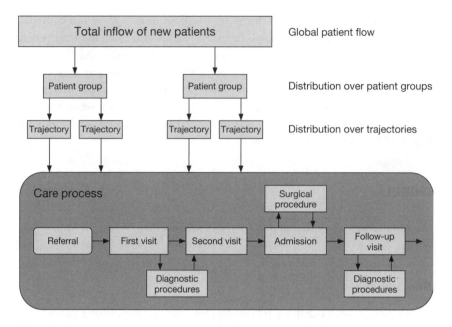

Figure 12.3 Outline for modelling demand.

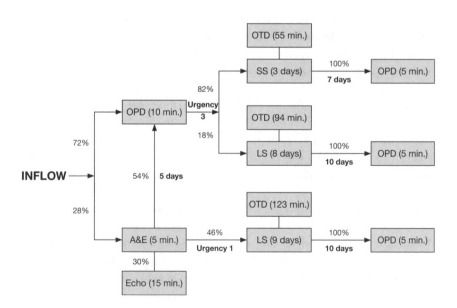

Figure 12.4 Process model of laparotomy or laparoscopy (OPD = outpatient department; OTD = operating theatre department; A&E = accident and emergency department; LS = long stay; SS = short stay).

with a duration of, on average, 55 minutes. Then after, on average, seven days the patient is seen once more at the outpatient department. The patient for laparotomy stays longer, has a longer duration of the surgical procedure, stays at the long-stay ward and returns for outpatient follow-up after, on average, 10 days. For the emergency patient the process starts at the emergency department. For 30 per cent of these patients, the next step is for an echo to be performed. Then 46 per cent of patients are admitted to a ward with urgency code 1, requiring immediate admission and short-term surgical intervention. Again the characteristics differ from the previous processes. The rest (54 per cent) can be seen on an elective basis as discussed before.

This process was carried out for all patient groups and trajectories distinguished. In total, seven patient groups were distinguished. See Table 12.1 for an overview of patient groups and trajectories.

The basis of description was provided by interviews with medical specialists and other professionals. The data provided by the interviews were checked with administrative data from the hospital information system.

The description in Figure 12.4 is more in the format of a decision tree than in that of trajectories. The contents of Figure 12.4 can be redrawn as five separate trajectories as shown in Figure 12.5. These will make it easier to look at the resource impacts of the processes.

Now we can analyse the different trajectories in terms of their demands of resources. This will make it possible to make the match later on between demand for and supply of resources. How this is done is illustrated in Figures 12.6 and

Table 12.1 Patient groups, trajectories and number of patients per year

Patient group	Trajectory	Number of patients
1 Abdominal complaints	15 trajectories, amongst others appendicitis, hernia inguinalis, cholelithiasis	1050
2 Mamma complaints	3 trajectories, amongst others mamma malign and benign	175
3 Vascular complaints	6 trajectories, amongst others varicose veins, aneurism	625
4 Fractures	8 trajectories, amongst others ankle ligaments, femur	175
5 Trauma	6 trajectories, amongst others ankle distortion, ruptures	175
6 Skin problems	2 trajectories, amongst others ganglion	75
7 Lung carcinoma	1 trajectory	25

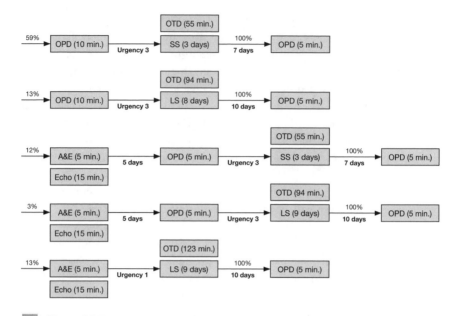

Figure 12.5 *Trajectories for the process of laparotomy/laparoscopy.*

(OPD = outpatient department; OTD = operating theatre department; A&E = accident and emergency department; LS = long stay; SS = short stay)

12.7 for a number of patients from different patient groups and different trajectories. First we present the demand on resources per week.

Figure 12.6 illustrates for patients 1–4 how the activities of the process are scheduled over the different weeks in the planning period. At this stage delays can occur in the process when resources are limited. If not all the patients scheduled for a specific week – according to the specification of the trajectory – can be dealt with, a proportion is rescheduled for the week after.

The way rescheduling is done depends on the resource considered. For the OPD, patients that have already been rescheduled will not be further delayed. Emergency patients are always scheduled. A part of the capacity is reserved for this purpose. The remaining capacity is used for planning patients. If capacity is not sufficient to meet all demand, a fraction of all patient groups following the same trajectory will be admitted; the fraction is equal to the available capacity divided by the required capacity. Rescheduling for the other departments is performed along similar lines, but in this case the urgency is used for the order in which patient groups are scheduled. This is performed for all the weeks in the planning period. Then the demand for capacity can be calculated as illustrated in Figure 12.7.

Figure 12.7 illustrates for a specified week T how the resources of the different units are utilised by patients 1–4. By aggregating the resource workloads over all the patients treated, the total demand for a resource can be calculated.

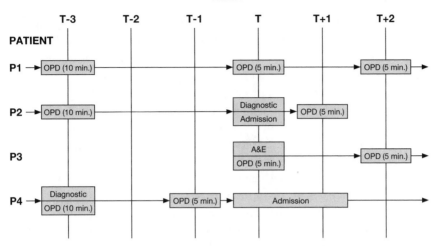

Figure 12.6 *Modelling the demand per week.*

(OPD = outpatient department; A&E = accident and emergency department)

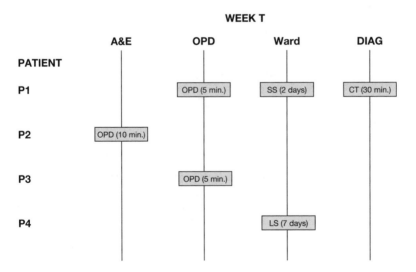

Figure 12.7 *Calculation of the demand for capacity for different units in week T.*

Supply side

To model the supply side in relation to the organisation of specialty practice for general surgery, we used different specifications, as illustrated in Table 12.2.

All demand is met in the A&E department, so we do not limit the resources available to handle the flow of emergencies for general surgery.

In the outpatient department the capacity is expressed in the number of minutes available each week in the planning period, and is further broken down into specialist, site and type of visit (first visit, follow-up visit, urgent visit referred from A&E, small procedure). Each of these visit types requires a specified amount of time.

The pre-operative screening unit has a number of slots available each week. This is further broken down into slots for elective patients and slots for urgent admission of patients that need to be admitted at a short notice (urgency codes 2 and 3).

The capacity for operating on patients is expressed in number of minutes available per week, and further broken down into specialists.

The capacity for admission is expressed in number of beds available, broken down into beds available: for day cases; for short-stay admission (up to five days); for long-stay admission (more than five days); and for IC stay. The number of available beds is not a limitation for admitting patients, as beds can be borrowed from other specialties. The number of beds borrowed from other specialties is counted as a 'logistic problem'.

Table 12.2 *Available capacity and specifications for resources*

Resourse	Available capacity	Specifications
Emergency department	no limitation	
Outpatient department	available minutes per week	per specialist per site per type of visit
Pre-operative screening unit	available slots per week	electives urgent
Operating theatre department	available minutes per week	per specialist
Wards	available beds	IC, day case, short stay, long stay

Assumptions

Modelling demand and supply according to the previous two sections involved many assumptions. The assumptions made are summarised for each of the components of the model in Table 12.3.

Table 12.3 *Assumptions made in modelling demand and supply*

Component	Assumptions
Inflow	average inflow per patient group per week; fixed routing per trajectory
Specialist	no change of specialist in route; no change of diagnosis
OPD	no change of site; deterministic duration per type of visit, independent of specialist
PSU	patients are seen according to urgency; results are valid for 13 weeks
OTD	scheduled according to urgency; fraction of urgency code 1 patients that are operated on during sessions within working hours; deterministic duration procedure, independent of specialist
Ward	deterministic length of stay; los daycase = one, shortstay if los ≤ 5 days, longstay patients can use also IC

The inflow of patients is based on an average number of patients per week, with a specified distribution over patient groups and trajectories. The trajectory defines a fixed routing for all patients. So deviations from this trajectory are not taken into account.

For involvement of specialist capacity in processes of patients, we assume that the patient will keep the same specialist throughout the trajectory. We also assume that the patient will keep the same diagnosis throughout the process.

For the outpatient department we assume that the patient will keep the same site for all outpatient visits. The length of the visit is deterministic per type of visit, and does not depend on the specialist involved.

Patients are seen in the pre-operative screening unit according to urgency (codes 2–4). Results of screening tests are valid for 13 weeks. If patients are delayed for a longer period, the patient needs to undergo tests once more.

Patients are scheduled in the operating theatre department according to urgency. Patients with urgency code 1 are operated on the same day. As many of these urgent admissions are operated on outside regular sessions during working hours (from 8 a.m. to 4 p.m.), the fraction of patients with code 1 that are using capacity of regular sessions needs to be defined. Then other patients are scheduled for operation, following the priority of the urgency code (codes 2–4). The duration of the operation is deterministic according to the length specified in the trajectory, and does not depend on the specialist involved.

The length of stay of patients at the ward is deterministic. For day cases the length of stay is one day. Patients are admitted on short-stay beds when the length of stay is less than or equal to five days, or to long-stay beds if the length of stay is longer. Only long-stay patients can use IC beds, as defined in the trajectory.

While the patient is in the IC unit the long-stay bed will also be kept available for the return of the patient. The period of using beds on the long-stay ward as well as on the IC unit is limited to seven days.

Simulation

The simulation model uses a week as the unit of time to follow the development of the state of the system. Results are produced over a period of a year, while the simulation can run over several years. To start with a stable system several measures were taken: waiting lists were initialised, patients with trajectories with a lead-time of over one year were generated and a warm-up period of one year was used to fill the system.

The inflow of patients was according to the description given in the 'Demand side' section earlier in the chapter. Patients were generated according to the distribution over patient group and the distribution over trajectories within patient groups. Once a patient was assigned to a trajectory, patients were further assigned to a specialist and to one of the two sites of the hospital.

A group of patients with the same combination of trajectory, specialist and site is called a patient cluster. The patient clusters were the basis for scheduling per week, according to the procedure illustrated in Figures 12.6 and 12.7. If no capacity was available in a specific week to accommodate the patient cluster, the cluster was split into two subclusters, one that is accommodated in the week asked for, and one that will be delayed to the next week.

Validation of the model was addressed in several ways. First of all, the outcomes of the model were compared to data from the hospital information system. It turned out to be possible to explain with the model 74 per cent of the outpatient output, 71 per cent of the day-case output and 80 per cent of the short-stay and long-stay output. This can be seen as a reasonable performance, as the 41 trajectories were meant to cover the most important processes, while the rest of the patients were considered too diverse in terms of routing to combine into more trajectories and were put into an 'all other patients' category. This nears the 20–80 rule of thumb, i.e. 20 per cent of all diagnoses account for 80 per cent of output. The second form of validation was to feed the results back to the general surgeons and the managers of departments involved. The third form of validation was to test the model's behaviour on manipulations in the input with predictable outcomes, for instance to increase the average length of duration of activities.

RESULTS

The model produces average results on use of resources and service levels, i.e. waiting times. We will now illustrate the results produced by the model in an evaluation of the current situation and illustrate its use for evaluating different scenarios.

Base scenario

The output of the model on use of resources can be presented in different ways. We will show these ways while showing the output on the current situation. The first example of output shown is the use of outpatient resources in Figure 12.8.

In this case the use of resources is broken down by hospital site as well as into used, non-used and overrun. Figure 12.8 shows that at the second site there is much under-use of available resources.

The second example of output is the use of resources at the emergency department, as shown in Figure 12.9. In this case the workload at the A&E department is expressed in the number of patients as the capacity available is assumed to be no limit and therefore not defined.

From Figure 12.9 one can see that the number of patients is well balanced throughout the year, but that in a few periods there seems to be a lower level of number of patients seen. The number of patients seen can be broken down into patient groups. Fractures and trauma are the largest specific groups in the general surgery patient flow at the A&E department, apart from the large group of patients that visit the A&E department for a minor problem and are discharged after this one visit, and patients allocated to the 'rest' group (other complaints).

Figure 12.10 illustrates the use of resources at the operating theatre department.

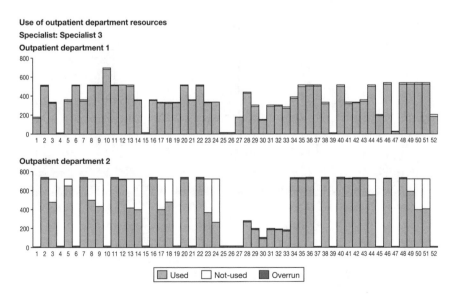

Figure 12.8 Use of outpatient resources in current setting, split into used, non-used and overrun.

Use of A&E department resources

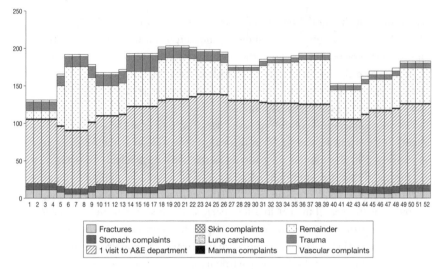

Figure 12.9 *Use of resources at the A&E department, expressed in number of patients seen and broken down into patient groups.*

Use of resources at Operating Theatre Department
Specialist: Specialist 6
Operating Theatre Department

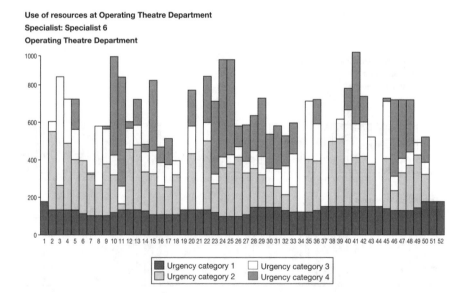

Figure 12.10 *Use of resources at the operating theatre department, broken down to urgency.*

From Figure 12.10 one can see that the use of OTD resources varies very much. The use of OTD resources is expressed in number of minutes, and is broken down into urgency categories. Urgency category 1 is always dealt with immediately. Then follow urgency category 2 (within one week) and category 3 (within 3 weeks). The category showing most variation is category 4 (when capacity is available).

Comparison of scenarios

The model was used to look at the impacts of different scenarios. The scenarios considered were:

- Scenario 1: better distribution of OPD patients and holiday and absence planning. This is a scenario that aims at improving the use of OPD resources by a better distribution of OPD patients over the two locations. Further it aims at improving the use of OTD resources by a better planning of the holidays and absence periods of general surgeons. The surgeons plan their holidays to coincide with a period of reduced capacity at the OTD. At all times, except during the first and last week of the year, four surgeons should be present.
- Scenario 2: trainee involvement. This is a scenario in which trainees are also used to treat patients in outpatient clinics and operating theatres. This scenario has the same assumptions as scenario 1. Instead of the surgeons, trainees treat less complicated patients in the OPD and OTD. Trainees take twice as long as surgeons take to treat such patients. To allow for this, OTD capacity is increased by 12.5 per cent and the OPD capacity by 4 per cent.

The results of these scenarios are summarised in Table 12.4.

For each of the scenarios, average results and standard deviations are shown for a number of critical performance indicators of resource use in the different departments. We will illustrate the results by discussing some of the outcomes of the scenarios.

Scenario 1 shows the impact of a better holiday planning of specialists, and a better distribution of patients over locations. The results illustrate that more outpatient capacity becomes available when patients are better distributed over the two locations. The pressure on location 1 becomes less and there is, relatively, less capacity loss in location 2. Compared with the base scenario this implies that more patients can be seen and waiting lists will be reduced. The operating theatre department also shows a better performance (more capacity used and less capacity overrun) due to a better planning of the holidays of specialists.

Scenario 2 illustrates the impact of trainee involvement in OPD clinic sessions. The results are of a comparable level with scenario 1, implying that involvement of trainees in OPD and OTD will not decrease the level of output of the specialty, provided some extra capacity is allocated as indicated before. The day case (DC)

Table 12.4 Comparison of the results of the scenarios with the base scenario

Resource	Indicator	Unit	2002 base scenario		Scenario 1 holiday planning		Scenario 2 trainee involvement	
			av.	std	av.	std	av.	std
OPD 1	capacity used	min. p.w.	2200	539	2017	484	2027	423
	capacity not used	min. p.w.	109	137	676	304	627	307
	capacity overrun	min. p.w.	24	38	0	0	0	0
OPD 2	capacity used	min. p.w.	518	250	987	232	999	218
	capacity not used	min. p.w.	89	91	121	82	289	143
	capacity overrun	min. p.w.	10	16	3	11	0	0
DC	average bed use	bed days p.w.	21.5	7	21.2	6.5	20.9	2.3
	logistic problem	bed days p.w.	2.9	5	2.2	4.2	7.1	4.9
Ward	average bed use	bed days p.w.	282	42	286	49	288	48
	logistic problem	bed days p.w.	1	7	1	6	1	6
OTD	capacity used	min. p.w.	2741	768	2930	608	2954	615
	capacity not used	min. p.w.	3	19	28	119	4	25
	capacity overrun	min. p.w.	580	187	522	248	547	229

ward requires some extra attention as logistic problems have increased because patients have to borrow beds from other specialties.

REFLECTION AND FURTHER DEVELOPMENT

We can conclude by drawing some preliminary conclusions and formulating some recommendations for follow-up research.

First of all we can conclude that the model does provide the insight looked for, i.e. the impact of resource use in the current situation and the impact of changes in available resources in units or in the design of processes. The use of patient groups is a big improvement as it improves insight into the functioning of the system and it allows a more precise definition of where changes are required.

Another interesting observation is that the new version of the model is simpler and more transparent compared with our previous models, which did not use a process description but instead were based on transitions between states (A&E department, outpatient department, ward, operating theatres). The patient flows between these departments were described in terms of the percentage of patients that continue from the A&E department or the OPD to the ward or operating theatres. Although these models (van der Lei, 1998; van Leeuwaarden and van der Linden, 2001) used less data, more calculations were required for producing results. The current model uses much more detailed information, as all the processes of patient groups, i.e. 41 patient trajectories, need to be described. However, having once described these processes, the calculations to be made for analysing resource use and patient throughput become quite simple. Apparently an investment in efforts to describe the processes of patient groups pays off in less complicated models.

Recommendations for development of the model and its use are to improve the quality of the data and to consider also processes of patients involving different specialties. Up to now only monodisciplinary processes have been considered. Processes of patients increasingly require more than one specialty. For instance, patients with vascular complaints can benefit from collaboration between specialists from internal medicine, cardiology, neurology and vascular surgery. There are already multispecialty treatment centres for specific patient groups (for instance patients with vascular problems) in which specialists from different specialties collaborate together in patient care processes. It would be interesting to develop the model further, and to include also these multidisciplinary processes.

QUESTIONS AND EXERCISES

1   Discuss the demarcation of the planning problem in Figure 12.2. What extensions would be possible? Present your proposal in a graphical way.
    Discuss the pros and cons of the demarcation in Figure 12.2 and your proposal for an extended model.

2   What is the difference between the representations of the process model of laparotomy or laparoscopy in Figures 12.4 and 12.5? When would you prefer to use the one above the other?

3   Discuss the impacts of the assumptions made (see Table 12.3) on the use of
     resources in the outpatient department and the operating theatre department. Do
     you think that the results with the current model overestimate or underestimate
     the performance in reality?
4   The results in Table 12.4 focus on the use of resources. What type of results are
     lacking? Can you mention a few items that it would be interesting to see
     supported by results from the model?

REFERENCES AND FURTHER READING

Beech R., R.L. Brough and B.A. Fitzsimons. The development of a decision support
     system for planning services within hospitals. *Journal of the Operational Research
     Society*, 41(11), 1990, 955–1006.

Bowen T. and P. Forte. Activity and capacity planning in an acute hospital. In S. Cropper
     and P. Forte (eds) *Enhancing Health Services Management. The role of decision
     support systems*. Open University Press, Buckingham-Philadelphia, 1997, 86–102.

Leeuwaarden J. van and S. van der Linden. Allocating specialist's capacity within a
     specialty. *Student report 01–04, Mathematics for Industry*, Stan Ackermans
     Institute, University of Technology, Eindhoven, 2001.

Lei H.M. van der. Business Planning voor Algemene Chirurgie in het Ziekenhuiscentrum
     Apeldoorn. *Mathematics for Industry*, Stan Ackermans Institute, Eindhoven
     University of Technology, 1998.

Roth A. and R. Van Dierdonck. Hospital resource planning: concepts, feasibility, and
     framework. *Production and Operations Management,* 4(1), 1995, 2–29.

Chapter 13

Scheduling appointments in outpatient clinics

Dave Worthington, Richard Goulsbra and James Rankin

SUMMARY

The appointment problem is well known and there have been numerous successful studies using a variety of modelling approaches over the last 50 years. The case study describes a study of ophthalmology clinics undertaken for a large UK hospital in the north of England.

Five different modelling approaches are described, of which three were used. Their relative strengths and weaknesses are discussed, and the general role of models in the context of improving health care delivery is highlighted.

KEY TERMS

- Appointment systems for outpatients clinics
- Waiting time in clinics
- Approaches for clinic waiting times: bottleneck analysis, simulation and queue modelling

INTRODUCTION

The problem of outpatient and general practice appointment systems will be well known to many students of health care management and health care managers, from accounts in the literature, patient feedback or personal experience. The fundamental problem is the case where patients are given appointments to see one or more doctors. The patients may arrive on time, early, late, or not at all and are seen by a doctor in order of arrival (or in order of appointment). The two primary performance measures are patients' waiting time and doctors' idle time.

Problems were recognised in health care appointment systems as early as a century ago. In 1908 when opening a new outpatient department at Cardiff Infirmary, Osler said:

> As one who has had a long hospital experience, may I mention one essential virtue for the members of the outpatients department staff to cultivate – namely, punctuality. It is not, of course, always possible, but it is remarkable how greatly it facilitates the work of an institution when men put in an appearance at the stroke of the hour. (Jackson *et al.*, 1964)

This problem was first modelled by Bailey (1952), and has subsequently been modelled by a variety of methods in a wide range of settings; see for example Jackson *et al.* (1964), Vissers and Wijngaard (1979), and Brahimi and Worthington (1991a). More complicated clinics in which patients receive more than one 'service' have also been considered by, for example, Rising *et al.* (1973), Cox *et al.* (1985) and Taylor and Keown (1980).

BOX 13.1   THE CASE STUDY SETTING

The Ophthalmology Department at the Royal Lancaster Infirmary, a major hospital in the north of England, operates five or six clinics per week, involving two consultants, three junior doctors and a senior house officer (SHO). The numbers of patients booked in for the clinics varied greatly, with some sessions finishing early, resulting in a considerable amount of 'lost' clinician time, and others finishing late, leading to over-running clinics and patients' appointments being cancelled at the last minute. As can be expected, waiting times at the clinics also varied greatly. It was not uncommon for patients to be waiting for well over an hour for a consultation that could take as little as five minutes.

The purpose of the study was to investigate the potential for re-organising the clinics so that more patients could be seen than at present. Although reducing patient waiting times at the clinics was not an explicit aim of the project, it was envisaged that an improved clinic schedule would also help reduce waiting times, or at least distribute them more equitably.

A further aim of the study (not described here) was to investigate the size of the waiting list, and to ascertain whether or not this would continue to grow, as was occurring at the time.

For further details of this part of the study, see Goulsbra and Rankin (2003).

A common finding is that, in practice, appointment systems are often designed massively in favour of reducing doctors' idle time at the expense of increasing patients' waiting time. However, as noted by Brahimi and Worthington:

> the impact of these studies has not been as widespread as might be hoped and many clinics today seem to be as badly run as those studied in the past. . . . hospitals tend to require their own individual studies rather than being able to adopt any general solution or guidance.
>
> (Brahimi and Worthington, 1991a)

Although this situation is disappointing it is not difficult to understand. Anyone involved in running a particular clinic knows very well that their doctors have their own ways of doing things and that their patients are highly variable in their needs, so that it is difficult to believe that 'solutions' devised elsewhere will fit the local circumstances. Indeed, even if the general nature of the solutions fits, they will almost certainly need tailoring to the local circumstances.

The next section provides more insight into the general nature of the planning problem by positioning it in the planning framework discussed in chapter 6, and by a review of the extensive literature published on this topic. The following section elaborates the specific case study planning problem and discusses data availability. Different modelling approaches to the problem and the results obtained are then presented. Finally, reflections on the contribution of operations management approaches to problems of this type are offered.

PLANNING PROBLEM

Provision of an outpatient clinic involves allocating doctors, nurses and other staff, plus clinic rooms, equipment and patient waiting areas for a specified period of time. It also requires that appropriate patients arrive at the clinic, preferably in such a way that the above clinic resources do not lie idle waiting for patients to arrive, but on the other hand so that the patients do not suffer unnecessarily long waiting times before seeing the doctor. An appointment system is the means used to control the arrival of patients.

This case study was concerned with investigating whether or not there was scope for improving the appointment system in use, and if so, suggesting and justifying improvements. While the case study problem is typical of outpatient problems faced in many hospitals, this account is unusual as it is written to enable the reader to see the contributions that can be made by a number of different operations management approaches.

The planning problem is familiar, and has been investigated much before. In the next subsection the planning issue is positioned in the planning framework for hospital production control presented in chapter 6, and a review of the literature is given in the following subsection.

Position in planning framework

As shown in Figure 13.1, the case study addresses the three lower levels of the planning framework, and focuses on the efficient scheduling of outpatients, trying to balance service for patients (waiting times) with a good use of clinic resources. It combines the perspective of units (outpatient facilities) with the perspective of chains (at the aggregate level of a specialty), although the emphasis is on efficient use of unit resources.

Although the case study spans a number of levels in the health operations management framework introduced in chapter 6, the emphasis lies on the level of 'resources planning and control' and on 'patient group planning and control'. An outpatient appointment system is used to provide resources to individual patients on a daily basis in such a way (it is hoped) that hospital resources are used efficiently (when viewed on a monthly or annual basis) while maintaining a good quality of service to the patient group (again when viewed on a monthly or annual basis). So, the choice of a suitable appointment system has to deal with the balance between service and resource use, which is a decision made at the level 'resources planning and control', and more detailed at the level of different patient groups at the level 'patient group planning and control'. However, the appointment system chosen does also provide guidelines for planning individual patients at the level 'patient planning and control'. In this particular case study it was also hoped that the exercise would help ascertain the capacity of the clinics to cope with future demands over the next couple of years. So in this case, there is also a link with the higher levels ('patient volume planning and control' and 'strategic planning') of the framework.

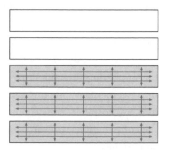

Network logistics application
Emphasis on unit logistics
Level: resources planning and control,
patient group planning and control,
and patient planning and control

Figure 13.1 *Scheduling appointments in outpatient clinics, and position in planning framework.*

Literature review

Well-documented studies of operations management of clinics in both hospitals and general practices have appeared for at least the last 50 years. In general terms the approaches can be labelled as bottleneck analysis, queueing models and simulation. A brief review of these approaches is presented here.

Early studies

One of the earliest applications of an OM approach to health care appointment systems was by Bailey (1952), who investigated the queueing process occurring in hospital outpatient departments. He came to the conclusion that 'a substantial amount of the patients' waiting time may be eliminated without appreciably affecting the consultant', a similar finding to the majority of studies that followed.

Simple analysis of the clinic bottleneck (i.e. the consultation with the doctor) revealed a number of characteristics of the clinics that also recurred in many later studies, including:

- disproportionate patient waiting time compared to actual consultation time;
- an over-riding consideration to the requirement that the consultant is kept fully occupied;
- a large amount of room (which is often in short supply) just for those waiting.

Bailey modelled the system with an input process (the appointment system), a queue discipline and a service mechanism (the consultation times). It was accepted that consultation times naturally vary, and hence that any purely verbal arguments based on average times would be unsound. Fifty separate series of 25 consultation times were sampled by hand (a pre-computer simulation) and were used to investigate what would happen for a clinic with equally spaced appointments, with spaces equal to the average consultation times. The number of patients present when the consultant arrives were varied and the relationship between patients' and the consultant's waiting times were determined.

The report also found that average waiting times increased during the clinic and it postulated as to whether a progressively longer appointment interval could be employed during the course of a clinic.

Later studies (1960s and 1970s)

The pioneering study by Bailey led to many further applications of OR in health care appointment systems. The problems he identified persisted, and technological advances resulting in increasing computing power made a wider range of approaches available to those investigating similar problems. This section outlines four studies that occurred over the following two decades.

A colloquium sponsored by the Operational Research Society and supported by the Ministry of Health was held in 1962; the subject was 'Appointment Systems in Hospitals and General Practice' (Jackson *et al.*, 1964), and three papers were given.

The first was by Jackson, an OR practitioner, who implemented an appointment system at his local general practice that reduced average waiting times from 90 minutes to 15 minutes. Queueing theory was used, and the effect of different intervals on patient and doctor waiting times was assessed. It was concluded that a traffic intensity (i.e. ratio of arriving work to service capacity) between 0.85 and 0.95 results in acceptable waits for both patients and doctors. Practical arrangements were also mentioned, such as setting appointments at five-minute intervals and booking slightly more patients at the start of sessions to reduce doctor waiting time.

The second paper was by Welch, a general practitioner, who adopted a bottleneck analysis style of approach. He claimed to show that an appointment system could be used to save the time of the patient without wasting the time of the consultant, and stated that punctuality and consulting time are the two main factors that affect the design of an appointment system. Data collected of the punctuality of 6,253 patients at 34 different clinics showed that patients were, on average, early for all but six of these clinics. Consultants, on the other hand, tended to be late, with only one clinic out of the 16 analysed having consultants arriving early; the sample of 101 consultants showed an average tardiness of 15 minutes. Nurses were always punctual, though, and the blame for the delay was clearly at the door of the consultants. He stated that the existing situation of patients being called at a rate in excess of that in which they could be seen was a great cause of excessive waiting, and needed to be changed, and came to the same recommendations as Bailey.

The third paper was by Fry, and was a report about the effects of – and opinions on – a successful appointment system for a general practice that also had a number of patients without appointments (walk-ins). While the paper does not document the analyses undertaken to the appointment system, it was reported to have resulted in virtually negligible waits. Gaps were left in the appointment system for the 25 per cent of patients who were walk-ins, and 97 per cent of 375 patients questioned were receptive of the new system. Other benefits of the system included a more even distribution of doctor workload, ability to plan better for meetings and holidays, much less rush and stress and an ability to give longer appointments to those who required more time.

Fetter and Thompson (1965) developed approaches to problems in the design and utilisation of hospital facilities, and aimed to provide hospitals with tools to help predict the operational consequences of alternative designs or policies. They modelled outpatient clinics, generating a daily appointment schedule for each doctor based on a predetermined traffic intensity (which they referred to as 'load factor'), appointment interval and total working hours. Three doctors were simulated for 50 days each. An input distribution determined whether patients were early, on time or late; walk-in patients arrived at random intervals, and the doctors' time was interrupted by emergency calls and scheduled breaks. One of the findings was that if the load factor was increased from 60 per cent to 90 per cent, then over the 50-day period 160 doctor hours would be saved (decrease in idle time), but at the expense of total patient waiting times increasing by 1,600 hours. Hence, it was argued, doctors' time would need to be considered as ten times more important than the patients' time for such an increase in load factor to be a rational decision.

Rising *et al.* (1973) also used a simulation approach to schedule more appointment patients during periods of low walk-in demand in order to smooth the overall daily arrivals at a university health service outpatient clinic. The system was conceptualised as a queueing system, and in this case patients could be routed from one service to another (e.g. consultation to X-ray to consultation). In a similar fashion to some of the earlier studies it was found that a queue at the beginning of a session results in the physicians' idle time being relatively insensitive to the subsequent arrangement of appointment periods.

They also noted three further system characteristics that (ideally) should be incorporated into further modelling exercises to avoid sub-optimal recommendations:

- the tendency for some of the walk-in patients to depart if they noticed a busy waiting room;
- the tendency of physicians to decrease their service times if the waiting room became crowded;
- the impact of the usage levels of other services (such as X-ray).

However such model refinement would have increased the model complexity significantly and required much more detailed data to be collected.

The trend of using simulation continued with a study by Vissers and Wijngaard (1979), who aimed to produce a general method for determining a suitable appointment system for outpatient clinics in hospitals. Their investigations concluded that only five variables were required for the simulation, reduced from 11 in the initial model. System earliness was used to encompass all the possible ways that allow patients to arrive, on average, earlier than their expected time of treatment, namely patients' earliness, block-booking, initial block-booking, doctors' lateness, and the frequency of appointment times relative to average consultation times. It was also determined that the effect of no-shows and walk-ins could be found by their influence on the mean consultation time and its coefficient of variation. The only five variables that the simulation needed to consider were:

- mean consultation time
- coefficient of variation of consultation time
- mean system earliness

- standard deviation of patients' punctuality
- number of appointments.

While this study did not incorporate the additional factors noted by Rising *et al.*, these parameters can be specified for any 'simple' clinic in order to find a suitable appointment system. Results can be expressed simply on a graph comparing the trade-off in patient waiting time and doctor idle time that occurs, and the most appropriate option can be selected.

More recent applications (1990s)

This section discusses two (from many) studies that have taken place over the last 15 years that demonstrate two different approaches.

Brahimi and Worthington (1991b) applied a queueing model to outpatient clinics at a local hospital. The problem was formulated as a time-dependent queueing system and involved approximating continuous service times by discrete ones. The model used the mean and standard deviation of consultation times plus the non-attendance rate of patients to produce graphs showing numbers of patients waiting and anticipated waiting times of patients throughout the clinic (in terms of average values and those that would occur on 95 per cent of occasions). The chance that the doctor became idle was also estimated.

The report showed that significant improvements in patients' waiting times were possible with very little increase in the risk of doctors having no patients to see. However the recommended appointment system clearly depended on the clinic characteristics, and hence it recommended that clinic behaviour should continue to be monitored and that further changes to the appointment system might be required if, for example, there was a change in doctor or in the mix of patients attending.

The report included a discussion of the relatively small impact such hospital studies appear to have had, often with individual clinics requiring their own studies to tailor the established general results to local circumstances.

A soft-systems-based approach incorporating some simulation modelling to improve the efficiency of a hospital outpatient clinic was taken by Lehaney *et al.* (1994). Flowcharts and a conceptual model were constructed that helped the participants – a group of medical staff from the hospital – to gain a greater under-standing of their own organisation. A model was required that would be simple enough for the medical staff to use themselves, and a computer simulation model was built representing the whole clinic environment (including the reception desk, waiting areas, two doctors and a consultant).

A need to front-load the appointment system to reduce the risk of doctor idle time due to non-attendees was realised. The proposed schedule was accepted and implemented, but the easily understood model was seen as key to convincing the group of its value. The insights the modelling process provided also led the hospital into tackling non-attendees by following up on missed appointments.

In summary

A number of studies have been considered in which the problems, in the main, were concerned with excessive patient waiting time. Problems that persisted 50 and even 100 years ago still seem to do so today.

Most of the investigations have come to the same sorts of conclusions – that patient waiting times can be reduced quite considerably while only slightly increasing the expected amount of time the clinicians will spend idle. In addition, many of the studies have had their results and recommendations implemented successfully.

A variety of approaches have been used, modelling processes in different ways:

- Bottleneck analysis typically uses available data to compare service capacity and demand at the bottleneck and can often identify clear mismatches and apparent scope for improvements.
- Steady-state queueing models can be used to give valuable insights into the general effects of certain changes to appointment systems, consultation durations and numbers of doctors – however, steady-state models have only limited applicability because clinic behaviour is typically very time-dependent.
- Time-dependent queueing models can be very effective for 'simple' clinics where patients only need to see the doctor once and either need to see a specific doctor or can see the first available doctor.
- Simulation models can in theory be used to model time-dependent behaviour for 'simple' and 'non-simple' clinics (for example, where patients also need to interact with other resources, or where patients' conditions dictate the doctors they are eligible to see). In practice such studies are limited by time and by data availability, and typically are used to improve understanding of the dynamics of clinic behaviour rather than to make precise predictions of the effects of changes.

While these models incorporate different levels of detail and focus on different aspects of clinic behaviour, they have all been used to provide better understanding of the systems involved and evidence to support changes that are likely to improve system performance.

ELABORATION

Understanding the department

The project initially required us to gain an understanding of the department and the way that review clinics operate. This was achieved through observing the department and the way the clinics worked, and discussions with nurses and clerical staff, leading to the construction of process maps showing the journey of a patient through the system – see for example Figure 13.2.

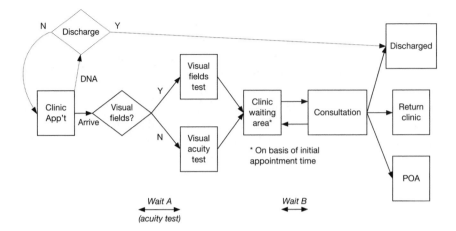

Figure 13.2 *A patient's journey at a clinic (DNA = did not attend; POA = pre-operative assessment).*

The black boxes and arrows indicate possible routes of patients through an ophthalmology clinic, from being given an appointment to final discharge, booking at another clinic or transfer to pre-operative assessment (POA). The grey arrows indicate the 'logical route' of patients who do not attend (DNA).

Observation and consultation with staff involved indicated that the fields and acuity tests did not cause patients any significant waits. The major waits were in the clinic waiting area, caused by a mismatch between the clinic appointment times and the capacity of the clinics to provide consultations with the doctors. Data collection therefore concentrated on this area of activity.

Primary data

Over a seven-week period 22 general review clinics were observed. At these clinics 657 patients were booked in for clinic appointments, 177 to see the consultant and the remaining 476 on the registrar's list to be seen by one of the junior doctors or the SHO. A total of 578 of these patients attended the clinics and 537 appointment durations were successfully recorded. Initially this data was used to establish the average length of appointment durations for consultants, junior doctors and the SHO, and was subsequently used to aid the model-building process.

Secondary data

Clinic sheets for the sessions observed provided us with information relating to the mix of new and follow-up patients on the three lists and the distribution of review periods for the follow-up patients. The number of patients booked on each list at each clinic was recorded as a basis for determining how many patients could (or should) be seen within the time available.

Comments relating to the previous behaviour of patients allowed us to distinguish between those patients who had a clean attendance record, those who informed the department that they were unable to attend their appointment (UTA/CNA), and those who, without prior notice, did not attend their appointment (DNA).

Past clinic sheets were used in a similar way, where a 12-month sample provided further information about the number of patients booked on each list. Further, this allowed us to gain an indication of the annual capacity of the review clinics (suggesting that the department has a capacity of 7,200 appointments). A sample of two of these 12 months contained follow-up patient review periods.

MODELLING APPROACHES

The choice of modelling approaches in this case study was strongly influenced by the practical context in which the project occurred, namely that of NHS modernisation.

NHS modernisation

In April 2001 the NHS Modernisation Agency was set up to help NHS staff and their partner organisations to improve services for patients. In 2002 the Modernisation Agency published a series of six Improvement Leaders' Guides to encourage and facilitate this process. The guides cover a series of topics, establishing a framework for 'improvement leaders' to follow. The first three guides look at how the departments can identify areas for change, in which the topics covered are: Process mapping, analysis and redesign (NHS Modernisation Agency, 2002a); Measurement for improvement (NHS Modernisation Agency, 2002b); Matching capacity and demand (NHS Modernisation Agency, 2002c). The last three guides focus more on implementation issues and cover: Involving patients and carers (NHS Modernisation Agency, 2002d); Managing the human dimensions of change (NHS Modernisation Agency, 2002e); and Sustainability and spread (NHS Modernisation Agency, 2002f).

Guides 1, 2 and 3 are of particular relevance to this case study and are summarised briefly in Tables 13.1, 13.2 and 13.3.

Modelling approaches

As can be observed from the previous section the improvement process envisaged in the Improvement Leaders' Guides is essentially one of 'wise' experimentation.

Table 13.1 *Guide One: Process Mapping, Analysis and Redesign*

Stage 1: Defining Project Aims

Stage 2: Defining Measurements for Improvement
It is recommended that these are agreed early in the project, to help focus the work, steer any data collection, and eventually monitor the success or otherwise of any changes. Guide 2, see Table 13.2, is also provided to give further more detailed help on this stage.

Stage 3: Construction of Process Maps
It is recommended that this involves all members of staff, with the aim being to gain a greater understanding of the problems within the system from the perspective of the patient. It is the use of these maps that identifies potential areas for improvement. Guide 3, see Table 13.3, is also provided to give further more detailed help on this stage.

Stage 4: Analysing the Journey
Stage 4 is to involve the investigation of all of the changes that are likely to make an 'improvement in line with the set aims' of the project, described as the process of analysing a patient's journey. The idea of analysing a patient's journey works on the basis of asking questions about why problems keep recurring, from which areas for improvement can be identified. It also encourages the team to look for examples of studies conducted in other health care services. Guide 3, see Table 13.3, is also provided to give further more detailed help on this stage, and emphasises how to focus on the 'bottlenecks' within the system.

Stage 5: Measuring Changes, Identifying Improvements
The testing stage sets up a system of experimentation. Make one change at a time, measure the effect that change has but keep in mind the knock-on effects that may cancel any advantages that the change has. This stage should be repeated for all the identified changes but is limited by the fact that combinations of changes are not tested. It makes the point that two or more simultaneous changes may have a non-additive effect on the system as a whole but the guide makes no suggestion that this should be tested, possibly as a means of keeping things simple.

Stage 6: Redesigning the Journey
The testing procedure leads into Stage 6 whereby positive changes are implemented and the way the system works is altered, termed as 'redesigning the patients' journey'. Once again emphasis is placed on carrying out this process with due consideration given to the second series guide relating to 'managing the complexities of change' and is a further example of how the two series should be used in parallel.

Stage 7: Congratulating, Monitoring, Reporting and Repeating
The final stage of the mapping process recommends that the team be congratulated on its achievements and that the improvements be sustained, commenting that the cycle should continue and that the findings of the study should be reported to support the practices of other improvement teams. Reporting establishes a collaborative process across the NHS with the sharing of ideas and expertise to achieve improvement.

Table 13.2 *Guide Two: Measurement for Improvement*

Stage 1: Identifying the Measurements

Stage 2: Reporting Progress

Table 13.3 *Guide Three: Matching Capacity and Demand*

Stage 1: Identifying Bottlenecks
Identifying bottlenecks within the system is imperative if the process is to be taken forward. It is important that measurements of demand, capacity, backlog and activity are taken at the bottleneck because it becomes a useful tool in convincing participants within the system that change is required.

Stage 2: Dealing with the Bottleneck
Once the bottleneck has been identified the team can begin to make changes to improve the situation. The use of measurements is encouraged to identify patterns in behaviour at bottlenecks such as seasonal variations and patterns of DNAs, and it is emphasised that the bottleneck will control patient flow throughout the system. Methods for alleviating the problems are suggested such as ensuring there is no idle time at the bottleneck. In addition it is suggested that if the bottleneck is the availability of an individual's 'expert skill' then the team should look for ways to lessen the burden on that individual, usually achieved through the sharing of skills.

Stage 3: Other Considerations
The way in which data can be collected and analysed to help convince the health care professionals and managers to change their practices is emphasised.

The underlying philosophy is essentially that research should be undertaken (i.e. stages 1 to 4 in Guide One) to improve understanding of the problem situation, and where appropriate the evidence from this research should be used to identify potentially beneficial changes in practices. However, whatever the nature of the research process, it cannot guarantee real and permanent improvements without some degree of practical testing. Hence stages 5 to 7 are also essential to test out these potentially good ideas in practice and to support any implementation.

In this context modelling can be seen to have a whole spectrum of possible roles. At one end of the spectrum minimal modelling might be undertaken simply to highlight problems and to interest people in the possibility of changing their processes. At the other end of the spectrum a much more thorough (and probably much more time-consuming) modelling exercise might highlight problems, generate possible 'solutions' and go on to produce compelling evidence that particular 'solutions' would indeed lead to significant improvements in performance. While this latter form of research is one towards which researchers often aspire, in reality projects are always constrained in terms of time and resources and can hope only to convince health care professionals and/or managers that it is worth giving something a try.

Given this context, three of the modelling approaches described in the 'Planning problem' section are applied to this case study, and two others are discussed briefly. The approaches applied are:

- simple bottleneck analysis
- 'partial' simulation
- time-dependent queue modelling.

The approaches not applied in this case are:

- steady-state queue modelling
- 'full' simulation.

Bottleneck analysis

This approach involves identifying the bottleneck(s) in the process, in this case the consultation with the doctor, and then investigating ways in which its processing capacity can be increased.

In general terms processing capacity of the doctors can be increased if either utilisation of doctors' time is increased or consultation times are reduced. In this case study the interest was in the former rather than the latter. Discussion with those involved, observation of clinics and analysis of available data was therefore undertaken to ascertain what scope there was for increasing utilisation. This approach eventually focused on clinic durations, patient attendance (and non-attendance) and appointment systems.

'Partial' simulation

Given the stochastic nature of the problem, simulation can be used to improve understanding of system behaviour. The term 'partial' simulation is used here to contrast with the more ambitious use of simulation that typically endeavours to model the 'full' system incorporating all the important stochastic aspects of the problem. A 'partial' simulation focuses on a particular aspect of the problem, knowingly ignoring other stochastic aspects, but nevertheless aiming to improve understanding.

In this case study partial simulation was used to address two different issues, to discover the practical clinic capacity and to test a proposed revised appointment system.

One method to calculate clinic capacity is simply to divide planned clinic duration by the average consultation time of patients. However, the random variation in actual consultation durations would mean that approximately 50 per cent of clinics would overrun. If the number of patients (and hence throughput) is reduced, the chance of overrunning will also be reduced. In order to decide on an acceptable compromise between reduced throughput and reduced risk of overrunning, the effects of the stochastic variation in consultation times need to be modelled. This is easy to do in a spreadsheet. So 1,000 runs of clinics with different numbers of patients were simulated, and the proportions of runs in which the clinics overran were calculated.

A BETTER APPOINTMENT SYSTEM?

In the light of the previous analysis new appointment systems were proposed that incorporated:

- a realistic number of patients;
- slight overbooking early in the clinic to maintain a small surplus of patients in the clinic waiting area to ensure that clinicians were rarely idle;
- patient groups with higher chances of non-attendance being given later appointments.

An indication of the likely benefits of this new appointment system was then obtained by hand simulations of five typical sets of patients, in which their consultation times were sampled randomly and the patients were put through the previous and proposed appointment systems. The performance of the two appointment systems for the matched sets of patients could then be compared.

Time-dependent queue modelling

The main disadvantage of the hand simulations of three clinics is that the relatively small number of randomly sampled patients may make the results unrepresentative, and that the number of simulations required to ensure that the results were representative would be impractically large. In contrast a time-dependent queue modelling approach can be used to ensure that statistically representative results are obtained very efficiently, although it is not able to incorporate the fine detail of the differential DNA rates that the proposed appointment system would imply.

This modelling approach was implemented using CLINIQUE software, which allows the user to investigate the impact of different appointment schedules on numbers of patients waiting at different times in the clinic and their associated waiting times. CLINIQUE is purpose-built software for modelling appointment systems and is based on the queue modelling research of Brahimi and Worthington (1991a) and Wall and Worthington (1999). It incorporates statistical information on patients' consultation times and overall DNA rates to predict system performance measures for appointment systems specified by the user.

Steady-state queue modelling

As recognised in the 'Planning problem' section, while steady-state queueing models can be used to give valuable insights into the general effects of certain changes to appointment systems, consultation durations and numbers of doctors, they only have very limited applicability because clinic behaviour is typically very time-dependent. Given the easy availability of the above time-dependent queueing model, nothing further would be learnt from applying steady-state models.

'Full' simulation modelling

As noted earlier, simulation models can in theory be used to model time-dependent behaviour of 'simple' and 'non-simple' clinics. General-purpose simulation software (for example, Witness) has this capability, and specialist clinic simulation software also exists (for example, CLINSIM – see Paul, 1995). However, in practice such studies are limited by time and by data availability, and this was very much the case in the present case study. Hence the use of simulation was restricted to the 'partial' simulations described above.

RESULTS

Bottleneck analysis results

Analysis of available data relating to the clinic capacity very quickly demonstrated scope for increasing clinic throughputs, initially simply in terms of clinic durations and then in terms of clinic throughputs and patient non-attendance.

Clinic durations

Of 22 clinics on which data was collected, only four began on time – of which three were early – but half started at least 15 minutes late. The average tardiness was 13 minutes and the worst clinic began 30 minutes late.

Departmental guidelines stated that the review clinics should last between 3 and $3\frac{1}{2}$ hours. However on only four of the 17 occasions (24 per cent) when a consultant was present did the clinic time exceed the recommended minimum duration of 3 hours. Similarly, in total 45 other doctors were present at the observed clinics but on only 16 occasions (36 per cent) did they work for over 3 hours.

Clinic throughputs

As doctors did not leave the clinic until they had seen all their patients who attended, the short clinic durations noted above essentially reflect the numbers of patients booked into clinics and patient attendance rates. The clinic guidelines upon which the current appointments are based are shown in the top third of Table 13.4. For the consultant's list various combinations of new and review patients are suggested. For the registrar's list only one combination of junior doctor and SHO patients is suggested.

Table 13.4 *Departmental guidelines and implications for clinic durations*

Consultant's list		Registrar's list	
New patients	Review patients	Junior doctor's patients	SHO's patients
Guideline appointments			
8	0	15	7
6	4		
4	8		
2	12		
0	16		
Average consultation duration (minutes)			
14.5	13.2	12.2	13.5
Expected clinic durations (minutes)			
115.7	182.6	94.5	
139.6			
163.6			
187.6			
211.5			
Expected clinic durations (with DNAs) (minutes)			
101.8	160.6	83.2	
122.9			
144.0			
165.1			
186.1			

Data collected on consultation times of patients seen at the 22 clinics are summarised next in Table 13.4. It can be seen that although the guidelines imply a marked difference between consultation times of new versus review patients, and of junior doctor versus SHO patients, these differences are not supported by the data. In particular the expected durations of clinics based on the guidelines are considerably shorter than the planned minimum clinic duration of 180 minutes for consultant clinics that have 4 or more new patients, and for the SHO's list at the registrar's clinic. When allowance is also made for the observed non-attendance (DNA) rate of 12 per cent, only consultant clinics with 16 review patients are expected to last the minimum of 180 minutes.

Patient attendance/non-attendance

The number of patients not turning up to their booked appointments is wasting approximately 12 per cent of available clinic time. Hence there was interest in the extent to which non-attendance could be predicted, and so allowed for by overbooking the clinic with extra patients.

Analysis of the data collected on the 22 clinics revealed that while it was not possible to predict whether or not any individual patient would attend, their chance of attending was dependent on their behaviour at their last appointment. These findings are summarised in Table 13.5.

Table 13.5 Non-attendance rates by previous behaviour

Behaviour at last appointment	Attended	Failed to attend	Total	Non-attendance rate (%)
New	68	8	76	10.5
Review	431	41	472	8.7
UTA/CNA	63	17	80	21.3
DNA	16	13	29	44.8
Overall	578	79	657	12.0

Note: UTA/CNA indicates 'unable to attend'/'could not attend', but that the patient contacted the hospital; DNA indicates 'did not attend' with no contact made with the hospital

If for example the percentages in the final column were used to predict the number of attendees at the 22 observed registrar's clinics as a basis for over-booking, on 20 out of 22 occasions (91 per cent) it would predict actual attendance to within +/− 2 patients, as shown in Table 13.6.

Table 13.6 *Accuracy of overbooking rule for registrar's list at observed clinics*

Predictive accuracy	Frequency
Correct	4
±1 patient	8
±2 patients	8
±3 patients	2

'Partial' simulation results

The previous bottleneck analysis clearly indicates scope for dealing with larger patient numbers on average than suggested by the departmental guidelines. However, this simple (average-based) analysis has not made any allowance for the stochastic variation in consultation durations. 'Partial' simulations were therefore used to investigate further the question of how many patients per clinic could be seen, taking into account the practical implications of the stochastic variations.

How many patients per clinic?

The combined data from the observed clinics was used to establish a distribution of appointment durations, representative of the consultants' contact with patients during the clinics. The distribution was then used to simulate the total consultation times of different numbers of patients – 1,000 runs for each – in order to recommend how many patients a consultant could see within a clinic. Similar exercises were also carried out for junior doctors and for SHOs. Experimentation with different numbers of patients suggested that 12 patients (new or review) would be appropriate for consultant clinics, with the predicted range of clinic durations shown in Table 13.7. Note that as clinics were planned to give the doctor a

Table 13.7 *Simulation summary statistics for 12 patient consultant clinics*

Time	Clinics completed by time (%)
2h 45	51.5
3h 00	73.6
3h 15	87.3
3h 30	96.0
2h 45–3h 15	35.8

15-minute mid-session break, a simulated duration of 3 hours 15 minutes would mean a clinic duration of 3 hours and 30 minutes.

A better appointment system?

As a result of the analyses so far, a revised appointment system was devised that it was hoped would lead to an increase in clinic throughput while not increasing (and preferably decreasing) patient waits. The revised system varied by day of the week to reflect the different combinations of doctors scheduled, and is summarised in Table 13.8.

These proposed schedules differed from the existing ones in terms of numbers of patients (generally more), and the appointments were spread more evenly between 9:00 and 11:30 for morning clinics and 13:30 and 16:00 for afternoon clinics.

These proposals were then tested using a 'partial' simulation of an example clinic (the Monday morning registrar and SHO's clinic) run under the proposed and existing systems. Because of the relatively complex nature of the booking rules it was much more convenient to do these simulations 'manually' in a spreadsheet (i.e. consultation durations were sampled using Excel functions, but the booking rules and patient queueing were controlled by the researcher). The simulation was repeated five times and the results are summarised in Table 13.9. Comparing like with like it can be seen that the new schedule resulted in a five-minute decrease in average patient waiting time (i.e. a saving of about 100 minutes of patient waiting time compared to a net increase of 3 minutes to the time that the two doctors spent at the clinic – which is even greater than Fetter and Thompson's (1965) tenfold effect) and an elimination of all patients having to wait over 45 minutes.

A similar process was used to evaluate the new schedule for consultant clinics, comparing an existing booking schedule with the proposed one, and the reduction in average waiting times was 5.6 minutes.

Time-dependent queue modelling results

The obvious disadvantage of the manual simulations described above is the time taken to perform them, and hence the limitation to just five experiments for just two of the schedules. The results from the time-dependent queue modelling approach do not suffer from this drawback, although they had to assume constant DNA rates throughout the clinics, whereas the above schedules are designed so that the DNA rates increase during the clinics. These results are shown in Figures 13.3 and 13.4.

Figure 13.3 indicates that under the existing appointment system in an 'average' clinic the number of patients in the queue (i.e. in the waiting room) will range between 1 and 3 for much of the clinic, and so patients will experience waits

Table 13.8 *Proposed appointment schedules*

Registrar and SHO clinics					Consultant clinics	
Mon/Fri	Thursday pm		Thursday am		Patients*	Mon/Thurs	Patients*
09:00	13:30	13:50	09:00	09:10	New and	09:00	New and
09:00	13:30	13:55	09:00	09:15	Review	09:00	Review
09:10	13:30	13:55	09:00	09:20		09:15	
09:15	13:40		09:00	09:20			
09:20	13:40		09:05	09:25			
09:25	13:45		09:10	09:25			
	13:45		09:10	09:25			
09:30	14:00	14:30	09:30	09:50	New,	09:30	New,
09:35	14:00	14:40	09:30	09:55	Review,	09:45	Review,
09:40	14:05	14:40	09:35	10:00	UTA and	10:00	UTA and
09:45	14:05	14:50	09:35	10:00	CNA	10:00	CNA
09:50	14:10		09:35	10:05		10:15	
10:00	14:15		09:40	10:10			
10:10	14:15		09:40	10:10			
10:20	14:20		09:45	10:15			
	14:25		09:45	10:20			
	14:30		09:50				
BREAK							
10:40	15:10	15:50	10:40	11:05	New,	10:45	New,
10:45	15:10	15:50	10:40	11:05	Review,	11:00	Review,
10:50	15:15	16:00	10:45	11:10	UTA,	11:15	UTA,
11:00	15:20		10:45	11:10	CNA and	11:30	CAN and
11:05	15:20		10:50	11:15	DNA		DNA
11:10	15:25		10:50	11:20			
11:20	15:30		10:55	11:20			
11:30	15:35		10:55	11:25			
	15:35		11:00	11:30			
	15:40		11:00				

*UTA/CNA indicate Unable To Attend/Could Not Attend, but that the patient contacted the hospital; DNA indicates Did Not Attend, with no contact made with the hospital

between 6 and 18 minutes. Under the proposed appointment system the 'average' clinic will have considerably shorter queues that range between 0 and 1 for much of the clinic, i.e. waits between 0 and 6 minutes. In addition, as not all clinics are average, Figure 13.3 also shows the estimated queue lengths that would occur in 1 in 10 clinics. For the existing system, queues range between 2 and 5 patients for much of the clinic, i.e. waits between 8 and 30 minutes; for the proposed system,

Table 13.9 *A simulated comparison of appointment schedules*

	Existing schedule	Proposed schedule	Change	% change
Waiting times				
Average wait	16 mins	11 mins	−5 mins	−31.3
0–15 minutes	8.4 patients	10.8 patients	2.4 patients	+28.6
16–30 minutes	6.4 patients	6.6 patients	0.2 patients	+3.1
31–45 minutes	2.8 patients	0.6 patients	−2.2 patients	−78.6
46–60 minutes	0.4 patients	0 patients	−0.4 patients	−100.0
Clinic times				
Doctor	2h 48	2h 52	4 mins	+2.4
SHO	3h 02	3h 01	−1 min	−0.5
Combined	2h 55	2h 56	1 min	0.6

queues range between 0 and 2 patients for much of the clinic, i.e. waits between 0 and 8 minutes. Clearly on both the average and the 1 in 10 measures the proposed system is much better for patients than the existing system. However, the model also indicates that the probability both doctors are busy is substantially lower in the proposed system, a point that was not so obvious from the hand simulations performed earlier.

Figure 13.4 tells a similar story of improvement due to the proposed schedule for consultant clinics. For example, 'average' queues drop from between 1 and 3 (i.e. waits between 7 and 34 minutes) to between 0 and 2 (i.e. waits between 0 and 21 minutes). In this case there are high probabilities in both systems that the consultant is busy.

REFLECTIONS

The appointment problem is long-standing and well known and there have been numerous successful studies using queueing and simulation models over the last 50 years. In general terms, the recommendations for the improvement of appointment systems are often similar. However, the impact of these studies has not been as widespread as might be hoped and many clinics today seem to be as badly run as those in the past. This suggests that hospitals tend to require their own studies rather than being able to adopt any general solutions or guidance.

In the UK, attempts to improve services are being led by the NHS Modernisation Agency, which is encouraging health care professionals and health care

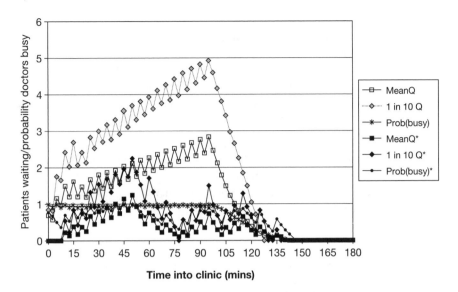

Figure 13.3 *Performance of registrar clinics under previous and proposed appointment systems.*

Note: * indicates proposed appointment system

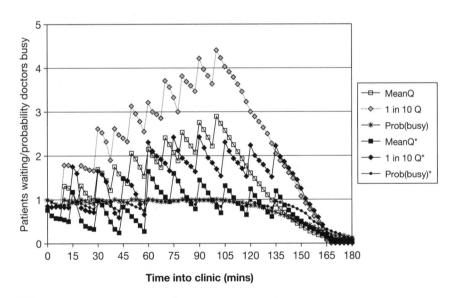

Figure 13.4 *Performance of consultant clinics under previous and proposed appointment systems.*

Note: * indicates proposed appointment system

managers to undertake studies to bring about service improvements. The initial role of these studies is to identify potentially beneficial changes in practices. Once identified, testing and evaluation is recommended. In the context of improving clinic appointment systems, modelling in general, and bottleneck analysis, simulation and queue modelling in particular, all clearly can be very useful.

However, whichever modelling approach is adopted, successful implementation of improvements will require a wise application of results that is sensitive to factors that it has not been possible to model. These include 'softer' factors (e.g. stakeholder involvement to achieve motivation and commitment to changes) and 'harder' factors (e.g. the removal of one bottleneck may simply move it elsewhere, or an appointment system designed for one doctor may be inappropriate for a new doctor or a new mix of patients).

QUESTIONS AND EXERCISES

1 Describe an outpatient clinic that you have observed or experienced using a diagram similar to Figure 13.2. What do you judge to have been its bottleneck?

2 Simulate the following clinic by hand or using a spreadsheet. There are 25 patients, three have appointments at 9 a.m., and the rest at 5-minute intervals thereafter until 10.50 a.m. Each arrives on time, and their consultation times with the doctor are 3, 12, 4, 10, 4, 13, 6, 4, 10, 8, 8, 8, 6, 4, 8, 13, 9, 4, 6, 2, 14, 6, 5, 4, 5 minutes respectively. Draw a graph to show how many patients have arrived, how many patients have left, and hence how many patients are in the clinic (i.e. patients in clinic = patients arrived − patients left) at 15-minute intervals throughout the clinic duration.

3 Rerun your simulation with what you believe would be an improved appointment system. Does it look as though you were correct?

4 What other factors do you think you ought to build into your simulation experiment(s) to make your test more valid, and hence (it is hoped) more convincing?

REFERENCES AND FURTHER READING

Bailey N.T.J. A study of queues and appointment systems in hospital outpatient departments. *Journal of the Royal Statistical Society – Series B*, 14(2), 1952, 185–199.

Brahimi M. and D.J. Worthington. Queuing models for out-patient appointment systems – a case study. *Journal of the Operational Research Society*, 42(9), 1991a, 733–746.

Brahimi M. and D. Worthington. The finite capacity multi-server queue with inhomogeneous arrival rate and discrete service time distribution: and its application to continuous service time problems. *European Journal of Operational Research*, 50, 1991b, 310–324.

Cox T.F., J.F. Birchall and H. Wong. Optimising the queueing system of an ear, nose and throat outpatient clinic. *Journal of Applied Statistics*, 12(2), 1985, 113–126.

Fetter R.B. and J.D. Thompson. The simulation of hospital systems. *Operations Research*, 13, 1965, 689–711.

Goulsbra R and J. Rankin. *A Study for the Ophthalmology Department General Review Clinics at the Royal Lancaster Infirmary*. MSc in Operational Research Dissertation, Department of Management Science, Lancaster University, Lancaster, 2003.

Jackson R.R.P., J.D. Welch and J. Fry. Appointment systems in hospitals and general practice. *Operational Research Quarterly*, 15(3), 1964, 219–237.

Lehaney B. and R.J. Paul. Using SSM to develop a simulation of outpatient services. *Journal of the Royal Society of Health*, 114, 1994, 248–251.

NHS Modernisation Agency. Improvement Leaders' Guides (series 1, guide 1). Process mapping, analysis and redesign, 2002a. Ipswich: Ancient House Printing Group.

NHS Modernisation Agency. Improvement Leaders' Guides (series 1, guide 2). Measurement for improvement, 2002b. Ipswich: Ancient House Printing Group.

NHS Modernisation Agency. Improvement Leaders' Guides (series 1, guide 3). Matching capacity and demand, 2002c. Ipswich: Ancient House Printing Group.

NHS Modernisation Agency. Improvement Leaders' Guides (series 2, guide 1). Involving patients and carers, 2002d. Ipswich: Ancient House Printing Group.

NHS Modernisation Agency. Improvement Leaders' Guides (series 2, guide 2). Managing the human dimension of change, 2002e. Ipswich: Ancient House Printing Group.

NHS Modernisation Agency. Improvement Leaders' Guides (series 2, guide 3). Spread and sustainability, 2002f. Ipswich: Ancient House Printing Group.

Paul R. The CLINSIM simulation package. *OR Insight*, 8(2), 1995, 24–27.

Rising E., R. Baron and B. Averill. A system analysis of a university health service outpatient clinic. *Operations Research*, 21, 1973, 1030–1047.

Taylor III B.W. and A.J. Keown. A network analysis of an inpatient/outpatient department. *Journal of the Operational Research Society*, 31(2), 1980, 169–179.

Vissers J. and J. Wijngaard. The outpatient appointment system: design of a simulation study. *European Journal of Operational Research*, 3(6), 1979, 459–463.

Wall A. and D. Worthington. Using the discrete time modelling approach to evaluate the time-dependent behaviour of queueing systems. *Journal of Operational Research Society*, 50(8) 1999, 777–788.

ACKNOWLEDGEMENT

We are pleased to be able to take this opportunity to acknowledge the contribution of the late Professor Brian Kingsman to this particular project, and to the development of operations management thinking in general at Lancaster University. Brian died suddenly towards the end of the project work on which this chapter is based.

We are also pleased to acknowledge the contributions of: Debbie Fielding of Morecambe Bay Acute Hospitals Trust for setting up the project; senior nurses Sue Howard and Liz Ashby for their interest and cooperation throughout the project; and all the staff of the Ophthalmology Department at the Royal Lancaster Infirmary for their enthusiasm, insights and suggestions.

Chapter 14

Cardio care units

Modelling the interaction of resources

Jan Vissers and Gijs Croonen

SUMMARY

Cardiology patient flows in hospitals are difficult to manage. Many patients are admitted via the emergency department, and go straight to the Cardio Care Unit (CCU). The bed capacity of the CCU is limited. If new patients arrive for the CCU, and the beds are full, the pressure on the cardiology subsystem increases. Decisions have to be made to transfer patients from the CCU to the regular ward, and to discharge patients from the regular ward to home or nursing home. These early transfers and discharges are a worry to those working in the system: emergency department, CCU staff, cardiologists and nursing staff. This chapter reports on a case study performed in a hospital in the Netherlands that was faced with this problem. A decision support model, CardioSim, was developed for the hospital to support decision making on improving the logistic management of cardiology patient flows. The chapter describes the model as well as the results of applying the model for different scenarios of improvement.

KEY TERMS

- Characteristics of cardiology patient flows
- Occupancy level of cardio care units
- Simulation approach for modelling patient flows and resources

INTRODUCTION

The cardiology inpatient flow is characterised by a high percentage of patients that are non-scheduled. These patients often arrive by ambulance at the emergency (A&E) department and need to be admitted immediately at the cardio care unit (CCU). When they have recovered sufficiently, they are transferred to a regular ward that specialises in the care of cardiology patients. After full recovery patients are discharged and seen at the outpatient department for follow-up.

Though physically separated, the units (A&E department, CCU, ward) are tightly linked by the cardiology patient flow. They act almost as 'a cardiology hospital' within the hospital. Through these tight linkages, even a small change can cause a disturbance and many knock-on effects. Suppose a cardiology patient arrives at the emergency department and needs to be admitted to the CCU. The CCU is full and there are also no beds available at the ward. Sending the patient away to another hospital is not a real alternative from the point of view of the patient (increase in anxiety, extra time required) or the hospital (poor quality of care, lost income). Within the 'cardiology hospital' the pressure increases, and there is much contact by phone between the units involved. The A&E department contacts the CCU and announces the arrival of the patient. The CCU says there is no bed available, but they will ask the ward whether there is a bed available for a patient that is 'most' ready for discharge from the CCU. The ward will say that all beds are occupied, but they will investigate whether one of the patients at the ward can be early discharged or whether a bed can be borrowed from another ward. This case study deals with this delicate relationship between the A&E department, the CCU and the ward within the 'cardiology hospital'. In Box 14.1 the case study setting is introduced.

BOX 14.1   THE CASE STUDY HOSPITAL

The specialty Cardiology in the case study hospital struggled with limited inpatient resources such as ward beds, cardio care beds and nursing staff. Over several years staff involved at the hospital (medical, nursing, management) have developed a number of *ad hoc* measures to tackle a range of problems. Examples are creating temporary over-capacity by placing beds in an examination room and discharging or transferring patients whenever there is no bed available. These measures were not satisfactory, as they tended to trigger negative side-effects such as unacceptable workloads for departments and transfer of patients during the night.

The hospital wanted to get more grip on this planning problem and not to have to resort constantly to *ad hoc* solutions. The request was to analyse the current practice and to give advice on how to improve the logistic management of cardiology patients.

The next section describes the planning problem, including the most important difficulties in handling the patient flow of cardiology and the different variables that play a role in the problem and the research questions. In the following section the planning problem is elaborated and the approach followed to tackle the problem is described. The model that has been developed is then described: its background, outline and assumptions, and the results of the simulation-experiments that were carried out with CardioSim are discussed; this enables an assessment of the effects of different scenarios for improvement to be offered. Finally, the conclusions of this project are given, along with recommendations for the further application and development of the model.

PLANNING PROBLEM

Admissions, transfers and discharges of cardiology patients constantly cause problems of a logistic kind. The different actors in cardiology differ in their interpretation of the problem. The CCU says that the inflow of patients stagnates: due to insufficient screening at the emergency department, non-cardiology patients are admitted to the CCU and cardiology patients are incorrectly placed at the CCU. This leads to excess demand for the CCU, causing patients to be transferred at inconvenient hours (evening and night-time). The emergency department says its throughput of patients stagnates, because they cannot get 'rid' of their cardiology patients. The wards complain over the untimely transfers and discharges and the inconveniences for patients. The cardiologists had accepted the inevitability of this situation and had learnt to cope with it – and in the beginning they did not have much confidence in the project and in finding a structural solution to the problem. Summarising, to cope with the patient flow, enormous flexibility was developed in creating an extra bed – in an examination room, in the day-unit or (when necessary) in the corridor. This led to an *ad hoc* work approach and no insight into the consequences of the measures taken.

Box 14.2 provides some background information on the patient flows of cardiology and the resources available to handle the flow.

BOX 14.2   CARDIOLOGY PATIENT FLOWS AND RESOURCES

The hospital had three cardiologists, who admitted in 1997 about 1,400 patients; 1,000 of these were emergency admissions while 400 were admitted as electives. At the Cardio Care Unit (CCU) 9 care beds were available for treatment of cardiology patients and 28 beds at the nursing ward F1. This nursing ward had three more beds that were in principle assigned to other specialties. This allocation of

---

beds was not used in a strict sense; sometimes cardiology occupied more than 28 beds and sometimes the other specialties occupied more than three beds. There were no limitations for emergency admissions – due to the large distance to other hospitals. Regarding elective treatment, coronary angiographies (CAGs) and percutane transluminal coronary angiographies (PTCAs) were performed at a neighbouring hospital. Patients undergoing these treatments stayed before and after treatment in the hospital. Due to governmental planning regulations the hospital was required to reduce its number of beds by 40 within a few years; therefore, extra beds for cardiology were unlikely to become available.

Position in the planning framework

In this section we position the planning problem in the framework for operations management introduced in chapter 6. This framework describes the different planning levels required for hospital operations management and allows us to define our planning problem in relationship with other planning issues in a hospital.

As shown in Figure 14.1, the planning problem addressed in this case study is positioned at the second and third level of the framework, i.e. 'patient group planning and control' and 'resources planning and control'. The approach followed is defined as a combination of a chain and unit logistics approach (i.e. network logistics approach), although the emphasis lies on unit logistics. We will provide some further information on the position of the case study in the framework, when describing the planning problem.

Literature review

The planning problem of cardiology patient flows has not often been studied before. However, analogies can be drawn with intensive care units and A&E depart-

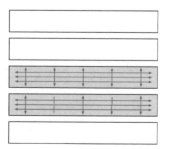

Network logistics application
Emphasis on unit logistics
Level: patient group planning and control
and resources planning and control

Figure 14.1 *Modelling cardiology patient flows, and position in planning framework.*

ments. A cardio care unit can be considered as a dedicated intensive care unit for cardiology patients. In both cases patients – once stabilised – are to be transferred as soon as possible to regular nursing wards. Patients stay at these specialised wards only as long as it is necessary for their condition. The temporary stay and short duration of stay is also a common feature with the A&E department. To be able to model the flow of patients, one needs to look at the state of the system in a more detailed manner, for instance at each hour of the day and night. To model regular wards, often a period of a day or half a day is sufficient detail for representing the flow. Queueing approaches, as well as simulation, are used for representing the behaviour of these units.

The modelling of intensive care units has been studied by Macfarlane (1996) and Ridge *et al.* (1998). Riley (1996) has developed a simulation model of an A&E department. Most of these studies focus only on the intensive care unit or the A&E department and do not include the flows from these units to the regular wards. Vissers *et al.* (1999) have looked at the interaction between the cardio care unit and the regular cardiology ward. This study is used for the current case study.

While the previous studies focus on the internal flow of patients within the unit or between units, other studies focus on the inflow of new patients and dealing with long waiting lists of cardiology patients who need to undergo a surgical procedure, for instance Akkerman and Knip (2004).

ELABORATION

The problems mentioned earlier had existed for a long time. The staff involved had discussed these matters frequently – but without result. It became necessary to develop a new perspective to the problem. By defining the problem as primarily a logistic issue it became possible to re-open the debate. The logistic approach followed is illustrated in Figure 14.2.

The uppermost box contains the inflow of cardiology patients, with a distinction between emergency and elective admissions. Within each type of admission different categories of patients are to be distinguished.

The next box refers to the care processes for cardiology patients. The most important variables describing the care process of a patient category are the routing, the treatment protocols used, the resources that are available and the available equipment.

The arrow from this box refers to the resource requirements resulting from these processes, expressed in the number of nursing days required at the CCU and the ward. The resource requirements combined with the available resources lead to the occupancy of resources for each type of resource involved.

Whenever occupancy rates rise above certain levels it produces logistic problems (lowest box). The most important logistic problems are logistic transfers

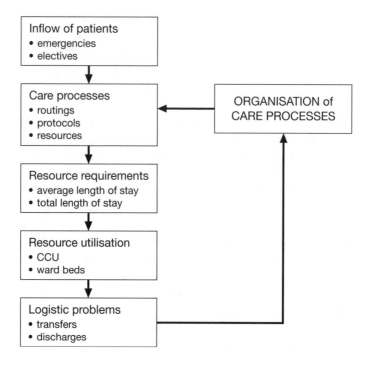

Figure 14.2 *Logistic approach followed in case study.*

(early transfers of patients from the CCU to empty a bed for a new patient) and logistic discharges (early discharge of patients from a nursing ward to empty a bed for other patients). It needs to be said that in practice logistic problems are disguised by the flexibility to create extra capacity temporarily. Moreover, the right moment for transfer or discharge is not a fact that can be determined in an objective way.

The most important arrow in Figure 14.2 is the connection between logistic problems and the box 'organisation of care processes'. This feedback signal can lead to a change in the way processes are currently organised. The added value of using a model such as CardioSim is that possible consequences of these changes can be assessed in advance.

Table 14.1 contains the characteristics of inflow, care process and resource requirements per patient category. For each of the patient categories distinguished, the table shows whether they are labelled as emergency or elective, what the annual number of patients is, what proportion is treated without prior admission, what the routing of the care process is, and what the average length of stay is at the CCU and the ward. Most elective categories do not use the CCU; some categories do use the CCU for half a day according to the protocol.

Table 14.1 Characteristics per patient flow

Inflow				Routing	Length of stay CCU (days)		Length of stay F1 (days)	
No. Description	Emergency/ Elective	Annual number	% external		Average	Standard deviation	Average	Standard deviation
1 unstable angina pectoris	Emergency	227	–	CCU-F1-discharge	1.8	2.2	5.3	4.5
2 myocardial infarction	Emergency	193	–	CCU-F1-discharge	2.6	1.9	8.2	4.6
3 arrhythmias	Emergency	159	–	CCU-F1-discharge	1.1	1.9	5.7	4.2
4 heart failure	Emergency	174	–	CCU-F1-discharge	2.1	1.7	10.8	5.3
5 others emergency	Emergency	183	–	CCU-F1-discharge	1.2	1.1	6.4	4.9
6 non-cardiac problems	Emergency	84	–	CCU-discharge	0.5^1	0	0	0
7 PTCA	Elective	60	67	external-CCU-F1	0.5^1	0	4.0	0
8 heart catheterisation	Elective	228	88	external-F1	0	0	1.0	0
9 cardioversion	Elective	108	100	CCU-discharge	0.5^1	0	0	0
10 pacemaker implantation	Elective	48	100	F1-discharge	0	0	4.0	0
11 observation arrhythmias	Elective	48	100	F1-discharge	0	0	6.0	0
12 observation heart failure	Elective	25	100	F1-discharge	0	0	8.0	0

[1] length of stay according to protocol

MODEL

To improve the insight into the development process of the model CardioSim we will first present the modelling problem; then we will present the outline of the model and the assumptions made during the process of developing the model.

Modelling of the planning problem

The departments cardio care unit (CCU) and the cardiology nursing ward (F1) constitute together the inpatient cardiology system in the case study hospital. We did not include the A&E department in the model, as we were focusing on the functioning of the CCU and the ward. However we did include the emergency patient flow from the A&E department to the CCU. The cardiology patient flow is the outcome of a complicated logistic process. The patients enter the system via CCU or F1 and can follow different routings through the system. As both cardiology departments have limited capacity the flow and throughput of patients is restricted. In practice a department can be fully loaded, causing an increased workload for medical and nursing staff. Moreover, sometimes patients need to be transferred or discharged at an early stage and not planned, as new emergency patients arrive and need to be admitted.

   The properties of this process are difficult to analyse without the support of a model. As the process is very complex, we have chosen a simulation model. In comparison to an analytical model (for instance a queueing model or a mathematical model) a simulation model offers more possibilities to experiment with different scenarios and to compare their results. A simulation model also imitates the reality of cardiology more realistically. First, a representative flow of patients (in terms of arrival times, length of stay, etc.) is generated by using the data collected on cardiology patients. Next, the generated flow of patients is processed by the system and we can determine some performance measures, such as the average occupancy and peak occupancies, the number of transfers that were forced by arrival of new patients, etc. The advantage of such a quantitative model is that the consequences of a wide range of policy decisions can be envisaged almost instantly. Moreover, the model allows for an objective assessment of different options; personal judgement is often not very reliable when it comes to the size of the impact of a change. Before we give a description of the model's structure it should be emphasised that a quantitative model also has its limitations. The model will strictly follow the rules that are implemented in the model's structure. In the reality of a hospital it can sometimes be better to deviate from the rules if a situation requires it.

Model description

The model presupposes the departments CCU and F1 and an inflow of emergency and elective patients. Figure 14.3 illustrates the structure of the model.

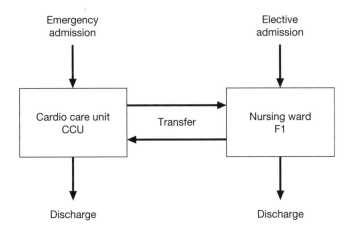

Figure 14.3 *Structure of the model.*

Unlike an elective admission, an emergency patient can arrive at any moment of the day. Table 14.2 contains information regarding the arrivals of emergency patients for the different periods of the day.

For each patient a length of stay is generated for CCU and F1 (one of either is allowed to be zero). When the length of stay of a patient at the CCU is completed, the patient is transferred to a nursing ward. When the length of stay at F1 is also completed the patient is discharged. If a patient arrives at a fully occupied department, the patient with the shortest remaining length of stay is transferred or discharged. The model developed is in fact a network of a number of stations linked by patient flows and limited due to the resources that are available.

The model is next defined by answering the following questions. How can the arrival pattern of emergency cardiology patient be described? How are the lengths of stay of a patient at the CCU and the ward determined? What happens when there is no capacity left at the CCU or F1? These questions were answered using data that were collected for the purpose of this project (sample data and standard statistics of the hospital). When answering these questions a distinction is made between different groups of patients based on their lengths of stay (see Table 14.1). A distinction is also made between daytime and night-time arrivals, to be able to

Table 14.2 *Arrival of emergency patients per time-period*

Time-period	Percentage of all emergency patients (%)	
	Daytime (8.00–18.00)	Night-time (18.00–8.00)
Monday-Friday	56.4	20.4
Saturday-Sunday	10.6	12.6

handle different levels of inflow during these hours (see Table 14.2). It is important to notice that the model uses stochastic routines to generate arrivals and lengths of stay. This implies that the current more or less random patterns in arrivals and lengths of stay are taken into consideration.

Assumptions

It is, of course, important that the model resembles reality as accurately as possible. However, it is also important to use a number of assumptions to make the model manageable. A very detailed model would require very large amounts of data to estimate the many parameters.

The assumptions used in the model are listed below.

- The length of stay at the CCU and F1 is determined by a random sample from distributions of the length of stay in the past.
- Moreover, the CCU and F1 are looked at separately, first, by generating the length of stay at the CCU and then (independent of this length of stay) by the length of stay at F1. However, it is likely that a long length of stay at the CCU will also be associated with a long length of stay at F1.
- It is also assumed that the routings of patients within a group are similar. Apart from the normal routing admission-CCU-F1-discharge, the routings admission-CCU-discharge or admission-F1-discharge are also possible. However, both options cannot be followed at the same time.
- A patient who returns to the CCU from F1 has travelled the route twice, and is treated in the model as two separate patients. Moreover, it is assumed that the number of re-admissions at the CCU is equally distributed over the different patient categories.
- The lengths of stay for CCU and F1 are supposed to be independent of the status of the system. In this way the degree of flexibility in transfer and discharge is limited. It is also assumed that the planning of elective admissions is independent of the workload status at the CCU and F1.
- Finally, it is assumed that the hospital cannot decide to use some spare beds. When all beds at a ward are occupied, any new admission inevitably leads to a forced transfer or discharge. In practice, nursing staff in such a circumstance can place a patient temporarily in a spare bed, while looking for a better solution. This, however, disguises the logistic problem and was thought not to be acceptable; attention should be focused on the structural dimensions of the planning problem.

These assumptions act sometimes as a limitation of the model. However, we do not see it as a failing of the model that it does not incorporate crisis measures (e.g. shortening lengths of stay when beds are full). This is because we want the model to support the development of strategies that reduce the need for crisis measures.

RESULTS

In using the model the following approach has been followed. First, ideas for changing the organisation of care processes to solve the problems have been generated by brainstorming. A number of these ideas were then elaborated as a scenario to be tested by the model. The parameters of the scenario were fed into the model. The simulation model was then run to give the results produced by the scenario. The model's results concern the occupancies of the CCU and the nursing wards, the number of logistic problems per day of the week (daytime and night-time) and the percentage of admissions that need to be transferred or discharged early for logistic reasons.

Simulated scenarios

The following example scenarios are presented to illustrate the use and possibilities of CardioSim:

- the current situation: this scenario will act as a reference point for the other scenarios;
- an increase in the number of beds at the nursing ward: suppose the number of available beds at F1 is increased by 4 beds;
- extension of the possibilities for monitoring (telemetrics) at the wards: this allows for an earlier transfer of patients from the CCU;
- shortening of the treatment programmes of patients with an acute myocardial infarct
- setting up a separate emergency heart unit: this includes among others: better triage (more precise selection of patients), better distribution of patients over CCU and F1, prevention of very short admissions (less than 6 hours).

Simulation results

The results of the simulation can be summarised in two tables. First, however, the output of the model is illustrated in Figure 14.4; for the scenario 'current situation' the occupancies of CCU and ward and the logistic problems (transfers and discharges for logistic reasons) are shown. Table 14.3 summarises for the different scenarios the occupancy of the CCU and F1, and Table 14.4 gives the logistic problems. The results are averages over 400 simulated days (about one year); this produces accurate results for the average: the deviation is less than 0.1 per cent at day level. The start-up period for the simulation is 28 days (about one month); after this period the cardiology system is filled with patients and the occupancy levels are stabilised.

In the current situation the CCU has an occupancy rate of almost 65 per cent and the nursing ward of almost 90 per cent; at the CCU 10 per cent of the transfers

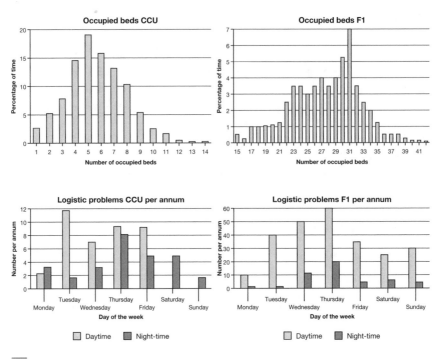

Figure 14.4 *Occupancies and logistic problems for 'current situation'.*

have a logistic reason and at the ward 16 per cent of the discharges are for logistic reasons.

Increasing the bed capacity at F1 by 4 beds results in a lower bed occupancy of F1 (82 per cent) and a decrease of the logistic discharges at F1 (6 per cent).

The use of telemetrics at F1 decreases the workload for the CCU (lower occupancy: 58 per cent; less logistic transfers: 6 per cent), but increases the workload for F1 (higher occupancy: 91 per cent; more logistic discharges: 20 per cent).

Shorter treatment at F1 relieves the workload for F1 (lower occupancy: 84 per cent, less logistic discharges: 9 per cent).

A separate emergency heart unit relieves the workload for both CCU and F1. The occupancy of the CCU goes down considerably from 64 per cent to 56 per cent and the occupancy of F1 decreases slightly (from 90 per cent to 88 per cent). The logistic transfers at the CCU decrease considerably (from 10 per cent to 5 per cent), and the logistic discharges at F1 also decrease considerably (from 16 per cent to 12 per cent).

Summarising: the intervention helps in the way it was intended to. Some scenarios produce better results for one department and worse results for other departments or vice versa. The last scenario produces better results for both departments, but this is probably also the most expensive solution.

Table 14.3 Bed occupancy of CCU and F1[1]

Scenario	CCU (9 beds)		F1 (31 beds)	
	Occupied beds	Occupancy rate (%)	Occupied beds	Occupancy rate (%)
Current situation	5.8	64.3	27.8	89.5
F1: plus 4 beds	5.8	64.3	28.6	81.8
Telemetrics at F1	5.2	57.8	28.2	91.1
Shorter treatment	5.8	64.3	26.0	84.0
Emergency heart unit	5.0	55.5	27.2	87.8

1. The occupancy figures for the CCU are to be interpreted with a margin of 4 per cent (standard deviation of 0.22); the F1 figures have a margin of 2 per cent (standard deviation of 0.54)

Table 14.4 Logistic problems (per week)[2]

Scenario	logistic transfers CCU (patients per week)			logistic discharges F1 (patients per week)		
	day-time	night-time	percentage (%)	day-time	night-time	percentage (%)
Current situation	1.15	0.79	10	4.03	0.92	16
F1: plus 4 beds	1.15	0.79	10	1.49	0.45	6
Telemetrics at F1	0.73	0.45	6	4.78	1.34	20
Shorter treatment	1.15	0.79	10	1.92	0.62	9
Emergency heart unit	0.47	0.32	5	3.09	0.70	12

2. The logistic problems have margins for CCU/daytime of 22 per cent (standard deviation 0.29), CCU/night-time margin 24 per cent (standard deviation 0.22) and F1/daytime margin 25 per cent (standard deviation 1.13), F1/night-time margin 20 per cent (standard deviation 0.24)

REFLECTION AND FURTHER DEVELOPMENT

The following conclusions can be drawn from the project. The problem is not solved yet, but it has become manageable. There is no straightforward solution presented, but instead a tool that supports the exploration of possible solutions.

The main learning point for the staff involved during the development process of CardioSim is to think in terms of (the organisation of) care processes, enabling one to rise above the level of *ad hoc* solutions for the short term and investigating lasting solutions for the future. The thinking in terms of processes also creates an awareness that it is not only concern with improvements that is sought but also the thinking through of consequences. In this, CardioSim proved to be a powerful tool. CardioSim did also contribute to a better understanding of the current situation. For example, non-cardiology patients at the CCU caused only minor stagnations in the system – a finding that was in contrast to the original problem perception.

The most important application of the model is to compare the results of different options to improve the logistics of cardiology patients. It is not so difficult to predict the direction of the impact, but the size of the impact is much more difficult to estimate correctly. Moreover, the simulation offers the possibility of combining different scenarios in the assessment.

To summarise: CardioSim helps the staff involved to analyse the current situation and to explore possible solutions, using an objective assessment of the consequences of alternatives.

We propose to increase our experience with further application of CardioSim in the hospital considered and, if the occasion arises, in other hospitals. It will be important to involve cardiologists in these applications. To formulate scenarios requires input from cardiologists; the consequences of, for instance, more telemetric facilities on the length of stay for the different categories of patients considered can only be taken into consideration by medical expert input. Based on this experience the model can then be further improved.

QUESTIONS AND EXERCISES

1   What arguments can be used to justify the boundaries drawn in this study for focusing the study on the CCU and the ward? What arguments can be used for a wider system modelling approach?

2   Formulate one or more other scenarios that could be tested with the current simulation model.

3   Formulate one or more other relevant scenarios for improving the patient flow of cardiology that would require an adaptation of the model. What would need to be adapted in the model to produce results for these scenarios?

4   Calculate the number of beds required at the CCU and the ward, using the data in Table 14.1 and average occupancy levels of 70 per cent for the CCU and 90 per cent for the ward.

5   Why are the target occupancy levels for the CCU and the ward different? What average occupancy levels would you suggest as targets for the CCU and the ward?

REFERENCES AND FURTHER READING

Akkerman R. and M. Knip. Reallocation of beds to reduce waiting times for cardiac surgery. *Health Care Management Science,* 7(2), 2004, 119–126.

Macfarlane J.D. Some problems in modelling intensive therapy units. In A. Kastelein, J. Vissers, F. van Merode and L. Delesie (eds) *Managing Health Care under Resource Constraints, Proceedings of the 21st meeting of the European Working Group on Operational Research Applied to Health Services,* Eindhoven University Press, Eindhoven, 1996, 99–104.

Ridge J.C., S.K. Jones, M.S. Nielsen and A.K. Shahani. Capacity planning for intensive care units. *Managing Health Care under Resource Constraints, Feature Issue European Journal of Operational Research,* 105(2), 1998, 346–355.

Riley J. Visual interactive simulation of accident and emergency departments. In A. Kastelein, J. Vissers, F. van Merode and L. Delesie (eds) *Managing Health Care under Resource Constraints, Proceedings of the 21st meeting of the European Working Group on Operational Research Applied to Health Services,* Eindhoven University Press, Eindhoven, 1996, 135–141.

Vissers J., G. Croonen, V. Siersma and H. Tiemessen. Simulation of the cardiology patients flow in a hospital setting. In V. de Angelis, N. Ricciardi and G. Storchi. *Monitoring, Evaluating, Planning Health Services.* World Scientific, Singapore-New Jersey-London-Hong Kong, 1999, 162–173.

Chapter 15

Service philosophies for hospital admission planning

Jan Vissers and Ivo Adan

 SUMMARY

The 'traditional' service philosophy underlying hospital admission planning has been one of optimising the use of scarce hospital resources without paying much attention to the level of service offered to patients. As patients nowadays do not accept long waiting times for hospital admission, it becomes necessary to consider alternative service philosophies. Waiting lists have also become a political issue, and alternative service philosophies have been advocated, such as giving all patients an appointment for admission. A simulation model was built to examine the impacts of extreme service philosophies in a simplified hospital setting. The alternative philosophies considered are the 'zero waiting time' philosophy (immediate treatment) and the 'booked admissions' philosophy (using an appointment for admission). The results of these service philosophies are compared with the results of the current philosophy, i.e. the 'maximising resource use' philosophy. The implications of the different philosophies in terms of patient service and resource use are discussed and used to feed the debate on more balanced philosophies for admission planning.

KEY TERMS

- 'Booked admission' and 'zero waiting time' as service philosophies
- Operationalisation of service philosophies
- Admission planning and service philosophies
- A modelling approach to compare service philosophies

INTRODUCTION

Admission planning refers to the operational planning of patients who need to be admitted as inpatients to a hospital (Kusters and Groot, 1996). Patients to be admitted to a hospital can be classified as elective, urgent or emergency. Elective patients do not have to be treated immediately and can therefore be put on a waiting list, to be called when it is their turn. Alternatively, elective patients can be given an appointment for admission. Urgent patients need to be admitted at short notice, which is usually as soon as a bed becomes available. Emergency patients need to be admitted immediately.

The current service philosophy that drives admission planning in hospitals is to utilise the available resources to the maximum, i.e. to treat as many patients as possible within the constraints of available resources. The waiting lists for elective patients are used as buffers for variations in the level of demand. Elective patients are scheduled by picking them from the waiting list in some priority order. This philosophy of 'maximum resource use' is increasingly viewed as unacceptable. In the current situation priority is given to optimisation of resource use without considering the consequences for the service level. As patients are increasingly aware of what is acceptable as waiting time, it becomes necessary to reconsider the trade-off between service level and resource use.

One of these alternative service philosophies currently in focus for admission planning can be labelled 'booked admissions'. The government in the UK promotes this philosophy to reduce waiting lists. Instead of putting patients on a waiting list, an appointment is made for the admission (Frankel *et al.*, 1991). In effect, the waiting time for admission may be the same as the waiting time with a waiting list, but the patient now knows the admission date in advance. On the other hand, a chance exists that elective patients will have to be deferred if there is an unexpected inflow of emergency patients. Alternatively, resources might be inefficiently used if not all resources are taken into account when scheduling appointments.

As a more extreme service philosophy for admission planning – one that would be favoured by the many politicians who would like to get rid of waiting lists – one could consider a 'zero waiting time' philosophy. This would imply that every patient is treated without delay, even when it requires extra resources. One may expect, therefore, that this philosophy will be resource-intensive.

In this chapter we discuss an approach for comparing these different philosophies in terms of their impact on the performance of hospital admission planning. The remainder of the contribution is structured as follows. The planning problem will be discussed in more detail in the next section, where it will be positioned in the planning framework used in the book, and where a short literature review will be provided. In the next section, the planning problem addressed in this study will be elaborated. Information will be given on the characteristics of the case study hospital, on the characteristics of the patients used in the study, and on the operationalisation of the philosophies. Information on the simulation model and the output produced by the model is then provided. The results of the simulation study together with a comparison of the performance of the different philosophies are then presented, and finally, conclusions of the study and implications for policy makers are formulated.

PLANNING PROBLEM

To support the political debate on alternative service philosophies for admission planning, there is a need to examine the effects of these philosophies in a systematic way and to compare them with the current performance. For each of these extreme philosophies we can foresee the direction of the results, i.e. better performance regarding service versus better performance regarding resource use. This contribution is not, therefore, about providing new insights into the possible effects of the individual philosophies; rather, it aims to offer a platform for comparing the effects of different philosophies currently discussed in health care management forums. By providing information on the effects of these extremes in the debate on waiting list management, it is hoped that the parties involved will develop more feeling for the underlying mechanisms and be able to discuss a more balanced service philosophy for hospital admission planning. For the purpose of illustrating our approach, we use a simplified case derived from a hospital setting. Although the data used are realistic, the results will mainly have an illustrative function.

Position in planning framework

As shown in Figure 15.1 the planning problem addressed in this case study is positioned at the 'strategic planning' level in the framework. Although chain logistics play a role, the emphasis is on unit logistics, as we are concentrating on the impact on resource use.

In chapter 6 the strategic level was presented as the highest level of planning in the planning framework. At this level decisions are made on: the range of services to be offered and the 'markets' in terms of product groups to which they are to be offered; the long-term resource requirements; the need to centrally coordinate scarce resources; the service levels to be aimed for; and the service philosophy.

The service philosophy used by the hospital is of extreme importance to the planning systems used within hospital departments. Essentially, it determines how important service is regarded in relation to the efficient use of resources, so the choice of the service philosophy has a big impact on the other levels in the planning framework.

Network logistics application
Emphasis on unit logistics
Level: strategic planning

Figure 15.1 *Service philosophies for admission planning, and position in planning framework.*

Literature review

The available literature on admission planning and waiting lists is rather extensive; see, for example, Gemmel and Van Dierdonck (1999) for a recent state of the art on admission planning and Mullen (1999) for a review on waiting lists and waiting list management. Many of the studies reported in Gemmel and Van Dierdonck (1999) are concerned with improving the scheduling of admissions and resources. For instance, Smith-Daniels *et al.* (1988) present an extensive literature review on capacity management in hospitals, and they conclude that most admission scheduling systems only consider bed capacity. This may lead to sub-optimal use of other resources such as nursing staff and operating theatre rooms. Fetter and Thompson (1969) introduced a patient classification system, diagnosis related groups (DRGs), that allows different resource requirements for patient groups to be taken into account when scheduling patients for admission. Roth and Van Dierdonck (1995) developed a Hospital Resource Planning system (HRP), based on a master admission schedule (borrowed from the theory on Materials Requirements Planning), that can be 'exploded' into plans for capacity requirements, while making use of the DRG system of patient classification. One other important issue in admission planning is how to deal with urgent and emergency admissions. In the HRP system (Roth and van Dierdonck, 1995) capacity for urgent and emergency patients is reserved, based on a prediction of demand. Groot (1993) uses a planning model for admissions that forecasts resource requirements, taking into account the occurrence of emergency patients. The focus of these studies is to improve the technique of scheduling patients for admission, by taking into account all resources involved, different resource requirements of different patient groups, and ways of dealing with urgent and emergency admissions. All the studies reported regard the level of scheduling of admissions, and do not address the level of the service philosophy behind the scheduling technique, which is the focus of our study.

Mullen (1999) gives a state of the art overview on waiting lists and waiting list management. Many of the studies reported deal with prioritisation, i.e. the order in which patients are selected from the waiting list. This is an important issue in waiting list management, but it is not the topic of this research. Worthington (1991) illustrates in his approach the impact of mechanisms in planning a specialty practice, for instance an extra clinic session, on waiting lists. Bowers and Mould (2002) investigate the effect of concentration and variability of orthopaedic demand on the performance.

In this study we do not aim at a contribution to improve the technique of scheduling admissions, but we aim at a contribution to the service philosophy that governs the technique of planning. The literature reports few studies with a focus on the service philosophy used for scheduling. Some studies investigate policies for a well-defined category of patients such as patients waiting for liver transplantation (Ratcliffe *et al.*, 2000), or cardiac surgery (Wright *et al.*, 1996) or a hip replacement (Saleh *et al.*, 1997). The focus of these disease-specific studies is often more on the rules of prioritisation and resource allocation, and not so much on the service philosophy driving the admission planning. In this study, we focus on generic and extreme philosophies rather than disease-specific admission policies.

ELABORATION

In this section we elaborate the planning problem that is addressed in this study. First, the simplified hospital setting that is used in the modelling approach is described. Then we investigate the characteristics of the patients used in the modelling approach. Finally, we operationalise the service philosophies.

Case study setting

In this case study we consider only one specialty (for instance general surgery) with one type of patients. We discuss later the consequences of these limitations in the study. The five resources considered include:

- regular beds in wards (denoted by 'Beds'), expressed in number of beds;
- beds in intensive care units (denoted by 'IC beds'), expressed in number of beds;
- operating theatre facilities (denoted by 'OT'), expressed in number of minutes per day;
- nursing capacity (denoted by 'NP'), expressed in nursing points (a measure of nursing workload) per day;
- specialists (denoted by 'SP'), expressed in number of minutes per day.

The amount of capacity available for each of the resources is given in Table 15.1. These amounts are chosen in such a way as to represent a system operating – in a

Table 15.1 Capacities available in case study hospital

Resource	Unit of resource	Available capacity
Beds	Number of beds	37
IC beds	Number of beds	2
OT	Minutes per day	300
NP	Nursing capacity points	140
SP	Minutes per day	675

high workload setting – with balanced occupancy levels. As we focus in this study on the impact of philosophies, we want to exclude problems due to there being unbalanced occupancy levels in the baseline situation. Although arbitrary, we have chosen an average occupancy level of 90 per cent for beds and other resources, but for IC beds an average occupancy level of 65 per cent occupancy. Intensive care units have smaller numbers of beds and more variation in workload, and can, therefore, only operate on a lower occupancy level than other resources (Macfarlane, 1996; Ridge et al., 1998). For a very high workload setting we use 95 per cent for beds. This is quite high for a setting with 50 per cent emergency inflow, but we allow for 20 per cent overflow for borrowing beds (see the 'Simulation' section below) and other resources and 70 per cent for IC beds.

The number of regular beds available matches roughly with a ward. The number of IC beds available for the specialty is an approximation of the number of beds available for general surgery from the total number of IC beds of the IC unit. The number of minutes of OT available matches an operating theatre session of 5 hours per day. The number of nursing points available per day matches very roughly with a staffing complement of 6 nurses during the day. The number of SP minutes per day matches very roughly with a situation with 3 surgeons.

Patient characteristics

In this chapter we combine urgent and emergency patients as both categories concern non-scheduled patients. We assume an annual inflow of 1,300 patients for a high load setting (or an equivalent of, on average, 5 patients per day), split arbitrarily into 50 per cent elective and 50 per cent emergency.

Elective patients do not need immediate treatment. We suppose that referrals for admission take place only during the working week. Once a decision is taken for admission, the patient is put on a waiting list to be called for admission at a later stage. Each working day patients are scheduled from the waiting list for a period of N working days ahead (notification period). No elective patients are admitted during the weekend.

We consider all inpatient admissions with a length of stay of more than one day. All patients are operated upon on the day of admission. We assume that the length of stay of patients is stochastic (for frequency distribution, see Figure 15.2) and that this stay can be split into different phases (day of admission/operation, day after operation, other days) that have different resource requirements. We assume an average resource requirement profile during the stay as shown in Table 15.2.

The operation takes 60 minutes of operating theatre time. After the operation 25 per cent of the patients require an IC bed, but only on the day of operation. The patient requires a regular bed for the whole stay. Even when a patient stays in an IC bed, the bed at the regular ward will be kept free for the return. The patient requires five nursing points of care during the day of operation and the day

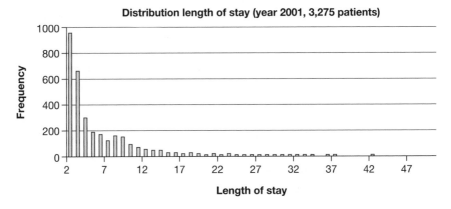

Figure 15.2 Distribution of length of stay.

Table 15.2 Average resource requirement profile during stay of patient

Resource	Phases in stay of patient		
	Day of admission/ operation	Day after operation	Other days
Beds	1	1	1
IC beds	0.25	0	0
OT (minutes)	60	0	0
NP (points)	5	5	3
SP (minutes)	70	10	10

Note: IC = intensive care; OT = operating theatre; NP = nursing capacity; SP = specialists

after – normally the days with most workload – and three nursing points of care on the remaining days.

Elective patients can be cancelled on the day of admission because there is no capacity available due to emergency arrivals. When the admission is cancelled the patient returns to the top of the waiting list.

Emergency patients need immediate treatment. We suppose that if an emergency patient arrives and no resources are available, the patient will not be admitted and will be moved to another hospital. Emergency patients follow the same resource requirement profile as elective patients. We assume a Poisson distributed arrival process with different arrival rates for the day and night (see the 'Simulation model' section below for more details).

Although the data used are not taken from a specific hospital setting, we tried to preserve the features that are illustrative for the functioning of hospital practice, and to use realistic data.

Philosophies

In this study we distinguish the following service philosophies for admission planning: maximum resource use (denoted by 'MRU'), zero waiting time (denoted by 'ZWT'), booked admission without coordination (denoted by 'BAWOC'), and booked admission with coordination (denoted by 'BAWC'). Table 15.3 summarises the characteristics of the different philosophies.

The philosophy MRU tries to maximise the use of resources without considering the impacts for patients. This philosophy resembles the current way of handling patients. First, we determine a certain percentage of the capacity of resources to be reserved for emergency patients. Next, as many elective patients are admitted as possible with the remaining resources, taking into account the expected resource utilisation levels for the next N days ahead. These N days correspond to the notification period used to call elective patients for admission.

Table 15.3 *Summary of characteristics of service philosophies*

	MRU	ZWT	BAWOC	BAWC
Reservation for emergency	Yes	No	Yes	Yes
Waiting list for electives	Yes	No	Appointment	Appointment
Notification period	Fixed	No	Variable	Variable
Cancellation of electives	Similar for all philosophies			
Rejection of emergencies	Similar for all philosophies			
Planning of resources	All resources	No	OT and SP	All resources

Note: MRU = maximum resource use; ZWT = zero waiting time; BAWOC = booked admission without coordination; BAWC = booked admission with coordination

The philosophy ZWT strives to admit all patients immediately, without any delay or waiting time. ZWT treats all patients like emergency patients, so no spare capacity is required for emergency patients. However, differences between 'real' emergency and 'pseudo' emergency remain, i.e. emergency patients have priority over elective patients. If the hospital is fully occupied, the elective patient will be put on a special waiting list to return next day.

BAWOC is a philosophy that gives a patient an appointment for admission without considering the availability of all resources that are required for the admission. Only the availability of operating theatre time and specialist time are considered. We suppose that this philosophy comes nearest to the practice of booked admissions where appointments are given in an outpatient setting where the specialist can consult only his or her own diary and the scheduling of operations in operating theatre sessions, and not the availability of beds, IC beds and nursing staff. For each arriving elective patient, we determine the earliest date of admission by taking into account only operating theatre capacity and specialist capacity. However, when not enough capacity is available on the day of admission/operation, the patient' admission is cancelled and they are given a new date for arrival.

BAWC is similar to BAWOC, but this philosophy considers all resources when the date for admission is determined. This philosophy resembles a practice in which the specialist can consult a computer support system with information on the availability of resources when making an appointment for the admission. For every patient the earliest admission date is determined, using information on the residual length of stay of patients who have already been admitted and information on the expected length of stay for all patients scheduled for admission prior to the patient considered.

MODEL

A simulation model was built to compare the impacts of different philosophies in a case study hospital setting, using specific performance criteria. We give more details of these aspects of the study.

Simulation model

The simulation model is built for a simplified hospital setting. For this model we have made several assumptions and we will give justifications for these assumptions. The general assumptions used for all philosophies include:

■ The number of patients arriving each day is Poisson distributed with an average of 5 patients per day (representing a setting with a high load) and

5.5 patients per day (representing a very high load level). Based on 50 per cent elective and 50 per cent emergency, the arrival intensity for each type of patients can be derived. The length of the day part and evening/night part was used to distinguish between the arrival rates for emergencies during the day and during the evening/night, respectively.

- The model interprets the capacity available for a specialty not in a very strict sense. We suppose for all resources except IC beds that 20 per cent extra capacity is available before the decision is taken to cancel or reject patients. Compared with the target capacities in Table 15.1, this corresponds with an extra capacity of, say, seven beds (that can be borrowed from another ward), an extra capacity of one hour OT capacity (in case the operating theatre session overruns), and equivalent amounts of extra NP and SP capacity (representing the flexibility of these personnel resources for dealing with extra work). The IC beds are interpreted in a strict sense, as one extra bed added to the two beds normally available would make the model insensitive for the different philosophies. Emergency patients leave the system when they are cancelled, while elective patients return to the waiting list when the admission is cancelled. Even with this less strict interpretation of available capacity, cancellation and rejection may occur in the model more often than in reality. The results should, therefore, be seen as illustrative.

- All patients have a fixed duration of operation of 60 minutes. In reality, the duration of the operation is stochastic, but in this study we are not interested in this feature of hospital operations. In reality, sessions may overrun if operations take longer than scheduled.

- At the time of scheduling an admission, it is known whether the patient will require an IC bed after the operation.

- Emergency patients arrive during the day and the night, while elective patients can be admitted only during the day.

- We assume that during the night operating theatre and specialist capacity is always available, and that in the beginning of the night all IC beds are available. Elective patients can be operated on only during the day, with restrictions on the number of operating theatre resources available as noted in Table 15.1.

The procedure for simulating events uses the following order for each day of the simulation: discharge of leaving patients; emergency admissions during daytime; admission of elective patients; determination of admission date for patients on the waiting list who do not have a date yet; and, finally, emergency admissions during night-time. The procedure for planning electives takes into account the patients in the hospital, the patients already scheduled within the notification period and the capacity reservation for emergency patients.

Performance criteria

The performance criteria considered are the utilisation of resources (beds, IC beds, operating theatres, specialists, and nursing staff), the average waiting time for patients, the percentage of cancelled patients at the moment of admission, the percentage of emergency patients that are rejected, as well as the percentage of days the target capacity use is exceeded. The waiting time calculated by the model is the time that is not spent in the hospital between the initial arrival of the patient in the outpatient or emergency department and their inpatient admission. If the admission of the patient is not cancelled, this is simply the time elapsed from the arrival to the scheduled admission date. For elective patients who are cancelled, the waiting time is the sum of all waiting times until the patient is eventually operated upon.

RESULTS

In Tables 15.4 and 15.5 we summarise the main results of this study for different load levels, and for two levels of reservation for emergencies and two periods of notification for the MRU philosophy. All service philosophies are simulated with the same patient flow. We assume no waiting list at the beginning of the simulation. The simulation is carried out over 11 batches of 1,000,000 days, which was long enough to produce reliable results (average results with standard errors less than 1 per cent for all results except waiting time, which may have a larger error of about 5 per cent; the first batch was used as the warm-up period and was disregarded in the calculation of results).

First, results are given for the utilisation of the different resources realised in the simulation. The realised utilisations can deviate a little from the target utilisation level. This is due to the setting of parameters for arrival intensity and due to the possibility of cancellation and rejection. Next, results are given for the average waiting time, the percentage of elective patients that are cancelled, the rejection of emergency patients during the day and during the night, and the percentage of days the target capacity use is exceeded. The average waiting times produced by the model are shorter than the waiting time common in practice. One explanation is a difference in the interpretation of waiting time. In practice, waiting time often also includes the visit to the pre-operative screening. In addition, we consider only one specialty with a proportion of 50 per cent emergencies. In many other specialties (for instance general medicine, cardiology, pulmonology), the percentage of emergency patients can be as high as 70–90 per cent). This will also result in longer waiting times.

At this level of resource occupancy, the philosophies MRU with N=1 and BAWC produce the same results. Maximising the resource utilisation of all resources involved, and booking admissions while considering all resources involved, does not make a difference. BAWOC produces similar or even shorter

Table 15.4 *Summary of simulation results for a high load level (IC=65%, other resources 90%)*

Philosophies	MRU with N=1		MRU with N=7		ZWT	BAWOC		BAWC	
Emergency reservation	R=0	R=1	R=0	R=1		R=0	R=1	R=0	R=1
Utilisation of resources (%)									
Beds	88	88	88	88	88	88	88	88	88
IC beds	66	68	66	68	66	66	66	66	66
OT	87	87	87	87	87	87	87	87	87
NP	86	86	86	86	86	86	86	86	86
SP	84	84	85	84	84	84	84	84	84
Average waiting time (in days)	1.8	3.3	8.4	9.5	0.8	1.8	2.0	1.8	3.3
Cancellation percentage electives (%)	8.7	3.7	8.7	3.7	0.0	11.9	7.6	8.7	3.7
Rejection percentage emergencies (%)									
Daytime	0.2	0.2	0.2	0.2	0.2	0.2	0.2	0.2	0.2
Night-time	1.8	1.6	1.6	1.5	1.8	1.7	1.6	1.8	1.6
Percentage days target capacity use is exceeded (%)									
Beds	19	18	19	18	19	19	19	19	18
OT	40	28	40	27	40	38	27	40	28
NP	18	17	17	16	18	18	17	18	17
SP	23	19	23	18	23	23	19	23	19

Note: MRU = maximum resource use; ZWT = zero waiting time; BAWOC = booked admission without coordination; BAWC = booked admission with coordination; IC = intensive care; OT = operating theatre; NP = nursing capacity; SP = specialists; N=notification period, R= number of reservations for emergency patients

waiting times (in the case of a reservation policy for emergencies) but with a higher level of cancellation of elective patients. The cancellation of elective patients can be reduced greatly for all philosophies by making a reservation for emergency patients. This increases the waiting time slightly. For the MRU philosophy, using a longer notification period results in a corresponding increase in the length of the average waiting time. When a patient is cancelled, under a MRU philosophy the patient needs to wait again at least as long as the notification period. ZWT has, of course, the shortest waiting time, and no cancellations. The BAWOC philosophy produces the most cancellation of elective patients, compared with MRU or BAWC. This is due to the fact that the BAWOC philosophy uses all capacity left (after reserving capacity for emergency patients) for elective patients. If it becomes very busy due to peaks in the arrival of emergencies, this will result in cancellation of elective patients. Rejection of patients during the day and the night is at a similar level for all philosophies. Apparently, the philosophies do not have much impact on the rejection of emergencies. The degree to which target capacity use is exceeded also does not differ much between philosophies. In the case of a reservation policy for emergencies, the chance of exceeding target capacity use is lower than in the case of the no reservation policy.

At a very high level of resource occupancy the results are most interesting. Now not all arriving patients can be treated and shortages of resources occur more often, not only for IC beds but also for regular beds. For all philosophies except BAWOC, waiting times substantially increase in the case of reservation for emergency patients. The explanation is that BAWOC does not consider all resources and, therefore, reservation policies do not have much impact. At this level of occupancy, reservation for emergency also leads to a slightly better occupancy of IC beds. Cancellations of elective patients and rejections of emergency patients occur more often. Again, the ZWT philosophy is best in waiting time but less good in relation to the rejection of emergency patients during night-time. The cancelling of elective patients occurs most often with the BAWOC philosophy. This illustrates the somewhat naive planning in the BAWOC philosophy that considers only OT and SP. For all philosophies, the chance of exceeding target capacity use is much higher than at a lower level of resource occupancy.

As we have chosen our parameter settings in such a way as to operate under comparable resource constraints, it is possible to tell something about the efficiency of resource use of the different philosophies. By supposing a setting with comparable service performance of the different philosophies, we can draw a conclusion on resource use. When, for instance, for a very high level of resource occupancy and a reservation for one emergency patient, we suppose a cancellation percentage for all philosophies to be 5–7 per cent, the BAWOC philosophy requires more resources than the MRU philosophy and the BAWC philosophy. The ZWT philosophy requires more resources to produce a similar level of rejection of emergency patients to the other philosophies.

REFLECTION AND FURTHER DEVELOPMENT

The conclusions of this study regarding the results of the different service philosophies for admission planning on performance measures such as resource use and waiting times can only be formulated tentatively, as it is not yet proved that the

Table 15.5 *Summary of simulation results for a very high load level (IC=70%, other resources 95%)*

Philosophies	MRU with N=1		MRU with N=7		ZWT	BAWOC		BAWC	
Emergency reservation	R=0	R=1	R=0	R=1		R=0	R=1	R=0	R=1
Utilisation of resources (%)									
Beds	96	96	96	96	96	96	96	96	96
IC beds	71	74	71	74	71	71	71	71	74
OT	95	95	95	95	95	95	95	95	95
NP	94	94	94	94	94	94	94	94	94
SP	93	92	93	93	93	93	92	93	92
Average waiting time (in days)	2.1	14.6	8.8	20.9	1.1	2.2	2.7	2.1	14.6
Cancellation percentage electives (%)	11.4	5.3	11.3	5.4	0	15.2	9.8	11.4	7.0
Rejection percentage emergencies (%)									
Daytime	0.2	0.2	0.2	0.2	0.2	0.2	0.3	0.2	0.2
Night-time	4.5	4.0	4.1	3.9	4.7	4.4	4.0	4.5	4.0
Percentage days target capacity use is exceeded (%)									
Beds	38	37	38	37	38	38	37	38	37
OT	52	38	51	37	52	49	36	52	38
NP	36	35	35	34	36	35	35	36	35
SP	42	36	41	36	42	41	36	42	36

Note: MRU = maximum resource use; ZWT = zero waiting time; BAWOC = booked admission without coordination; BAWC = booked admission with coordination; IC = intensive care; OT = operating theatre; NP = nursing capacity; SP = specialists; N=notification period, R= number of reservations for emergency patients

model developed is robust to the simplifications made. At this stage of development it is only possible to formulate a number of possible conclusions provided that the model has passed the test of robustness. Therefore conclusions are presented as an illustration of the type of conclusions that can be drawn:

■ Simulation can help in the study of the effects of different service philosophies for admission planning of hospitals by visualising consequences in a comparative way.

- The simplification of the case study hospital (one specialty and one patient category) does not necessarily harm the generalisable nature of the findings, as long as essential characteristics are included (e.g. emergency flow, stochastic length of stay). The simplicity of the case allows for a better focus on the analysis of performance of different philosophies. Some of the simplifications make the model differ from reality but still make it possible to draw conclusions in a comparative way.

- The results of the simulation show that the philosophies have a different impact on the performance. The scenario with very high occupancy levels produces longer waiting times, higher cancellation percentages and more frequent excess of target capacity levels – as can be expected. The cancellation of electives can be reduced by reservation of capacity for emergency patients. Reservation for emergency patients proves to be very effective, although at a very high level of occupancy it increases the waiting time substantially. This effect is more prominent with the MRU and BAWC philosophies than with the BAWOC philosophy.

- It is important for policy makers to see that MRU as a current philosophy does not perform badly at all. The waiting times under MRU are not longer than the ones under the philosophies BAWOC or BAWC, and cancellations of elective patients and rejections of emergency patients do not occur more often. The advantage of the BAWOC and BAWC philosophies is that patients know in advance the date of admission. However, for the BAWOC philosophy this seems to be more a marketing point than reality as many appointments need to be cancelled due to the variability in the number of emergency patients per day. The BAWC philosophy performs better in this respect, and illustrates the advantage of coordination. The ZWT philosophy is best in waiting time but less good in rejections of emergency patients during nighttime. This does make the ZWT philosophy less acceptable as a philosophy. The MRU or BAWC philosophies show the best performance for a hospital operating on a high level of resource occupancy.

The results and approaches of this study can be helpful for policy makers who are discussing alternative service philosophies for hospital admission planning and attempting to find an appropriate balance between resource utilisation and service levels. The 'maximum resource use' philosophy is where we come from, and its performance in a hospital with a high load on resources is not bad at all, as shown earlier. The major drawback of this philosophy is that the patient does not know the exact admission date in advance. In addition, waiting times in a real world situation might be longer. The 'zero waiting time' philosophy sounds attractive but shows serious drawbacks in the handling of emergencies. Because of the stochastic nature of the emergency patient flow, the workload will show huge variations in time. These can be handled only by deferring patients in the case of a fully occupied hospital or by creating over-capacity. The popularity of booked admissions philosophies is due to its patient friendliness, but coordination of resources should not be neglected. The 'booked admissions without coordination' philosophy has as a major drawback the many cancellations of elective patients, which is not patient friendly at all. The 'booked admission with coordination' philosophy can overcome this drawback. The right handling of the emergency patient flow, for instance by making a sufficient reservation of capacity, is the key to a successful philosophy. The best philosophy is probably a mix between the extreme philosophies discussed before: booked admissions for certain well-defined categories of patients, for instance day-surgery patients, a reservation of capacity for emergency patients and a waiting list system for other categories of elective patients with a sufficiently long notification period to allow the patient to prepare for the admission.

The approach is illustrated for a specific case setting. The approach can also be used for other specialties with different characteristics, or for a whole hospital. Depending on these characteristics the outcome may differ for each setting. For instance, a specialty with hardly any emergency patients could benefit from choosing a booked admissions policy, as cancellation of patients due to inflow of emergencies will not happen. To use the approach for a whole hospital with a range of specialties would make it possible to compare the outcomes for the different specialties and to show that the best philosophy might be different for each specific setting.

As other recommendations for further study, more service philosophies for admission planning could be included in the study. An alternative philosophy, for instance, would be to have a number of patients on call for 'last minute' admissions when other patients have been cancelled. Furthermore, we could also evaluate the philosophies on their effectiveness in clearing long waiting lists. It remains also to be investigated whether the philosophies that perform best under the purely stochastic scenario of this study, would remain best under circumstances with periods of time when demand exceeds capacity, perhaps due to seasonal effects, ward closures, sickness of personnel, etc.

Another extension might be to include more resource areas in the BAWC analysis, for example rehabilitation services for hip replacements. Delays in access could extend patient stay.

QUESTIONS AND EXERCISES

1   Give an estimate for the mean and standard deviation of the length of stay (see Figure 15.2). What would be the impact on the performance of the different policies if mean and standard deviation increase or decrease?

2   We used a fixed duration for the operation duration. What will be the impact on the performance of operating theatres (cancellations, utilisation, etc.) in the case where the operation duration is stochastic and shows high variation?

3   Formulate one or more alternative philosophies. What are their expected performances on service as well as utilisation of resources?

REFERENCES AND FURTHER READING

Bowers J. and G. Mould. Concentration and variability of orthopaedic demand, *Journal of the Operational Research Society*, 53, 2002, 203–210.

Fetter R.B. and J.D. Thompson. A decision model for the design and operation of a progressive patient care hospital. *Medical Care*, 7(6), 1969, 450–462.

Frankel S., J. Coast, T. Baker and C. Collins. Booked admissions as a replacement for waiting lists in the new NHS. *British Medical Journal*, 303, 1991, 598–600.

Gemmel P. and R. Van Dierdonck. Admission scheduling in acute care hospitals: does the practice fit with the theory? *International Journal of Operations & Production Management*, 19(9), 1999, 863–878.

Groot P.M.A. *Decision Support for Admission Planning under Multiple Resource Constraint*. Published doctoral dissertation, Enschede: Febo, 1993.

Kusters R.J. and P.M.A. Groot. Modelling resource availability in general hospitals. Design and implementation of a decision support model. *European Journal of Operational Research*, 88, 1996, 428–445.

Macfarlane J.D. Some problems in modelling intensive therapy units. In A. Kastelein, J. Vissers, G.G van Merode and L. Delesie (eds) *Managing health care under resource constraints*, Eindhoven University Press, Eindhoven, 1996, 99–104.

Mullen P.M. Waiting lists in the post-review NHS. *Health Services Management Research*, 7(2), 1999, 131–145.

Ratcliffe J., T. Young, M. Buxton, T. Eldabi, R. Paul, A. Burroughs, G. Papatheodoridis and K. Rolles. A simulation modeling approach to evaluating alternative policies for the management of waiting lists for liver transplantation. *Health Care Management Science*, 4(2), 2000, 104–117.

Ridge J.C., S.K. Jones, M.S. Nielsen and A.K. Shahani. Capacity planning for intensive care units. *European Journal of Operational Research*, 105(2), 1998, 346–355.

Roth A. and R. van Dierdonck. Hospital resource planning: concepts, feasibility, and framework. *Production and Operations Management*, 4(1), 1995, 2–29.

Saleh K.J., K.C. Wood, A. Gafni, *et al.* Immediate surgery versus waiting list policy in revision total hip arthroplasty. *Journal of Arthroplasty* (United States), 12(1), 1997, 1–10.

Smith-Daniels V.L., S.B. Schweikhart and D.E. Smith-Daniels. Capacity management in health care services. *Decision Sciences*, 19, 1988, 898–919.

Vissers J.M.H., J.W.M. Bertrand and G. de Vries. A framework for production control in health care organizations. *Production Planning and Control*, 12(6), 2001, 591–604.

Worthington D. Hospital waiting list management models. *Journal of the Operational Research Society*, 42, 1991, 833–843.

Wright D. and H. Arthur. An analysis of the impact of a management system on patients waiting for cardiac surgery. *Canadian Journal of Cardiovascular Nursing*, 7(1), 1996, 5–9.

Chapter 16

Services for older people

Finding a balance

Paul Forte and Tom Bowen

SUMMARY

In this chapter we describe a whole systems approach to planning services for older people. This involves defining the system of interest in terms of the make-up of the client group, the components of services that are (or might be) provided for them, and how these two aspects can be connected in terms of models of service delivery. A computer model supports this approach, enabling decision makers to explore many different planning scenarios quickly and easily. Integral to this process is an understanding of the potential impact their plans will have for the balance of service provision, both across the client group as a whole and across the different agencies supplying the services. For the agencies in partic-ular – public or private sector – the approach indicates potential types of service to develop in terms of their costs and volumes, and the analyses can be used in the development of a commissioning strategy and the implications for workforce recruitment and development.

Two UK case studies are presented – at national and local levels – that illustrate recent applications of the approach and model.

KEY TERMS

- Developing services for older people
- Whole systems approach
- Decision support system for scenario planning
- Modelling workforce implications of services

INTRODUCTION

It is axiomatic that the strategic planning or operational management of health care services is complicated. Many different people – with many different views – contribute to both processes: users, carers, care professionals and non-clinical managers. Reliable data and information on which to undertake planning and management tasks are often not routinely available or are scarce and difficult to locate. There may be diverse outcomes for different groups of people or parts of the system depending on decisions taken in allocating resources. Identifying which of these factors are most important or significant (and which criteria to judge them against), and comparing them with each other as well as a backcloth of targets and resource constraints – is a daunting task.

In the UK, in the field of elderly care, these problems are increased by having many players in the system. As well as health service organisations, social care services (run by local authorities) are important and there is a large role for the independent sector in providing care homes. A relatively large number of people require services and, increasingly, these services have to be flexible in their provision as client choice becomes more important.

With this general picture it is not surprising that, in any given locality, the easiest route in terms of planning services is to attempt only marginal changes to the existing patterns of services in keeping within the local culture of organisation and delivery. It is very difficult for individuals – or groups – to develop a new strategic vision outside the limits of existing local frameworks, let alone develop an implementation path for that strategy.

Given this background, 'whole systems' approaches – which attempt to define and make connections between the main elements of the system of interest – are crucial to gaining a comprehensive understanding of the nature of that system. They can also offer means by which the implications of potential planning and management actions can be assessed in a systematic and quantifiable manner; moving the planning and management agenda beyond discussion and towards action based on evidence.

The 'Balance of Care' approach has this wide-embracing view: bringing together appropriate people to define local planning issues, employing available local data and using computer-based decision support systems to support the interpretation of analyses. The aim is to support local decision makers in exploring both wider and deeper analyses of planning options than might otherwise have been undertaken across a wide range of planning issues. Its perspective puts the requirements of the client group – and not the structures of the organisations – at the centre of the planning process. This, in turn, means that the approach also focuses attention on relevant information needs, helps to clarify responsibilities for setting a strategic direction and provides a framework for the effective management of operational services.

283

In this chapter the Balance of Care model and approach is described, illustrated with examples drawn from UK applications. The next section outlines the background to the issues and the trends and pressures that characterise the planning of services for older people. The basic form of the Balance of Care approach and associated computer model is then described, and this is followed by two case studies. The first of these describes an application of the approach that was used to support policy development work at a national level; in the other case study a local health and social care community application is the focus. Finally, some concluding remarks are offered.

PLANNING PROBLEM

Trends and potential demand for elderly care services: a brief review

The provision and management of care and treatment services for older people is taking place against a background of an increasing older population in the UK, an expectation that further investment and expenditure is needed, and a complex 'mixed economy' of public and independently funded service purchasing and provision. This makes the establishment and coordination of local policy often difficult to achieve.

Elderly people in the UK, in common with other developed economies, make up an increasing proportion of its population – currently about 16 per cent is over 65, and this is projected to rise to 22 per cent by 2031. The rate of increase is even more marked in the over-75 group (currently 7 per cent of the population, rising to about 11 per cent in 2031) and over-85 group, who typically place the most significant demand on health and social care services. However, increasing longevity of itself does not necessarily lead to greater morbidity and health care demand. There is some indication of increases in the number of years with chronic diseases (Impallomeni and Starr, 1995) but improvements in approaches to managing these conditions may reduce individual dependency on services. Work in the US indicates improvements in age specific disability levels over time (Manton et al., 1997) and recent analyses in the UK (Dixon et al., 2004) support findings from other countries that the number of acute hospital bed days in the last 3 years of life does not increase with age. In other words, as people live longer so their major demands for care treatment are also deferred to older ages.

Hunter (1996) considers that the management and planning of services is of more importance in controlling costs than the numbers of elderly people. Nevertheless there are rising expectations from older people about the health and social care they can expect, and in the UK there is increasing investment in this area, covering the range of service provision from acute hospital provision, through intermediate care (see the case study later in this chapter) to community-based provision of health and social care, including significant contributions from 'informal' sources: family, friends and neighbours.

As much as 80 per cent of total care hours for elderly people may be provided by 'informal support' from family and friends (Morris and Wilsdon, 1996), but demographic and social changes may also be reducing the pool of this source of support. Over the period 1981–1991 the numbers of people aged 80 and over living alone increased by 10 per cent, with a similar reduction in the proportion living in their children's homes (Murphy and Berrington, 1993).

The planning issues

As in most countries, responsibilities for care and treatment services in the UK are spread across a number of agencies, including primary and secondary care organisations within the National Health Service (NHS), social care departments, usually within local authorities, and a range of independent sector organisations providing complementary services.

This can provide significant challenges when addressing strategic issues, including determining the boundaries of responsibilities and the mutual interests. There are no national guidelines, so any arrangements have to be established locally and can vary from place to place. The boundaries are also significant for clients; long-term care provided by the NHS is free, whereas that funded by social services are usually means-tested and require a contribution from the client.

Complexity also stems from the range of 'care packages' that may be provided to an individual, each potentially requiring different combinations not only of services but of providing (and sometimes funding) agencies. At the operational level it is important to ensure some degree of choice, but at the strategic level of service commissioning the issue is to establish the broad direction for service provision to ensure there are no gaps in coverage of the elderly population and that the highest quality service is being provided for the lowest possible cost.

The simple reason, therefore, why the strategic planning perspective is not well established is that it is a difficult, time-consuming and 'messy' task, and it is impossible for one person – or even organisation – to maintain a coherent overview. The usual difficulties created by a lack of information are compounded by the number of interested parties involved (statutory, private and voluntary sectors; client and carer groups). This, in turn, makes people unwilling to take the lead in strategic planning and helps to promulgate the idea of strategy as remote from reality and not of immediate importance. Difficulty in finding a common language between agencies makes it hard to translate general care statements of intent (such as 'more care in the community') into strategic and subsequent operational plans. It rapidly becomes impossible to try to keep an overall picture of how plans will impact on the quantity and quality of the services different agencies will have to provide, the quality of care that will result and who will have to pay for it.

THE BALANCE OF CARE MODEL

At its simplest, the Balance of Care model can be considered as a framework that enables 'demand' and 'supply' elements of a care system to be defined and the links between them to be described and modelled – both reflecting existing connections and enabling completely new ones to be expressed. This simplicity is an important feature of the model as it means that it can be tailored to particular local interests. The ability to reflect these interests is important for the credibility and acceptance of the approach. The examples below illustrate this.

We start by illustrating the basic principles of the model with reference to a large client group: people aged 75 years and older (see Figure 16.1). This is an age group where demand for health and social care services typically increases. Questions facing planners and managers may include assessing the resource implications of developing new models of care, which agencies this might impact upon, and what the target populations for different types of services might be.

The first stage is to describe the demand for services, and this needs to be defined in more detail than just 'the local population over the age of 75'. The most useful way of doing so is to divide the client group into subgroups (or 'patient categories') differentiated in terms of their dependency levels and consequent requirements for health and social care services. The basis of this connection has a clear pedigree (Canvin *et al.*, 1978).

Earlier versions of the model used a definition of dependency with two principal dimensions: the incapacity of the individual and the level of 'informal support'

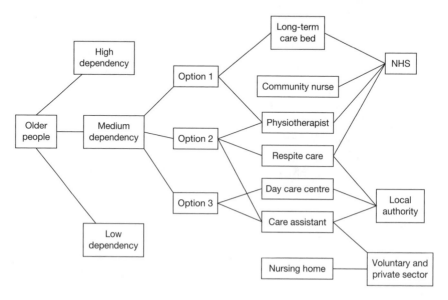

Figure 16.1 *Structure of the Balance of Care model.*

(from family and friends) available to them. 'Incapacity', in turn, had three dimensions: physical ability (mobility and an ability to carry out activities of daily living); mental ability (including dementia or behavioural disorder); and incontinence. Different combinations of these characteristics generate different patterns of service requirements.

Levels of informal support are not directly linked to these and are more difficult to assess, but they do have an important mediating effect on whether, or to what degree, statutory services provision becomes involved. Informal carers often absorb much, if not all, of an individual's social care requirements and their presence or absence will have a significant impact on the response demanded of statutory services.

Table 16.1 presents a list of 16 different patient categories derived from relevant combinations of the above characteristics used in some model applications. Note, however, that the category definitions can be tailored according to requirements.

It is important to populate the patient categories with estimated numbers for planning purposes. In the ideal case data are available that can be directly related to the category definitions, but in most localities they do not exist. The options are then either to undertake special data collection – for example, a survey – or,

Table 16.1 Patient categories

	Description
1	Very severe physical disability
2	Severe physical disability; behavioural disorders
3	Severe physical disability; dementia
4	Severe physical disability; incontinence; poor support
5	Severe physical disability; incontinence; good support
6	Severe physical disability; good support
7	Moderate/minor physical disability; behavioural disorder
8	Moderate physical disability; possible dementia; incontinence
9	Moderate physical disability; possible dementia
10	Moderate physical disability; good support
11	Minor/no physical disability; possible dementia; incontinence
12	Minor/no physical disability; dementia
13	Minor physical disability; poor support
14	Minor physical disability; good support
15	No physical disability; poor support
16	No physical disability; good support

as has been done on a number of applications, to take data from detailed surveys that have taken place in other localities and modifying these using local demographic data. This is achievable as, with the exception of informal support, the other characteristics are age-sex related and can be derived, at least as a first estimate, from Bond and Carstairs (1981) and the World Health Organisation (1983). The patient categories illustrated in Table 16.1, for example, were derived from a large-scale survey in part of central England. This approach has demand for services driven by the characteristics of the population. This is particularly meaningful to clinical and social care professionals and the perspective encourages their participation in the planning process.

On the service provision side, the list of services does not need to be exhaustive but to account for those elements that are significant locally in terms of their cost or volume. These service elements, in turn, can be linked to the different agencies responsible for them, and unit costs and current volumes assigned to provide a baseline against which to compare future planning scenarios (Table 16.2).

Table 16.2 Key service elements

	Service description	Measurement unit	Unit cost	Annualised summary units
1	Continuing care bed	weeks pa	£652.00	Beds
2	Mental health continuing care	weeks pa	£543.00	Beds
3	Day hospital	days pw	£70.00	Places
4	Mental health day hospital	days pw	£58.00	Places
5	Community nurse	hours pw	£18.00	'000 hrs
6	Comm. psychiatric nurse	hours pw	£19.00	'000 hrs
7	Nurse advisor	hours pa	£12.00	'000 hrs
8	Domiciliary physiotherapist	hours pm	£20.00	'000 hrs
9	Independent residential home	weeks pa	£220.00	Beds
10	Independent nursing home	weeks pa	£320.00	Beds
11	Day care centre	days pw	£40.00	Places
12	Home carer	hours pw	£9.45	'000 hrs
13	Occupational therapy	hours pm	£20.00	WTE
14	Night home care	nights pm	£85.00	'000 hrs
15	Domiciliary laundry	sets pw	£0.01	Sets
16	Meals on wheels	meals pw	£2.00	'000 meals

Note: pw: per week; pm: per month; pa: per annum

Finally, there is the 'planning component', which links demand and supply. Here, views and experience of appropriate combinations of service types and volumes – 'care options' – can be defined, which match the needs of patients in a particular patient category. There may well be more than one potentially appropriate care option for a given category – the list is not exhaustive – and views of what constitutes 'appropriate' may vary according to who is making the definition. Moreover, the actual care options do not currently have to exist locally; the opportunity is there to model the resource impact of introducing new forms of care – perhaps building on the results of experience elsewhere – and to test out the potential local impact (see Table 16.3).

Once an initial set of care options is specified, the population of each patient category can be allocated across one or more care options for that category and, after viewing the results, revised allocations can be made or other model parameters altered as required. Thus the model can enable a wide range of different views and assumptions of health and social care professionals to be viewed alongside – or amalgamated with – those of users and carers.

This is the crucial aspect of the Balance of Care model that, in its computerised version, acts as a decision support system for planners, policy makers and managers to test out a huge range of different assumptions quickly, easily and transparently.

Table 16.3 illustrates five care options for patient category three (there is an equivalent table for every patient category). The estimated planning population of this category in this example is 85, allocated in different percentages across the care options columns. Each of these is defined in terms of 'per person, per year' and is made up from a combination of different quantities of services. The important aspect is that all of these options will have been specified locally with the dependency characteristics of the people in this category in mind and, in principle, will be interchangeable for this particular population.

For each patient category, costs are automatically calculated on-screen, but other areas of the model enable a variety of summary and detailed views of the results across all patient categories and care options to be seen.

Starting with an overall summary of the plan compared with the current baseline (Figure 16.2 and Table 16.4), users can obtain an overall impression of the potential impact of a particular planning scenario in various graphical and table forms, and then 'zoom in' on this view to see how it impacts on individual patient categories or services and implications that this might have for the agencies providing the service (see Table 16.5; note that due to space limitations the table here shows only the total and breakdowns for the first four patient categories. In the computer model there is an individual column for every patient category defined).

At this point users are likely to have to start reconciling conflicting objectives of cost efficiency and service effectiveness while, at the same time, taking into

289

Table 16.3 *Example care options for a patient category*

	P3 – Severe physical disability; dementia						No. of patients: 85	
Unit cost:	£33,904	£22,812	£19,484	£24,175	£27,224		£	Totals
Allocation (%):	2	5	30	23	40		0	100
Allocated patients:	2	4	26	20	34		0	85
Service description	Opt 1	Opt 2	Opt 3	Opt 4	Opt 5		Opt 6	Cost
Continuing care bed (wks pa)	52			8				£159,610
Mental health continuing care (wks pa)								
Day hospital (days pw)								
Mental health day hospital (days pw)		0.15	0.15					£13,459
Community nurse (hrs pw)			2	2	2			£147,982
Community psychiatric nurse (hrs pw)								
Nurse advisor (hrs pa)								
Domiciliary physio. (hrs pm)								
Ind. residential home (wks pa)			52					£437,580
Ind. nursing home (wks pa)		52						£95,030
Day care centre (days pw)				2	5			£434,928
Home carer (hrs pw)				18	30			£674,152
Occupational therapy (hrs pm)								
Night home care (nights pm)				4				£79,764
Domiciliary laundry (sets pw)				3	3			£84
Meals on wheels (meals pw)					2			£7,072
Total cost:	£57,637	£96,953	£496,852	£472,617	£925,601			£2,049,659

Note: pw: per week; pa: per annum

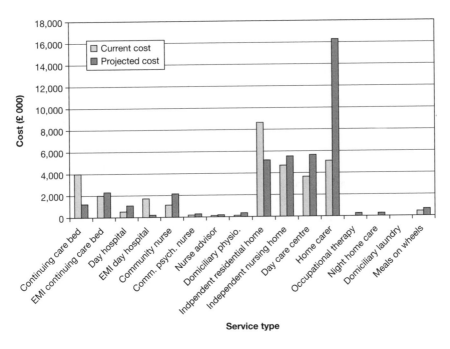

Figure 16.2 *Graph of summary comparison between current baseline and projected costs of scenario.*

account other constraints that may be imposed by existing patterns of service delivery and workforce. Using the model, they can then return to, for example, care options or allocations, make adjustments as desired and recalculate the results in a few seconds. Thus they can enter an iterative cycle of testing assumptions until satisfied that all strategic objectives and constraints have been recognised.

Meanwhile these analyses can be used as supporting material for discussion and debate locally about the direction of planning and the potential impact of different assumptions and decisions. They enable assessments to be made of what are regarded as appropriate services in terms of volume and costs, and how they relate to dependency and locality issues under consideration.

The computer-based model has seen several transformations in its structure and technological platform over the years, with the trend being towards decreasing its complexity, and increasing its flexibility. It currently operates as a stand-alone MS Excel spreadsheet. Data requirements of the model are geared to the management issue under consideration. In theory at least, many data will be routinely collected or available (apart from patient dependency data as noted above). However, the ability to access them can vary quite significantly from agency to agency. While, in principle, data on the quantity, location and costs of services should be straight-forward to obtain, in practice, data are often held on different systems (not all of

Table 16.4 Summary results table

Service	Annual units	Current units	Projected units	Current cost	Projected cost
Continuing care bed	Beds	123.0	37.1	£3,961,682	£1,195,716
Mental health continuing care bed	Beds	75.0	85.2	£2,011,815	£2,284,510
Day hospital	Places	30.0	61.8	£525,000	£1,081,659
Mental health day hospital	Places	120.0	9.4	£1,740,000	£136,451
Community nurse	'000 hrs	65.0	116.4	£1,170,000	£2,095,295
Community psychiatric nurse	'000 hrs	9.0	11.1	£171,000	£210,148
Nurse advisor	'000 hrs	5.0	12.6	£60,000	£151,488
Domiciliary physiotherapist	'000 hrs	2.0	13.2	£40,000	£263,213
Ind. residential home	Beds	800.0	316.3	£8,694,400	£5,156,857
Independent nursing home	Beds	300.0	260.9	£4,742,400	£5,541,814
Day care centre	Places	366.0	564.2	£3,660,000	£5,641,667
Home carer	'000 hrs	540.0	1729.1	£5,103,000	£16,340,239
Occupational therapy	WTE	0.0	6.1	£0	£189,154
Night home care	'000 hrs	0.0	2.1	£0	£176,052
Domiciliary laundry	Sets	0.0	1548.1	£0	£805
Meals on wheels	'000 meals	200.0	298.9	£400,000	£597,725
Total cost				£32,279,297	£41,062,794

which are computer based), and there may be different data definitions to contend with as well.

Importantly, the Balance of Care model aids this process, first, by focusing attention on data relevant to the planning issues and, second, by enabling people to progress in their planning without having to wait for every last item of data to be gathered and verified first. As it is very easy to enter data into the model, initial estimates or 'best guesses' for data items can always be used to start with and quickly updated as and when they become available. The model encourages users

Table 16.5 *Service volumes for scenario by patient category*

Service	Annual units	Total	P1	P2	P3	P4
Continuing care bed	Beds	37.1	14.5	0.0	5.0	17.7
Mental health continuing care bed	Beds	85.2	0.0	60.7	0.0	0.0
Day hospital	Places	61.8	0.0	0.0	0.0	25.6
Mental health day hospital	Places	9.4	0.0	0.0	0.9	0.0
Community nurse	'000 hrs	116.4	1.2	0.0	8.2	80.2
Comm. psych. nurse	'000 hrs	11.1	0.0	7.1	0.0	0.0
Nurse advisor	'000 hrs	12.6	0.0	0.0	0.0	0.0
Domiciliary physiotherapist	'000 hrs	13.2	0.5	0.0	0.0	9.4
Independent residential home	Beds	316.3	0.0	0.0	26.8	7.9
Independent nursing home	Beds	260.9	94.3	52.2	4.5	27.7
Day care centre	Places	564.2	0.0	11.6	43.5	62.6
Home carer	'000 hrs	1729.1	23.3	21.3	71.3	496.6
Occupational therapy	WTE	6.1	0.3	0.0	0.0	0.0
Night home care	'000 hrs	2.1	0.5	0.6	0.9	0.0
Domiciliary laundry	Sets	1548	67.2	55.8	160.7	864.8
Meals on wheels	'000 meals	299	0.0	0.6	3.5	107.5

to use local information whenever possible, but estimates or data from other localities or projects can be used as well if required.

APPLICATIONS OF THE BALANCE OF CARE APPROACH

The scope of the Balance of Care approach means that it is not always straight-forward to define an 'application', as this can encompass everything from people basing their work on the general philosophy of the approach (for example, wide-ranging stakeholder involvement) to more detailed quantitative analyses using the Balance of Care model. Some applications have been published (Boldy *et al.*, 1982; Forte and Bowen, 1997), but we are also aware of others that have been undertaken and remain in a local reporting (unpublished) domain only.

Here we report on two recent applications of the approach: one at a national level in England focusing on the resource implications of 'intermediate care' for older people; the other on a local level in East Berkshire – a locality to the west of London.

Intermediate care case study

In this example, the Balance of Care approach was used in connection with work on the National Service Framework for Older People, focusing on 'intermediate care' (Department of Health, 2001). This form of care carries different definitions but, essentially, refers to services for older people that provide alternatives to admission to, or early discharge from, existing acute care settings. This requires more in the way of community-based care services, and the single most important element in realising this is the workforce. The range of skills required to provide these services is extensive, including medical, nursing, therapy and home care. New forms of intermediate care imply changes not only to the number of people required to deliver such services but also to their skill-mix. 'Multi-skilling' is seen as increasingly important.

The Department of Health commissioned work to make an initial estimation of these implications based on available data and expert advice, and this was achieved using the Balance of Care approach and model. The work focused on an 'expert workshop' in which an appropriate classification of intermediate care users was developed and, based on this, the types and volume of workforce elements required to provide care in an intermediate care setting. This was used in conjunction with the few existing data available to calculate workforce requirements and estimate the additional impact on them that new forms of intermediate care might have, bearing in mind that some might potentially be re-deployed if large-scale intermediate care service development were to take place.

The starting point was to identify the population who might be eligible for particular phases of intermediate care. The client group base was people aged 75 years and older and they were divided into five 'phases of care' (see Table 16.6). These were all short term (the longest being six weeks) but the results were subsequently annualised using data derived from a survey of patients conducted in a locality west of London.

Although care options for each of these phases of care would include a range of inputs, the particular focus was on workforce so care options were then described in terms of those elements only. In the time available at the workshop, the essential 'skills components' of four different care options – relating to different intensities of need – were defined (with one of the care options broadly applicable to two of the phases of care). A key purpose of the workshop was to define at least one relevant 'ideal' care option for each phase of care in detail. These are presented in terms of 'per person, per week' in Table 16.7.

The role of the care coordinator was particularly noted as having a crucial role in the timely coordination of different intermediate care service inputs and hence

Table 16.6 *Patient categories for intermediate care*

	Patient phase of care	Description
1	Alternative to admission	Mild confusional state and/ or slightly frail. A medical diagnosis has been made, but the person can be in an alternative to hospital care setting
2	Post-acute intensive (up to 7 days)	A more severe medical condition, but patient is making a good recovery
3	Supported discharge (up to 14 days)	Severe arthritic patient recovering from a fall or fracture (for example). Patients often have multiple pathologies
4	Rehab/ recovery (up to 28 days)	Stroke
5	'Slow stream rehab' (up to 42 days)	Severe stroke

its significant role across all phases of care. Also prominent are the inputs from therapy staff for people in earlier phases of care, including those in phase 1 (avoiding admittance to the acute sector) and the role of the health care assistant.

To assist in the policy decisions the data were converted to an annual basis and into whole time equivalents (WTEs). The conversion factor used to translate the total number of hours into WTEs is important. Its value depends on the number of hours worked and on how many of these hours are spent in direct patient contact, as opposed to travelling, training or other activities.

Of particular interest was the difference between the total estimates of people required and existing workforce levels in intermediate care. As is often the case, data enabling precise current WTE estimates of people providing services for clients over 75 was difficult to come by for several reasons. Most of the workforce also provides services for clients under 75 years (and it is difficult to ascertain the division of workload on an age-related basis) and, as health and care workers are often employed by organisations with different operating territories, it can be difficult to map services provided to patients in a specific geographical area. However, data from a special Department of Health survey provided some estimates that could be used in the analysis.

The conclusions were quite clear: a large-scale shift in care provision across the country towards intermediate care would be likely to lead to significant demands in particular skill areas (see Table 16.8).

The degree to which individual care workers can themselves become 'multi-skilled' is limited, but anecdotal evidence suggests that it is a knowledge of the skills that other members of a multidisciplinary care team have rather than possession of that knowledge that is important in making intermediate care work well.

Table 16.7 *Potential care options for intermediate care patients*

Hours and measurement units of service	Phase 1 No acute care MILD	Phase 2 7 days post acute MILD	Phase 3 14 days post acute MODERATE	Phase 4 28 days post acute SEVERE	Phase 5 42 days post acute LONG TERM
Community nurse (day/ evening) hrs/wk	2	2	7	7	2
Physiotherapist hrs/wk	2	2	5	4	2
Occupational therapist hrs/wk	2	2	5	4	2
Speech therapist hrs/wk	0	0	0	2	2
Care coordinator hrs/wk	3	3	3	3	3
Care manager/ key worker hrs/wk	1	1	1	1	1
Chiropodist hrs/wk	0	0	0.5	0.25	0.16
Health care assistant hrs/wk	21	21	42	42	21
General practitioner hrs/wk	1	1	1	0.5	1
Specialist geriatrician/physician hrs/wk	0.75	0.75	0.75	0.5	0.5
Health visitor hrs/wk	1	1	1	1	1
Community psychiatric nurse hrs/wk	1	1	0.5	0.25	0.5
Dietician hrs/wk	0	0	0	0.25	0
Pharmacist hrs/wk	0	0	0	0.25	0
Occupational therapist technician hrs/wk	0	0	0.5	0.25	0

Table 16.8 *Actual and estimated total whole time equivalents (WTEs) for selected care staff groups across England*

	Total required (Table 16.3)	Estimated shortfall (68%)	Total available (Sep 99)	% increase
Physiotherapists	3,453	2348	15,030	15.6
Occupational therapists	3,453	2348	12,560	18.7
Speech and language therapists	1,179	802	4,250	18.9

This is reflected by the importance placed on the role of the 'nurse advisor' as described by the expert panel at the workshop. It was also clear that the viability of the care packages appears to be dependent on large numbers of relatively low-skilled care assistants.

East Berkshire: potential levels of services required

In this application the main object was to quantify the overall levels of non-acute beds and associated community services that would enable emerging local care policies in East Berkshire (near London) to be delivered. As with the previous example the focus here was on 'intermediate care' provision but the difference was that the estimation work could be derived from a detailed point prevalence survey that had been carried out earlier to examine how beds were being used.

This provided an already established classification of patients based on their potential to be in an alternative care setting to the one in which they were currently receiving care. Client group age was not a discriminating factor, although, inevitably, the majority of the patients surveyed were people over the age of 65.

The survey included all adult inpatients on that particular day in both acute and community hospitals (except for paediatric, maternity and psychiatric patients). The validated Appropriateness Evaluation Protocol (AEP) tool (Lang *et al.*, 1999) was used to assess the need for acute hospital care both at admission and on the day of the survey. For the community hospitals, experimental survey protocols were agreed to allow the assessment of alternative ways of meeting needs for rehabilitation and other non-acute services.

To identify non-acute bed and other community services, subsequent additional data on all patients surveyed had to be obtained in order to identify how long their hospital episode of care was and their eventual discharge outcomes following their hospital stay. The following key points emerged: bed usage at the main community hospital was dominated by patients with relatively long lengths of stay; only

297

six patients completed their stay within one month, and the dominant pattern was for stays of two or three months; for patients waiting to move to long-term placements in care home places, the stays were even longer.

Current intermediate care schemes were targeted at patients requiring care for up to 21 days, and these had not been extended to meet the needs of those patients who need longer-term rehabilitation and where care based in their own home was possible. The majority of patients receiving rehabilitation as the main form of care in the community hospitals were eventually discharged home (after an average length of stay of 66 days). The stays were longer for patients who were waiting for care home places or who were in for other reasons and not receiving rehabilitative services. Relatively few of the acute patients went directly to care homes, and the majority of those requiring rehabilitation were eventually discharged home without transfer to a non-acute bed.

Although alternative care locations were identified for a large number of acute patients on the survey day, this does not imply that alternative services are needed on this scale. Many of these patients were discharged soon after the survey and for others recovery was not necessarily expedited by a hospital transfer. Furthermore, alternative care pathways are only likely to be viable if they can be anticipated prospectively. For example, consideration of risk factors may help preventive approaches to avoiding admission, and, similarly, enhancements to discharge planning may be able to identify patients at an early stage for whom alternative services, when established, could shorten length of stay.

For the purposes of identifying future capacity requirements, we developed a scenario based on a subset of those patients surveyed for whom alternatives were identified. This subset comprised patients who had been identified as potentially able to be in alternative care settings to the one they were in at the time of the survey and who were medically fit to move on from the acute hospital but were still there at least a week later (or two weeks if they had been identified as moving on to a long-term care home placement).

The preferred alternative care sites for these 119 patients are summarised in Table 16.9, which also expresses the potential for adjustment to current bed utilisation. Note: 'interim care' patients are receiving non-acute care; the majority are waiting for a care home placement to become available.

The shift in capacity implied by these figures amounts to a 'cascade' whereby some patients currently treated in acute beds would spend part of their stay in non-acute beds (these will be patients requiring rehabilitation), while some patients who, on current practice, would stay in non-acute beds would now be treated in the community (i.e. in their own homes). The switches in bed usage implied by the calculations in Table 16.9 are shown diagrammatically below in Figure 16.3.

Given the existing hospital and care home bed capacities, there was negligible change in the total requirement for non-acute beds. To the extent that care home

Table 16.9 *Potential for change in bed utilisation by current location of beds*

Current patient type	Acute beds	Non-acute beds	Care home beds	Community places
Acute hospital patients	-73	22	32	19
Interim care patients		-22	22	
Community hospital patients		-24	2	22
Total	-73	-24	56	41

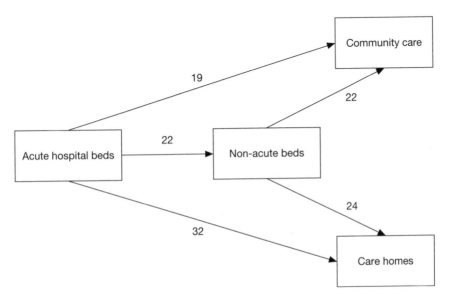

Figure 16.3 *Potential changes in care location shown graphically.*

placements could be increased (or prevented altogether), acute beds could be freed up either directly (through faster discharge of patients) or indirectly (through release of the 'interim care' beds for the transfer of acute patients).

Turning to the resources required to support the additional community-based placements implied, this meant defining, in broad terms, the staffing inputs required according to patient dependency types. These correspond to the types of potential alternative services that were used in the survey (see Table 16.10).

Staff groups are not separated by skill mix and grade and, in practice, relatively junior staff can provide significant parts of the work required. Rehabilitation assistants, working under the direction of physiotherapists and occupational therapists as required can provide much of the delivery of therapy services. Similarly basic

299

Table 16.10 Care options related to patient dependency in East Berkshire

Dependency	Care alternative definitions used in the bed usage survey
High	Home with intensive rehabilitation; home with intensive domiciliary care
Medium	Home with specialist nurse; home with non-specialist care (i.e. general nursing); home with limited care
Low	Home with outpatient/ day hospital; home

nursing may be provided by health care assistants, with involvement of community nurses and, in some cases, specialist nurses, as required (other care staff who may be involved in the assessment and delivery of care, such as geriatricians, GPs, health visitors, etc., are not considered here).

Table 16.11 illustrates some of the calculations. Care options (without any description of skill mix) are described in the top row and the total input per week is shown in the bottom row.

We concluded that, subject to the social care requirement discussed above, the various intermediate care schemes introduced in East Berkshire were sufficiently resourced to meet the additional demand identified in the bed capacity scenario described earlier, and indeed to allow developments beyond this. However, the benefits of the changed capacity across the system will depend on equivalent changes in care pathways for patients. In turn this requires earlier discharge of patients with rehabilitation needs from the acute hospitals, and substitution of home-based care for some patients currently transferred to community hospitals.

Table 16.11 Inputs to community-based staffing requirements

Care packages	Dependency level	Therapy	Nursing	Care assistants
	High	1 hr per day	1 visit per day	3 × 1hr per day
	Medium	3 × 1hr p.w.	3 visits p.w.	1–2 × 1hr per day
	Low	1 × 1hr p.w.	–	3 × 1hr p.w.
Weekly input per care package	Dependency level	Hours per week	Visits per week	Hours per week
	High	7	7	21
	Medium	3	3	10.5
	Low	1		3

Enabling changes to care pathways

The changes to the mix of services outlined above implies changes to care pathways and, in turn, changes to clinical processes to enable these to happen both effectually and successfully. Put simply, this means, at the hospital level, expediting the patient's journey through the hospital both as quickly as appropriate and to an appropriate community-based setting. From the community level perspective, this means 'actively receiving' those patients and including both those who require 'fast stream' and those who require 'slower stream' rehabilitation. The latter group currently make a much greater demand on beds, and the extension of the scope of intermediate care is the most important factor in enabling these patients to get home more quickly (Foote and Stanners, 2002).

Our analyses indicated that, broadly, capacity requirements were either in place or would shortly be so. Current services were focused on patients with shorter-term care needs (typically up to three weeks). This means 'joining up' existing services as much as the development of new capacity – for example, more nurse-led care provision and greater geriatrician input to the intermediate care framework in a case advisory role. Increased communication between different professional groups was seen as an important step forward in enabling this to take place and permitting earlier intervention by the intermediate care services and to ensure appropriate levels of clinical responsibility at different stages in the care processes.

CONCLUDING REMARKS

The Balance of Care approach enables people to gain insights into the implications for resources of policy directions they may be taking, and can support the development of subsequent, more detailed, implementation strategies. The modelling approach aims to support a whole systems focus. In practice organisations find difficulty in addressing all parts of the system at once, and planning activity and associated analyses will often concentrate on key issues across the organisations involved, as instanced by the case studies.

The approach can be applied at different levels of detail appropriate to the particular problems faced locally. This can range from a simple demonstration of the approach – which has been enough in itself to stimulate thoughts on ways of improving existing systems – to more complex and detailed examination of local care policies and their quantification.

We have found that a workshop environment helps the various stakeholders to reach shared views, both on the nature of the problems faced and the potential solutions. In practice, the level of interaction between the components is substantial, and the presentation and exploration of 'what if' scenarios can stimulate and support decision processes. In practice, a 'workshop' can range from a short session within a relevant business meeting to a sequence of full-day workshops involving all stakeholders. They can be a stand-alone introduction to whole system issues for a local health economy or be closely integrated into the existing decision processes. In practice, the approach is issue driven, and determined by the level of involvement of key managers and clinicians and other care professionals.

Both the approach and the system are designed to be easily tailored to different local circumstances. However, although the Balance of Care approach can help build involvement in whole systems working, no decision support system alone can substitute for a lack of local commitment to pursue the implications of the analyses and introduce necessary changes to local systems that will not only be effective but sustainable, i.e. that will entrench any new ways of working beyond any individual managerial or clinical regime. This is a valuable goal in a health system often subject to re-organisation and, in many places, a high degree of turnover in senior management and a tendency for a consequent loss of organisational 'memory'.

Where a robust partnership between agencies is active, the Balance of Care approach can support the search for effective solutions to local service developments and enable more scope for imaginative and innovative solutions to problems facing health and social care communities.

QUESTIONS AND EXERCISES

1 Though this case study goes beyond the scope of the planning framework for hospitals presented in chapter 6, try to position this contribution in terms of the level of planning and to label it in terms of unit, chain or network logistic approach.

2 Taking Figure 16.1 as a template, try adapting the Balance of Care approach to a client group in a health and social care system with which you are familiar. It does not have to be older people – any client group of interest can be substituted. We have, for example, applied the model to dialysis patients, HIV/AIDS patients and paediatric gastroenterology patients. Follow these steps:

   1 Develop a simple diagrammatic model of your system of interest. This forms a useful base on which to then consider:
   2 classifying the client group into mutually exclusive patient categories that are meaningful in clinical management terms;
   3 listing the current service elements that apply to these groups (such as types of workforce and facilities) and elements that you might want to apply in the future that may not currently exist;

4   identifying the agencies that supply these services (there may be more than one for each service type);

5   considering the sort of care options that connect the services with the client groups both currently and potentially.

3   Given the analysis undertaken in East Berkshire, which showed the potential for a shift towards more community-based service provision, what are the potential additional therapy, nursing and care assistant staff requirements to accommodate this?

The data in Table 16.11 and the following information on numbers of additional patients previously in hospital beds given below form the starting point for the calculations:

High dependency patients:	19
Medium dependency patients:	12
Low dependency patients:	10
Total:	41

Calculate:

■   hours per week required of different staff types given this extra demand;

■   additional staffing requirements (in WTEs), given that a therapist can see on average 25 patients per week, nursing staff 40 patients per week and care assistants 30 clients per week.

REFERENCES AND FURTHER READING

Boldy D., J. Russell and G. Royston. Planning the balance of health and social services in the United Kingdom. *Management Science*, 28, 1982, 1258–1269.

Bond J. and V. Carstairs. Services for the elderly. *Scottish Health Service Studies no. 42.* Scottish Home & Health Department, Edinburgh, 1981.

Canvin R., J. Hamson, J. Lyons and J. Russell. Balance of care in Devon: joint strategic planning of health and social services at AHA and county level. *Health and Social Services Journal*, 18 August 1978, C17-C20.

Department of Health. *National Service Framework for Older People*. Department of Health, London, 2001.

Dixon T.M. Shaw, S. Frankel and S. Ebrahim. Hospital admissions, age, and death: retrospective cohort study. *British Medical Journal*, 328, May 2004, 1288–1290.

Foote C. and C. Stanners. *Integrating Care for Older People: New Care for Old – A Systems Approach*. Jessica Kingsley, London, 2002.

Forte P. and T. Bowen. Improving the balance of elderly care services. In S. Cropper and P. Forte (eds) *Enhancing Health Services Management*. Open University Press, Milton Keynes, 1997, 71–85.

Hunter D. New line on age-old problems. *Health Service Journal*, 20 June 1996, 21.

Impallomeni M. and J. Starr. The changing face of community and institutional care for the elderly. *Journal of Public Health Medicine*, 17, 1995, 171–178.

Lang T., A. Liberati, A. Tampieri, G. Fellin, M. Gosalves, S. Lorenzo, M. Pearson, R. Beech and B. Santos-Eggiman. A European version of the Appropriateness Evaluation Protocol. *International Journal of Technology Assessment in Health Care*, 15, 1999, 185–197.

Manton K., L. Corder and E. Stallard. Chronic disability trends in elderly United States populations: 1982–1994. *Proc Natl Acad Sci* USA , 94, 1997, 2593–2598.

Morris N. and T. Wilsdon. Who pays for long-term care? *London Economics Newsletter* 1, 1996, 1–3.

Murphy M. and A. Berrington. Household change in the 1980s: a review. *Population Trends*, 73, 1993, 18–26.

World Health Organisation. The uses of epidemiology in the study of the elderly. Report of a WHO Scientific Group on the epidemiology of ageing. *Technical Report 706.* WHO, Geneva, 1983.

Part III

Conclusion

Chapter 17

Challenges for health operations management and change management

Jan Vissers, Roger Beech and Guus de Vries

As we stated in our preface, this is the first book with an explicit focus on health operations management. We would therefore like to conclude this book with a short review of its content, the challenges we see for health OM and some observations that can be helpful when implementing changes as part of an OM approach.

HEALTH OM CONCEPTS, FRAMEWORK AND CASE STUDIES

The overall structure of the book is given in Figure 17.1. We have introduced in the first part of this book a number of concepts that are derived from the domain of general operations management and made them applicable to the domain of health care. This allowed us to describe the delivery of health care in terms of processes, consisting of different operations to be performed to deliver a service to a client, and in terms of the resources that are required to deliver these services.

We defined health OM as the analysis, design, planning, and control of all of the steps necessary to provide a service for a client. Analysis refers, among other things, to the relationship between each step in a process, and the resources required, and between the different steps in a process. In these analyses we have learned in chapter 3 to distinguish between different types of operation, different types of processes and different types of resource. We have also seen that some problems need to be approached as a unit logistics problem (often focusing on the optimal use of resources in a department) and others as a chain logistic problem (in which the focus is on optimal flow of patients). However, often a network approach is advisable, in which (a part of) a hospital is represented as a number of different units, connected by chains of care for specified groups of patients. The specific concepts for the unit logistic approach and for the chain logistics approach were discussed in chapters 4 and 5.

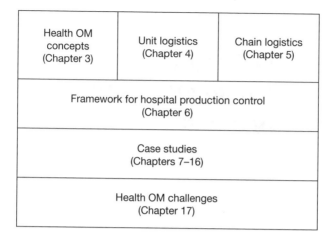

Health OM concepts (Chapter 3)	Unit logistics (Chapter 4)	Chain logistics (Chapter 5)
Framework for hospital production control (Chapter 6)		
Case studies (Chapters 7–16)		
Health OM challenges (Chapter 17)		

Figure 17.1 *Outline of book.*

These different health OM concepts were brought together in a framework that described the way hospital activities need to be coordinated to realise the objectives of the hospital as an organisation. In an analogy to frameworks used for production control in industrial settings for manufacturing organisations, we distinguished a number of levels of planning. At each of these levels a number of decisions have to be taken to ensure that demand for services and supply of services is matched, that the conditions shaped by the higher level of planning are taken into consideration, and that the conditions for the lower level of planning are created. This framework can be used as a reference framework for developing hospital production control systems.

We use the framework in this last chapter to discuss the different case studies that were presented in the second part of the book (see Figure 17.2). This serves two main purposes. The first is to illustrate the usefulness of the framework for discussing different issues of planning in a hospital context. The second is to illustrate how each of the case studies can be positioned in terms of the level of planning addressed. Furthermore, this provides an opportunity for us to discuss the links between the different cases.

Figure 17.2 presents an overview of the case studies on two dimensions: the level of planning (ranging from operational, and tactical to strategic) and the focus on type of logistics approach (unit and/or chain within a hospital system context; care chain management within a broader context of planning services).

This allows us to make some observations on the position of each of the case studies and on the links between case studies. Although the case studies are not selected with a predetermined design, we can see that they represent a good range of studies, covering different areas within the framework. We see that the case

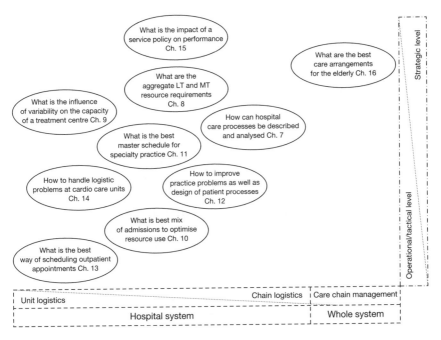

Figure 17.2 *Overview of case studies in production control framework perspective.*

studies differ in the level of planning that is primarily addressed and in their focus on unit logistics versus chain logistics.

The case study in chapter 16 on the planning of services for the elderly must be set apart, as this study has the extended (whole system) health and social care system as its setting while the other case studies are limited to the hospital system. Nevertheless, the case study can be equally well positioned in the framework. It sits somewhere between 'strategic planning' and 'patient volume planning and control'. If we regard the different health organisations that contribute to the chains of health services delivery as the units, the case study illustrates that the planning framework can also be used outside the context of a hospital. This case study demonstrates that the 'hospital' can be the whole system for health and social care. Hence, the case study demonstrates the flexibility of the framework and the importance of thinking 'outside the box'.

If we concentrate on the hospital case studies, we see that the case study on the impact of alternative service policies on the performance of a hospital (chapter 15) is the most strategic one. This is because the choice of a service concept for an organisation is the starting point for the development of planning approaches and planning systems at the other levels of the framework.

The decision for a service concept determines the target levels for resource use. In the case study in chapter 8 on long-term (more than 3–5 years) and medium-term (1–2 years) resource requirements, these target levels were used to analyse whether there is enough capacity available to tackle future patient flows. Because of the aggregated hospital-wide character of such a planning task, it can be labelled as a network logistics approach. It will involve all types of resources and all specialties. The outcome will focus on the overall hospital resource requirements.

The case study in chapter 9 illustrates a unit logistics approach at a strategic/tactical level, to take into account the variability of the process of a unit when planning its capacity. This can be a refinement on the unit's role in the hospital-wide capacity plan at strategic level as discussed in chapter 8.

The case studies in chapters 8 and 9 also determine the resource setting for case studies at lower levels of planning. The case studies in chapters 10–15 focus more on how to make best use of the available resources. This applies especially to the case on developing a master schedule for medical specialists (chapter 11), the handling of logistic problems for cardio care (chapter 14) and the best mix of admissions for optimising resource use (chapter 10). These studies focus most on the tactical level of planning and show little variation in the degree to which patient groups are distinguished within the approach followed. This explains their relative position on the horizontal dimension of unit versus chain logistics.

The position of the case study on outpatient appointment scheduling in chapter 13 requires some explanation. It is classified as a unit logistics approach, although the emphasis of an appointment system is on the level of service provided to waiting patients. The reason for its classification is that its reach is limited to the unit of the outpatient department, and to the service the unit delivers to all patients visiting the unit, irrespective of the other steps in the process of the patient. This illustrates that a focus on service does not necessarily imply a chain type of approach.

There are two case studies with an emphasis of focus on chain logistics, i.e. the case study in chapter 7 (how to describe and analyse hospital processes) and the case study in chapter 12 (how to solve practice problems, e.g. inefficiencies in the use of resources, and improve at the same time the design of processes for patient groups). Including all the chains of a specialty offers opportunities to improve the level of performance of a specialty. The case studies in chapters 7 and 12 represent typical illustrations of logistic approaches in which a combination of unit and chain logistics is sought that can be tailored to the central issue that needs to be addressed.

Though there are many other case studies that could have been presented in the case study part of this book, the selection of case studies shows the wide range of application of operations management approaches to hospital practice.

HEALTH OM CHALLENGES

All but one of the case studies presented in this book had the acute hospital as their setting. This reflects the fact that the acute hospital consumes the majority of the resources devoted to health care. In addition, the analysis, design, planning and control of these resources are probably the most complex and challenging within the acute sector. Hence, there is an ongoing need for the more widespread development and adoption of health OM approaches and techniques within this sector. However, the agenda of responsibilities addressed by health OM stretches beyond the boundaries of the acute hospital. There is an increasing need for practitioners to extend the development and application of their approaches and techniques to these other parts of the health and social care economy.

In most western economies the proportion of the population aged over 65 years is increasing. This will increase overall demands for health care. In the UK, one response to this anticipated rise in demand is the development of community-based schemes for delivering care that has traditionally been supplied in acute hospital beds, for example, the use of community-based rehabilitation teams for the ongoing care of stroke patients. The rationale for these developments is provided by research that has estimated that at least 20 per cent of acute bed use by older people is 'avoidable', i.e. their care could be delivered in non-acute settings (McDonagh *et al.*, 2000). The 'avoidable' use of beds also exists elsewhere in Europe (Fellin *et al.*, 1995; Lorenzo *et al.*, 1995). Hence, community-based schemes are seen as service alternatives that either prevent 'avoidable' acute admissions or facilitate timely acute discharge.

From the health OM perspective, this means that the planning of the 'unit' needs to be extended beyond the boundaries of the acute hospital: in the UK professionals are being encouraged to think in terms of the 'whole system' of health and social care (Department of Health, 2000; Light and Dixon, 2004). For example, the strategic analysis, design and planning of 'ward' nursing care will need to make allowance for the fact that some aspects of nursing care might more appropriately be delivered in other settings. Hence, the concept of the 'ward unit' will need to be extended to embrace elements of care delivered both within the hospital and elsewhere. This extension of their boundaries is in keeping with the primary goal of units: to make optimal use of the resources within their control.

This need for a broader definition of the unit is relevant to the strategic planning of other patient groups (for example, cancer patients, where the focus might be on changing the balance of care delivered within networks of hospitals, nursing homes and patients' homes) and service areas (for example, rehabilitation departments where the focus might be on extending the supply of services to non-acute settings). Health OM practitioners will need to develop approaches that are capable of supporting such 'whole system' thinking. The case study by Paul Forte and Tom Bowen represents an example of such an approach: the Balance of Care model. Other approaches will need to be developed and/or applied.

There is also an increasing need to extend the concept of health care chains beyond the boundaries of the acute hospital. Again, the rising demand for care from older people will be one driver for this development in the scope of health

OM. For conditions such as stroke, for example, after the period of acute care, patients can require inputs for their ongoing rehabilitation and/or continuing care from professionals working in other sectors of the health and social care economy. Delays in the supply of care from these other sectors can extend the acute stay of patients and, as a result, lead to the sub-optimal use of acute hospital resources. In addition, the scope of clinical guidelines and initiatives such as the UK's National Service Framework for Older People (Department of Health, 2001) can extend beyond the boundaries of the acute hospital. Although the primary focus of such initiatives is to improve the quality and clinical outcomes of patient care, their implementation can require changes in the design and organisation of services. Hence their implementation falls within the remit of health OM.

A difficulty that the health OM practitioner will face in responding to such requests for their services is that the complexity of care chains increases as they are extended within and beyond the acute sector. For example, inputs from an increasing number of departments and professionals need to be accommodated. This makes it more difficult and, possibly, less desirable to develop approaches and techniques that draw upon results from the types of computer models presented in the case studies of this book. The chains described in case studies were relatively small, involving, for example, outpatient departments, operating theatres and beds. More sophisticated models are required to analyse longer care chains, and even if they can be developed, such models are usually less easily understood by users. This means that they are more difficult to validate and that their results are less readily accepted by users.

However, the relevance of health OM concepts and approaches remains, regardless of the length of the care chain. In the absence of computer models, analytical frameworks might be developed for supporting the design and planning of services along care chains. Such frameworks could help professionals to identify, for example: the key planning questions that need to be addressed; the types of analysis that need to be undertaken; the potential sources of the data required to support analysis; and the ways in which these data should be analysed in order to generate useful information for decision making. Such a framework was developed by one of the authors to support the development of acute and community-based services for stroke care (Beech and Bell, 2003). The chain covers services for primary and secondary stroke prevention, acute-based care, and community-based care and rehabilitation. The framework aims to help professionals to generate information that clarifies, for each aspect of the chain, the types of stroke services required and the nature and numbers of patients who need these services. Given this information professionals are then able to specify the amount of resources required.

Finally, regardless of the need to extend the concepts of units and chains beyond the boundaries of the acute hospital, there is a need for the development and application of health OM approaches and techniques in other sectors of the health and social care economy. These other sectors include, for example, primary care centres, nursing homes, and mental health units. Professionals in all of these sectors are concerned with delivering a service for a client and all are faced with the tasks of analysing, designing, planning and controlling health services. In addition, 'inadequate' services in any of these areas may have knock-on consequences for other service areas.

CHANGE MANAGEMENT PERSPECTIVE

If you consider the challenge for change in the case studies, health OM can be characterised as functioning within a setting in which:

- different actors play a role with often different interests (managers, clinical staff, clerical staff, boards of directors);
- aspects of service (access time, waiting time) need to be balanced with aspects of efficiency (occupancy of resources);
- short-term interests at the operational level need to be balanced with long-term interests at the strategic level.

How can these different balances of interests be addressed? What change management perspectives can help to implement changes in a health OM project? First we address the position and interests from the management perspective and then we focus on the service perspective.

In general, hospitals and other health service institutions have a traditional hierarchical, pyramid-like organisational structure. Most managers have a position in this structure as a unit manager, i.e. the manager of the nursing department, operating theatre department, radiology department, intensive care unit and so on. In other words, their main task is the planning and control of the resources (staff, beds) of their unit. Their focus is more on efficiency aspects than on service aspects. For a unit manager, flow control is reduced to the patient flows into and out of his or her unit, between the unit borders, to monitor the unit's performance on resource utilisation. This will be especially the case when shared resources are involved. To focus on all sources of origin of flows and all specialties referring patients is rather complex for a unit manager.

From a service and chain point of view, a balance is required between service and efficiency aspects. However, in a fragmented structure – as is often the case in a hospital – the unit managers undertake their positions and responsibilities, without a countervailing equivalent represented by a function such as a 'chain' manager. To address and balance service and efficiency issues adequately, a countervailing power is required, but in practice there is an inequality in power and influence. We come across a fundamental ownership problem: who is, who feels, and who acts like the owner of a chain, or the owner of a patient group from start to finish? And if the chains cross the hospital's border (as described in the previous section), the ownership problem is even more complex.

To handle this problem, we mention some measures that can be taken. Performance indicators must be formulated not only for the aspects of efficiency (resource use) but also for service aspects, i.e. access time, waiting time and throughput time, preferably specific indicators at the level of patient groups. All links in the chain must specify what range of products and services they contribute, including the service levels that are distinguished.

At a structural level the balance between supply and demand must be guaranteed. In the framework for hospital production control, the 'resources planning and control' level is 'the level of truth' to guarantee this structural balance, as a link between 'patient volume planning and control' and 'patient group planning and control'. Chain logistics for a patient group starts at the moment of entering the hospital, i.e. the outpatient department (or the A&E unit for emergency care). From this point onwards, the service aspects of the chain must be controlled. Outpatient staff or a planning department are charged with the operational coordination of resources at the level of individual patients. This task will always be difficult if those responsible for coordinating access to resources are dependent on the authority of the unit managers. Operational coordination can only be successful when secured in structural coordination. If you want control over the performance of a chain, you cannot leave it to the discretion of individual professionals at operational level to solve all problems of coordination. The coordination that is required should also be incorporated in an organised form of coordination at a higher level. Moreover, unit managers should be held responsible for their contribution to chain service as well as their resource performance.

The solution to balancing efficiency and service aspects is not only dependent on technical or structural changes. It also requires changes in the mindset of unit managers. They must shift from a strongly internal orientation to the broader perspective of the chains they are contributing to. In other words, they must shift from positional to transactional leadership, focused on the interfaces between the units in the chains. In an organisational network configuration consisting of hospitals and other care providers, coordination must be guaranteed at the operational level, the structural/organisational level and the strategic level. In such extended chains, in addition to tensions between an efficiency oriented unit manager and the service aspects for a patient group, tensions will exist between common 'network' interests and the interests of each participating organisation. For example, budgetary pressures in participating organisations might reduce their motivation to improve the coordination of services, particularly if they then become responsible for financing a greater proportion of a patient group's care. Hierarchical leadership principles will not work because the organisations are at the same level; no one organisation can overrule another. Specifying common missions and interests, goal setting and monitoring performance at all the levels mentioned will be necessary to arrange for commitment.

The professionals, and especially medical specialists, are also confronting a shift to a broader orientation. The increasing ageing of the population involves an increase in the complexity of care, in comorbidity and in chronic diseases. It is becoming less and less true that the individual professional has 'total professional ownership' of their patient. More and more they are team workers, accepting that they are part of the team around the patient, with their own unique and highly skilled contribution. This loss of autonomy can be threatening, and it can appear even worse when logistic experts come into hospitals, analysing and redesigning the processes that traditionally have been the exclusive domain of the doctor. Moreover, in logistic resource models, the specialist is just one of the resources from a logistic point of view. We have to realise that the specialist is the owner in content and the person who is ultimately seen as responsible for the care of patients. Hence, in applying the principles of health OM, the professionals must be involved and play their roles as director and leader in the chain. Besides, professionals, like many others, are also providers of care within chains. A participative approach is the way to involve the professionals; cooperation and collaboration are important keywords. From our own experience we know that specialists can react with resistance when an outsider tries to open the 'black box' of medical practice by discovering the patterns in, for example, clinical paths. We have to pay attention to this and jointly make the voyage of discovery for developing new perspectives that contribute to patient services. In several cases in this book, the principle of a participative approach and involvement is practised, e.g. in defining patient groups that are 'meaningful' from both a medical and a logistical point of view.

What makes people change? A statement from the field of change management asserts that people are willing to change but they are not willing to be changed. A second statement, based upon multiple case studies, suggests that there is no such thing as 'resistance to change' but many change processes have shortcomings in communication. A lack of communication is a source of uncertainty and distrust. So these are two important lessons.

Finally, we pay attention to some key elements in change management: a sense of urgency, interests of actors, a common perspective, a plan, competences and means.

A sense of urgency can come from both external developments, as mentioned in the previous section, and the internal situation. The actions of boards of directors might be proactive and 'belief driven', trying to influence their environment, or reactive and 'action driven', following external developments. The sense of urgency generally will not be the same for directors, managers and professionals.

Here we have the first assignment for the board of directors: to communicate the need for change to all the stakeholders inside the organisation. Their message may not be an attractive one to everyone. The first question people may ask themselves is: what is in it for me? In the case of differing interests – and we have already referred to some of the tensions that have to be balanced – the board of directors must give transparency in their mission, their choices and their priorities. All managers should be aware of how the balance between 'pain' and 'gain' works out for employees, professionals included. A participative approach can be a good tool to help people, as the directors of their own processes, to set their own goals and interests within the context of external developments and organisational goals and interests. Together with a clear and shared mission, it indicates the direction from pain (if any) to gain. Finally, to be credible in their mission and assignment, the board of directors has to create the conditions and the means for the change processes to be successful. Part of this is to invest in communication, but it also involves training and learning new skills for all key players in the organisation, and creating a solid plan and project organisation during the transformation process. The approach to change can be design ('blueprint') or development ('voyage of discovery') oriented – in practice it is commonly a mix of both. And, as we all know, despite the transformation plan, the organisation will meet both planned and unplanned changes and effects. And that is why change processes are always fascinating!

REFERENCES

Beech R. and J. Bell. The 'What, who for, how much, in what way' approach to implementing the National Service Framework for Stroke: a working paper to support the development of business plans for stroke services. *Keele papers in Geriatric Medicine and Gerontology*, 8, 2003.

Department of Health. *National Services Framework for Older People*. Department of Health, London, 2001.

Department of Health. *Shaping the future NHS: Long term planning for hospitals and related services*. Consultation document on the findings of the national beds inquiry. London, Department of Health, 2000. Available http://www.dh.gov.uk/assetRoot/ 04/02/04/69/04020469.pdf; accessed 26 October 2004.

Fellin G., G. Apolone, A. Tampieri, L. Bevilacqua, G. Meregalli, C. Minella and A. Liberati. Appropriateness of hospital use: an overview of Italian studies. *International Journal for Quality in Health Care*, 7(3), 1995, 219–225.

Light D. and M. Dixon. Making the NHS more like Kaiser Permanente. *British Medical Journal*, 328, 2004, 763–765.

Lorenzo S. and R. Sunol. An overview of Spanish studies on appropriateness of hospital use. *International Journal for Quality in Health Care*, 7(3), 1995, 213–218.

McDonagh M.S., D.H. Smith and M. Goddard. Measuring appropriate use of acute beds: a systematic review of methods and results. *Health Policy*, 53, 2000, 157–184.

Index